Behind
Closed Doors

Violence in the American Family

Behind Closed Doors

Murray A. Straus
Richard J. Gelles
Suzanne K. Steinmetz

With a new introduction by
Murray A. Straus and Richard J. Gelles

Transaction Publishers
New Brunswick (U.S.A.) and London (U.K.)

Second printing 2007

New material this edition copyright © 2006 by Transaction Publishers, New Brunswick, New Jersey. Originally published in 1980 by Anchor Press / Doubleday.

This book is printed on acid-free paper that meets the American National Standard for Permanence of Paper for Printed Library Materials.

Library of Congress Catalog Number: 2006044645
ISBN: 1-4128-0591-0
Printed in the United States of America

Library of Congress Cataloging-in-Publication Data

Straus, Murray A. (Murray Arnold), 1926-
  Behind closed doors : violence in the American family / Murray A. Straus, Richard J. Gelles, Suzanne K. Steinmetz ; with a new introduction by Murray A. Straus and Richard J. Gelles.
      p. cm.
  Originally published: Garden City, N. Y. : Anchor Books, 1980.
  ISBN 1-4128-0591-0 (alk. paper)
  1. Family violence—United States. I. Gelles, Richard J. II. Steinmetz, Suzanne K. III. Title.

HV662632.S87   2006
306.87—dc22   2006044645

CONTENTS

INTRODUCTION TO THE
TRANSACTION EDITION

When *Behind Closed Doors: Violence in the American Family* (*BCD* from here on) was published in 1980, it was favorably reviewed in the *New York Times* and a number of other newspapers and magazines. However, it was not extensively or enthusiastically reviewed in academic journals. Nevertheless, it became a standard reference and was widely cited by academics. That continues to this day. In fact, we were prompted to consider a twenty-fifth anniversary reprinting by receipt of a notice from Questa Media (an organization that provides on-line access to out-of-print books). In 2004, they filled over 33,000 "page views." Not long after that, the book exhibit at the 2005 meeting of the American Sociological Association provided an opportunity to see if it was cited in textbooks for Introductory Sociology, Criminology, and Family courses. Glancing through these books showed that even though *BCD* was published twenty-five years ago it is still widely cited.

THE REVIEWS

BCD was intended as a contribution to the field of sociology, and specifically to provide evidence that family violence was more a product of the nature of the American family and society in the 1970s than a consequence of psychological problems. For a book with this objective, perhaps the most important place to have a favorable review would be in *Contemporary Sociology*, as it is the book review journal published by the American Sociological Association. The review of *BCD* in that journal (Boudouris, 1982) was, at best, lukewarm. The primary theoretical focus of the book—the social causes of family violence—was not mentioned. There were numerous criticisms, as is appropriate in a book review, but not one positive contribution was noted. Boudouris complained that the "interpretations" were *ex post-facto*. Apparently, he did not realize the meaning of "interpretation" (as compared to a result). He then went on to state, "There has been enough discovered about victimization surveys...to question many of the findings of this survey." Boudouris cited the National Crime Survey (now referred to as the National Crime Victimization Survey) as a study that "contradicted" what was in *BCD*, but did not identify any finding that was contradicted. At the time, we checked the findings from that survey and found only two contradictions:

(1) The National Crime Survey found a partner violence rate of only two tenths of one percent, whereas *BCD* found 16 per cent, which is 80 times greater. The problems with the National Crime Survey that produced this vast undercount are discussed elsewhere (Straus, 1999), and the need to correct these errors was one of the factors that led to a major revision of the National Crime Survey, in order to achieve a more complete assessment of domestic assaults. In fact, the National Crime Victimization Survey was redesigned in 1989, with its results published in 1993 (see, Bachman and Saltzman, 1995). Criticism of the pre-1993 surveys' capacity to gather information about certain crimes, including sexual assaults and domestic violence, prompted the redesign.

(2) The second way in which the National Crime Survey "contradicted" what was reported in *BCD* was in regard to domestic assaults perpetrated by women. The National Crime Survey, like tabulations of crimes known to the police, found that men perpetrated 93 per cent of domestic assaults, whereas *BCD* found that men committed only 50 per cent of domestic assaults. The finding that women physically assaulted their partners at about

the percentage men came as a surprise to us because, like almost everyone else at the time, we believed that domestic violence
was almost exclusively a crime committed by men (see, Straus,
1976). The approximately equal rates of assault on partners by
men and women was subsequently confirmed by more than a hundred studies showing equal or greater rates (Archer, 2000; Fiebert,
2004; Straus, 2005). However, even the redesigned National Crime
Victimization survey finds that men reportedly commit acts of domestic violence at higher rates than do women (Rennison, 2003).

Despite the overwhelming evidence, the findings on intimate
partner violence perpetrated by women resulted in twenty-five
years of bitter controversy that still has not yet been resolved.
The main focus of the debate has shifted somewhat from denying
the reportedly equal rates of physical assaults by male and female
partners to arguing that when women use violence it is in self-
defense, in retaliation for violence initiated by men, or an act of
desperation to end male oppression. The empirical evidence, however, reveals just the opposite. It demonstrates the following:

1. There are as many, and possibly more, couples where the
   female partner is the only one to use physical violence as
   there are couples where the male partner is the only one to
   use violence (see, page 37; and, Straus and Ramirez, in press);
2. Women initiate acts of intimate violence as often as men
   (Straus, 2005);
3. Male *and* female partner violence is overwhelmingly utilized
   as a method of coercive control (Fiebert and Gonzales, 1997;
   Medeiros and Straus, 2006).

There is one large and extremely important difference—the
rate of physical injury resulting from male partner violence is
about three times greater than injuries inflicted by female partners. As stated,

> "Even though wives are also violent, they are in a weaker, more vulnerable
> position in respect to family violence. This applies to both the physical, psycho-
> logical, and economic aspect of things. That is the reason we give first priority to
> aiding wives who are the victims of beatings by their husbands"

Important as is the greater degree of victimization of women, the other side of the coin is also significant, namely that men are the victims of about a third of the injuries and a quarter of the deaths from partner violence (Archer, 2000; Straus, 2005).

BCD is like the proverbial cat with nine lives. Given the few and unenthusiastic reviews in scholarly journals, it should have quickly moved to the remainder bins. Although it escaped that fate (*BCD* sold 12,400 copies in clothbound and nearly 24,000 copies in the paperback edition), there were other threats ahead. One was the exponential growth in research on family violence in the decade after *BCD* was published (Straus, 1999), including other national surveys. The flood of new data should have displaced the presumably outdated results in *BCD*. Another potentially fatal threat arose because *BCD* first reported the phenomenon of gender symmetry in partner violence. These findings on violence by women made our research the object of bitter denunciations by feminist scholars (see, Straus and Gelles, 1990, p. 11; Straus, 1992; Straus, 1999).

What then might explain the continuing relevance of this book? Put simply, *BCD* was one of the first books that shed light on a once hidden but significant personal trouble. It laid the foundation for much of the research on family violence that has been carried-out over the last twenty-five years. *BCD* provided groundbreaking, scientific evidence that frames many of the debates that still occur in the field of family violence. Finally, it identified and proposed ways of reducing family violence that are valid today—some of which yet remain to be implemented.

METHODOLOGICAL INNOVATIONS

The Pioneer National Survey of Family Violence

BCD was the first survey of family violence based on a nationally representative sample of families in the United States. Previously, studies of family violence were based on relatively small or geographically restricted samples or samples that represented special populations, particularly women who had sought assistance from battered women shelters, batterers, or parents reported to Child Protective Services.

These "clinical populations" are very important because shelters, police departments, and child protective services need information about those whom they serve. However, as a basis for prevention efforts, information is needed on a representative sample of the general population because the general population, not clinical populations, is the target for prevention efforts. Primary prevention strategies cannot be based on results from clinical population studies as they are usually systematically different from the general population with the same problem, as has been shown for depression and alcoholism (Room, 1980). In respect to family violence, the sample of women surveyed in *BCD* was assaulted by their partner an average of six times in the previous year. That is a high number—about once every two months—but it pales by comparison with the more than once a week found by two studies of women in shelters for battered women (Giles-Sims,1983; Okun, 1986). Moreover, in the general population, most of the violence among intimates is mutual, whereas among clients of services for battered women it is primarily asymmetrical. A final example is the belief based on clinical samples that once a man starts hitting his partner, it will not stop, and it will escalate to more serious and frequent violence. This fact is likely to be true for women who seek battered women services, as that population consists *only* of women for whom the violence did not stop. However, in the general population, the typical pattern, over time, is cessation (Feld and Straus, 1989).

Most family violence is enacted within the average relationship, such as the angry husband or wife who slaps or kicks an unfaithful partner, or an exasperated parent who spanks a child after exhausting all other alternatives. Two-thirds of physical abuse cases dealt with by child protective services in the U. S. began as corporal punishment, which then escalated (Straus, 2000). These are not "mentally ill" parents; they are acting out one of the socially legitimate roles of a violent society. These differences could only be discovered by a general population survey. The differences between extreme and brutal assaults and less severe patterns of violence are extremely important because they indicate a need for utilizing different methods for aiding victims, treating offenders, and different approaches for primary prevention.

The Conflict Tactics Scales

Before the 1975 National Family Violence Survey proved otherwise, few people would have believed it possible to knock on the door of a random sample of households and be able to obtain data on the incidence and extent of violent acts between members of that household. Although one of us had demonstrated that such information can be obtained from the general population by personal interviews through the use of in-depth qualitative interviews (see, Gelles, 1974), this method is unsuitable for a national survey. However, the insights gained from the 1974 study, and from exploratory interviews conducted in 1971, provided the basis for an instrument to measure family violence that is suitable for use in large-scale surveys—The Conflict Tactics Scales (CTS; Straus, 2004; Straus, 2006 in press; Straus and Hamby, 1997; Straus, Hamby, Boney-McCoy, and Sugarman, 1996). The CTS made *BCD* possible. Since then, the CTS, and its second iteration, the CTS2, have become the most widely-used measure in family violence research. More than 400 papers have been published based on data obtained using the CTS and CTS2. Currently, four to five such papers are published every month.

The extensive use of the CTS is all the more remarkable because it has also been the most widely criticized measure in family violence research. The main basis of the criticism is the previously noted fact that use of the CTS in these hundreds of studies has consistently shown that women assault their partners at about the same rate as men. Advocates for battered women, whose knowledge is mainly based on clinical samples, found this so completely at odds with their experiences that they simply have reject the resultant evidence, and thus the measure and the measurers. The results provided by studies employing the CTS also contradicted the feminist theory that partner violence is almost exclusively committed as a means to dominate women. Consequently, the National Family Violence Surveys results of gender symmetry in rates of partner violence are taken as virtual proof that the CTS is not a valid instrument. Ironically, the CTS has also provided some of the strongest evidence for the feminist theory of partner violence; for example it confirmed the link between male dominance and partner violence (see Chart 23; and, Straus, 1994), but this has not shaken the belief that the CTS is an invalid instrument. Perhaps this is because evidence provided by the CTS shows that when female partners are dominant, there is also an increase in the probability of violence. It is a classic case of ideology triumphing over evidence, even among scientists.

Another irony is that, despite these denunciations, many feminist researchers use the CTS in their own research. To deal with the contradiction of using the CTS, they tend to employ two strategies. One strategy utilized in the recent World Health Organization cross-national study of intimate violence (García-Moreno, Heise, Jansen, Ellsberg, Watts, and World Health Organization, 2005) is to omit questions about female perpetration; or if those questions were asked, not to report the results. The second strategy is to atone for the sin of using a "forbidden" instrument by inserting a paragraph repeating some of the erroneous criticisms. These criticisms are then cited in other articles as though based on empirical evidence. This gives the impression that there is a large body of scientific showing the invalidity of the CTS, where in fact, there is only endless repetition of the same unproven opinions.

Perhaps the most frequently mentioned erroneous limitation of the CTS is the claim that it only measures violence that occurs in the course of rational conflict. It is true that the theoretical basis of the CTS is conflict theory. However, the introductory explanation to participants specifically includes expressive and malicious violence. It asks respondents to answer about the times when they and their partner "...disagree, get annoyed with the other person, want different things from each other, or just have spats or fights because they are in a bad mood, are tired, or for some other reason." This "limitation" of the CTS have been cited for twenty-five years in perhaps a hundred or more publications. However, none of these publications provide empirical demonstrating that only conflict-related violence is reported. In fact, where there are both CTS data and qualitative data, as in Giles-Sims (1983), it shows that the CTS elicits malicious violence as well as conflict-related violence.

Data from Both Perpetrators and Victims

Still another way in which *BCD* broke new ground was by obtaining data from perpetrators in the general population, as well as from victims. Previously, the pattern was to base partner violence research on data from either battered women or men convicted of battering. But, as indicated by the above discussion of differences between clinical and general populations, it is critically important to also gather information about perpetrators in the general population. *BCD* provides data obtained from both male and female perpetrators. About half of the respondents reported in *BCD* were husbands and half were wives (although none were marital partners). However, just the fact that we were able to obtain data from men and women who had physically assaulted their partners resulted in unique and important, but controversial, findings.

The Risk Factor Index

Still another innovation of *BCD* was the "Risk Factor Index" in the next to last chapter. This provided empirical data on our theoretical commitment to the principle that family violence could only be explained by taking into account a multitude of casual factors. The early chapters in *BCD* had followed the standard research approach of examining the effects of these risk factors one-by-one. For the chapter on "Putting the Pieces Together," we created a scale to indicate how many of twenty-five risk factors characterized each couple in the study.

Studies of risk factors for partner violence and child maltreatment usually focus on a small number of correlates. They estimate the "net effect" of each of the risk factors after controlling for their overlap with each other. This is a necessary research strategy because it permits an in-depth examination of those risk factors, such as examining variables that mediate or moderate their effect. But the price of doing that is not being able to see the whole picture. Consistent with our multiple causation theoretical orientation, we wanted to examine the cumulative effect of the many risk factors measured for *BCD* and to estimate the probability of violence when a family had only one of the twenty-five risk factors, when they had two of them, three of them, etc.

If a program to compute logistic regression had been available in the late 1970s when the statistical analyses for *BCD* were done, we could have used it to create a graph showing the cumulative effect the number of risk factors had on the probability of violence accruing in a family. In the absence of such a program, we used simple check lists to achieve the same end. Each family was given a score consisting of the number of risk factors. We then computed the percent who were violent that year for the families in each risk factor score category. The results shown in Chart 26, for severe partner violence, demonstrate that the percent of partners who were severely violent goes from under 1 per cent for partners with none of the risk factors, to over 70 per cent for those who had 14 or more of the risk factors. Moreover, the plot lines are parallel for male and female perpetrators.

SUBSTANTIVE CONTRIBUTIONS

The Theoretical Framework

The theoretical framework of *BCD* had been laid out in several previous publications, such as (Gelles and Straus, 1979; Steinmetz and Straus, 1974; Straus, 1973; Straus, 1974; Straus, 1977). A core assumption is that violence in each family role is interrelated with violence in other family roles. Until *BCD*, research on family violence tended to be focused on either child abuse or spousal abuse. Studies did not seem to exist that gathered data on both, despite the obvious theoretical links. *BCD* broke new ground by describing the full range of family violence in the U.S., including child, spousal, sibling, and elder abuse. It also provided evidence that, although it may at times be necessary to study each form separately, a more accurate understanding of family violence also requires studying its interrelatedness. *BCD* showed that this holistic approach to understanding family violence was both possible and fruitful. Unfortunately, except for our 1985 National Family Violence Survey (Gelles and Straus, 1988) no study since *BCD* has provided similar evidence, even though much still remains to be learned about the types and interrelatedness of family violence.

The Social Causes of Family Violence

A major contribution of *BCD* was that it provided evidence that demonstrated that the "causes" of family violence lie in the fabric of the American family itself, and on a broader level, throughout society-at-large. Among the many possible explanations for the high rates of family violence are social norms and economic arrangements that create and justify male dominance within the family and in society. The devastating effects of poverty and the violent child-rearing practices experienced by over 90 per cent of American children in the form of spanking by parents are just some of the precursors of violence in families.

This is not to say that *BCD* provided the first empirical description of the social causes of violence. There had been a long tradition of such research in sociology (see Gil, 1970; Elias, 1978; Loftin and Hill, 1974; Wolfgang and Ferracuti, 1967). Examining the possible social causes of violence has been at the theoretical core of our research since 1970, as illustrated by numerous articles on the social causes of both ordinary physical punishment of children (Straus, 1971) and child abuse (Gelles, 1973), male dominance, and female intimate partner violence (Straus, 1974; Straus, 1976), and an entire book devoted to partner violence, *The Social Causes of Husband-Wife Violence* (Straus and Hotaling, 1980). However, these studies either were theoretical analyses or used empirical data with important threats to the validity of the data. *BCD* changed that radically. The results in Parts III and IV, and the results from the "Risk Factor Index "in Part V, (which consists almost entirely of social characteristics such as unemployment, early marriage, multiple children, inequality between partners, and the lack of participation in organized religion) are examples of social causes. They show that a few social characteristics can go a long way toward explaining the high rates of violence in American families.

Trends

The findings in *BCD* are both dismal and hopeful. They are dismal in the sense that they provided overwhelming evidence that the family is the location where the typical American child or adult is more likely to be the victim of a physical assault than in any other normal social setting. We believed the findings were also hopeful because the risk factors identified in *BCD* that may lead family to violence are changing in a direction that will lower rates of violence within families in the future, such as a growing proportion of college-educated Americans, later marriages and fewer children, the torrent of information about all aspects of child-rearing in newspapers, magazines, and TV, greater equality between men and women, and less reliance on spanking children. Moreover, cultural norms are changing that reduce the threshold for what is an "acceptable" or "tolerable" level of violence. These and other social changes (Straus and Gelles, 1986) led us to predict a decrease in all forms of family violence. Research by a number of investigators shows that this prediction has been borne out for all forms of family violence from spanking children, to partner violence, and intimate homicides (Finkelhor, 2005; Rennison 2003; Straus and Gelles, 1986; Straus and Kaufman Kantor, 1995; Straus, Kaufman Kantor, and Moore, 1997). Some of these trends are shown in Charts I.1, I.2, I.3, and I.4.

There is continuing grounds for optimism because these social trends are continuing; for example, the trend toward greater equality between intimate partners and the reduction of hitting teen-agers from about two thirds of to "only" one third. There is still a long way to go in regard to both of these risk factors for family violence as men continue to earn more than women, and as nearly all American parents continue to use physical violence against pre-school children (Straus and Stewart, 1999). Interpersonal violence in society as a whole, and within the family,

Chart I.1
Percent of Parents who Spanked or Slapped in Past Year

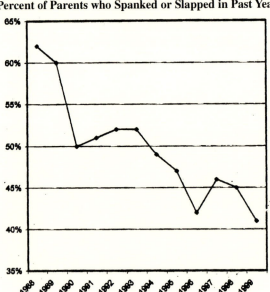

Chart I.2
Trends in Severe Violence by Parents National Family
Violence Surveys 1975-1995

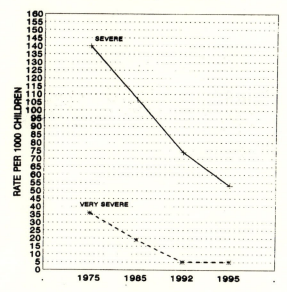

Chart I.3
Partner Violence Reported to the National Crime Victimization Survey

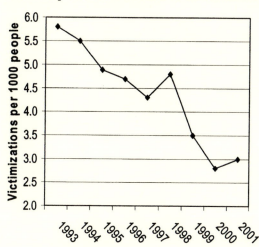

Chart I.4
Trends in Intimate Partner Homicide Victimizations, USA, 1976 to 1998,
data from Rennison & Welchans, 2000, Appendix Table 2

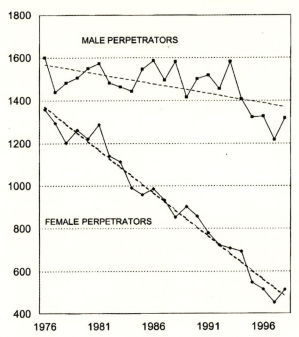

has been decreasing since the late Middle Ages (Eisner, 2001; Elias, 1978; Straus, 2001b). Bit-by-bit, and with many steps backward as well as forward, the world is becoming more civilized. The reduction in violence in and outside of the family is a key part of that social evolution.

Risk Factors for Partner Violence Confirmed by Numerous Studies

In the twenty-five years since the publication of *BCD*, there have been hundreds of studies of risk factors for family violence. These studies have confirmed the factors in our "Risk Factor Index." For example, the chapter on partner violence in the World Health Organization report on Violence and Health

(Krug, Dahlberg, Mercy, Zwi, Lozano, and World Health Organization, 2002), which many regard as the current definitive statement, included the list of risk factors, which follows below. The "+" signs indicate a risk factor reported in *BCD* and also in the WHO report. "NS" indicates factors we did not study. The only differences from the *BCD* and the WHO list are five items that we did not study, and items that are in the *BCD* risk factor list and not in the WHO list.

• Young age	+
• Heavy drinking	+
• Depression	NS
• Personality disorders	NS
• Low academic achievement	NS
• Low income	+
• Witnessing or experiencing violence as a child	+
• Marital conflict	+
• Marital instability	NS
• Male dominance in the family	+
• Economic stress	+
• Poor family functioning	+
• Weak community sanctions against domestic violence	NS
• Poverty	+
• Low social capital	+
• Traditional gender norms	+
• Social norms supportive of violence	+

What Will It Take to End Family Violence?

At several points in *BCD* we emphasized the evidence demonstrating that a major part of the explanation for violence in the family can be found in the effects of the structure of society and in the family as it was in the 1970s. *BCD* provided evidence showing that male dominance and power is related to partner violence within a representative sample of ordinary American families. It was also the first of several studies to demonstrate that the more corporal punishment was experienced as a child, the greater the probability of hitting a partner later in life for both men and women (Straus, 2001a; Straus 2006; in press). There has been progress in reducing these violence-generating aspects of society. Nevertheless, gender inequality still exists, women continue to have less financial power than men in a society where "money talks," and spanking is still the norm in child-rearing (Straus and Stewart, 1999).

BCD uncovered evidence to suggest that the prevention of the risk factors for family violence that are the focus of much public concern and remedial efforts—violence toward women and physical abuse of children—has to go beyond providing interventions for battered women and abused children, and arresting and educating assaulting partners and abusing parents. Although these are important ameliorative steps, which are discussed in the concluding chapter, they will not solve the basic underlying characteristics of the family and of the society that lead to violence and abuse. These are primarily socially created factors. Therefore, they require steps to create a different society and family system. Five of these steps are the focus of the final pages of *BCD*:

- Eliminate the norms that legitimize and glorify violence in society and family.
- Reduce the violence-provoking stressors created by society.
- Integrate families into a network of kin and community.
- Change the sexist character of society and the family.
- Break the "Cycle of Violence" in the family (including, ending the practice of spanking children).

These are not the only steps, however, to achieve primary prevention of family violence, but they remain as important today as they were twenty-five years ago.

There is a painful irony that tempers our pride in having identified the social causes that provide the clues to preventing family violence. Although there are important exceptions, such as the home-visitor program developed by David Olds (Eckenrode, Ganzel, Henderson, Smith, Olds, Powers, Cole, Kitzman, and Sidora, 2000) and the "Safe Dates" program for high school students (Foshee, 2004), almost all the current research on family violence is focused on the treatment or psychopathology of male perpetrators. In addition, despite a torrent of polemics on partner violence by women, there is almost no empirical research on preventative steps needed to address the fact that half of all family violence is initiated by women (Straus, 2005). Research on treatment is crucial. But it does not deal with prevention. Psychopathology is an important risk factor, but probably applies to, at most, 10 per cent of cases of family violence (see, for example, Cavanaugh and Gelles, 2005; Gelles, 1973; Holtzworth-Munroe, 2000). Although *BCD* may have led the way in defining the underlying social causes of family violence, except for the research on gender inequality, few social scientists have followed.

Fortunately, as pointed out when we discussed trends in family violence, the process of social evolution is gradually changing the social causes, and families are becoming less violent. The European Union has taken steps to have all member states that have not yet done so, to make corporal punishment illegal (Council of Europe, 2005). The United Nations and the World Health Organization are working worldwide to enhance the status of women. These are important examples of societal changes that will eventually transform the family from being the most violent institution in which individuals participate. We hope the family will eventually become a safe and nurturing environment for all of its members—women, men, and children alike. We firmly believe this process could be accelerated if more of the efforts of social scientists addressed the social causes of family violence.

Richard J. Gelles   Murray A. Straus
University of Pennsylvania   University of New Hampshire

REFERENCES

Archer, John. 2000. "Sex differences in aggression between heterosexual partners: A meta-analytic review." *Psychological Bulletin* 126:651-680.

Eckenrode, John, Barbara Ganzel, Charles R. Henderson, Elliot Smith, David L. Olds, Jane Powers, Robert Cole, Harriet Kitzman, and Kimberly Sidora. 2000. "Preventing child abuse and neglect with a program of nurse home visitation: The limiting effects of domestic violence." *Journal of American Medical Association* 284:1385-1391.

Eisner, Manuel. 2001. "Modernization, self-control, and lethal violence: the long-term dynamics of European homicide rates in theoretical perspective." *British Journal of Criminology* 41:618-638.

Elias, Norbert. 1978. *The civilizing process*, vol. 1 and 2. Oxford: Oxford University Press.

Feld, S. L. and M. A. Straus. 1989. "Escalation And Desistance Of Wife Assault In Marriage." *Criminology* 27:141-161.

Fiebert, Marin S. and Denise M. Gonzalez. 1997. "College women who initiate assaults on their male partners and the reasons offered for such behavior." *Psychological Reports* 80:583-590.

Fiebert, Martin S. 2004. "References examining assaults by women on their spouses or male partners: an annotated bibliography." *Sexuality and Culture* 8:140-177.

Foshee, V.A. 2004. *Safe Dates: An Adolescent Dating Abuse Prevention Curriculum*. Center City, MN: Halzelden Publishing and Educational Services.

García-Moreno, Claudia, Henrica A.F.M. Jansen, Mary Ellsberg, Lori Heise, Charlotte Watts, and. 2005. *WHO Multi-countryStudy on Women's Health and Domestic Violence against Women Initial results on prevalence, health outcomes and women's responses*. Geneva: World Health Organization.

Gelles, R. 1974. *The violent home: A study of physical aggression between husbands and wives*, Beverly Hills, CA: Sage.

Gelles, Richard J. 1973. "Child abuse as psychopathology: A sociological critique and reformulation." *American Journal of orthopsychiatry* 43:611-621. Also reprinted in Suzanne K. Steinmetz and Murray A. Straus (eds.) *Violence in the Family*. New York: Harper and Row.

Gelles, Richard J. and Murray A. Straus. 1979. "Determinants of Violence in the Family: Towards a Theoretical Integration." Pp. 549-581 in *Contemporary Theories About the Family: Volume 1*, edited by W. R. Burr, F. Rueben Hill, I. Nye, and I. L. Reiss. New York: The Free Press.

Gelles, Richard J. and Murray A. Straus. 1988. *Intimate violence*. New York: Simon and Schuster.

Giles-Sims, Jean. 1983. *Wife battering: A systems theory approach*. New York: Guilford Press.

Holtzworth-Munroe, A. (2000). A typology of men who are violent toward their female partners: Making sense of heterogeneity in husband violence. *Current Direction in Psychological Science*, *9*, 140-143.

Krug, Etienne G., Linda L. Dahlberg, James A. Mercy, Anthony B. Zwi, Rafael Lozano, and World Health Organization. 2002. *World report on violence and health*. Geneva: World Health Organization.

Loftin, Colin and Robert H. Hill. 1974. "Regional subculture and homicide: An examination of the Gastil-Hackney Thesis." *American Sociological Review* 39:714-724.

Medeiros, Rose A. and Murray A. Straus. 2006. "Gender differences in risk factors for physical violence between dating partners by university students." in *Intimate Violence Intervention Study Group meeting.* New York University.

Okun, L. 1986. *Women abuse: Facts replacing myths.* Albany: State University of New York Press,

Rennison, Callie Marie. 2000. "Intimate partner violence." Bureau of Justice Statistics, Washington, DC.

Room, Robin. 1980. "Treatment sampling populations and larger realities." Pp. 205-224 in *Alcoholism treatment and transition,* edited by G. Edwards and M. Grant. London: Croom Helm.

Steinmetz, Suzanne K. and Murray A. Straus. 1974. *Violence in the family.* New York: Harper and Row.

Straus, M. A. 2004. "Cross-cultural reliability and validity of the revised Conflict Tactics Scales: A study of university student dating couples in 17 nations." *Cross-Cultural Research* 38:407-432.

Straus, Murray A. 2006 in press. "The Conflict Tactics Scales." in *Encyclopedia of domestic violence,* edited by N. A. Jackson: Routledge/Taylor and Francis (also available at http://pubpages.unh.edu/~mas2).

Straus, Murray A. 1973. "A General Systems Theory Approach to a Theory of Violence Between Family Members." *Social Science Information* 12:105-125.

—. 1974. "Cultural and Social Organizational Influence on Violence Between Family Members." Pp. 53-69 in *Configurations: Biological and Cultural Factors in Sexuality and Family Life,* edited by R. Prince and D. Barrier. Lexington, MA: Lexington Books/D.C. Health.

—. 1976. "Sexual inequality, cultural norms, and wife-beating." Pp. 543-559 in *Victims and Society,* edited by E. C. Viano. Washington, DC: Visage Press.

—. 1977. "A sociological perspective on the prevention and treatment of wife-beating." in *Battered Women,* edited by M. Roy. New York, New York: Van Nostrand-Reinhold.

—. 1994. "State -to-State differences in social inequality and social bonds in relation to assaults on wives in the United States." *Journal of Comparative Family Studies* 25:7-24.

—. 1999. "The Controversy over Domestic Violence by Women: A Methodological, Theoretical, and Sociology of Science Analysis." Pp. 17-44 in *Violence in Intimate relationships,* edited by X. Arriaga and S. Oskamp. Thousand Oaks, CA: Sage.

—. 2000. "Corporal punishment and primary prevention of physical abuse." *Child Abuse and Neglect* 24:1109-1114.

—. 2001a. *Beating the devil out of them: Corporal punishment in American families and its effects on children, 2nd Edition.* New Brunswick, NJ: Transaction Publishers.

—. 2001b. "Social evolution and corporal punishment." Pp. Chapter 11 in *beating the devil out of them: Corporal punishment in American families and its effects on children, 2nd Edition,* edited by M. A. Straus. New Brunswick, NJ: Transaction Publishers.

—. 2005. "Women's violence toward men is a serious social problem." Pp. 55-77 in *Current controversies on family violence, 2nd Edition,* edited by D. R. Loseke, R. J. Gelles, and M. M. Cavanaugh. Newbury Park, CA: Sage Publications.

—. 2006, In Press. *The primordial violence: Corporal punishment by parents, cognitive development, and crime*. Walnut Creek, CA: Alta Mira Press.

Straus, Murray A. and Richard J. Gelles. 1986. "Societal Change and Change in Family Violence From 1975 to 1985 as Revealed by Two National Surveys." *Journal of Marriage and the Family* 48:465-479.

Straus, Murray A. and Sherry L. Hamby. 1997. "Measuring physical and psychological maltreatment of children with the Conflict Tactics Scales." in *Out of the darkness: Contemporary research perspectives on family violence*, edited by G. Kaufman Kantor and J. Jasinski. Thousand Oaks, CA: Sage.

Straus, Murray A., Sherry L. Hamby, Susan Boney-McCoy, and David B. Sugarman. 1996. "The revised Conflict Tactics Scales (CTS2): Development and preliminary psychometric data." *Journal of Family Issues* 17:283-316.

Straus, Murray A. and Gerald T. Hotaling. 1980. *The social causes of husband-wife violence*. Minneapolis: University of Minnesota Press.

Straus, Murray A. and Glenda Kaufman Kantor. 1995. "Trends in physical abuse by parents from 1975 to 1992: A comparison of three national surveys." in *The Annual Meeting of the American Society of Criminology*. Boston, MA.

Straus, Murray A., Glenda Kaufman Kantor, and David W. Moore. 1997. "Change in cultural norms approving marital violence: From 1968 to 1994." in *Out of the darkness: Contemporary perspectives on family violence*, edited by G. Kaufman Kantor and J. L. Jasinski. Thousand Oaks, CA: Sage Publications.

Straus, Murray A. and Ignacio Luis Ramirez. In press. "Gender symmetry in prevalence, severity, and chronicity of physical aggression against dating partners by University students in Mexico and USA." *Aggressive Behavior*.

Straus, Murray A. and Julie H. Stewart. 1999. "Corporal punishment by American parents: National data on prevalence, chronicity, severity, and duration, in relation to child, and family characteristics." *Clinical Child and Family Psychology Review* 2:55-70. Also as "Prevalence, chronicity, and severity" 2006, In Press, in *Murray A. Straus, The primordial violence: Corporal punishment by parents, cognitive development, and crime*. Walnut Creek, CA: AltaMira Press.

Wolfgang, M.E. and Franco Ferracuti. 1967. *The subculture of violence: Towards an intergrated theory of criminology*. London: Tavistock.

FOREWORD

The eight years since we first started to do research on physical violence in families has seen a radical shift in concern with this aspect of the family. At the beginning of this period almost the only aspect of family violence which commanded attention from either the general public or the scientific community was child abuse. Even in respect to child abuse, there were only two or three books. There was nothing in book form on physical violence between spouses.

The situation today is almost the opposite. There are many books, and even more articles. Just as an example, one of us personally owns twenty-nine different books on child abuse, nine on spouse abuse, and three which cover both child abuse and spouse abuse. It is unfortunate that the latter category is least well represented because we believe that neither child abuse nor spouse abuse can be adequately understood outside of the entire context of violence in the family. Therefore, one of the distinctive contributions of this book is that it focuses on violence in the family as a whole.

What do we mean by "violence in the family as a whole"? It is more than just including materials on both child abuse and spouse abuse between the same covers. To start with, it means carefully considering the relationship between the two. But even that does not truly address the issue of violence in the family as a whole. It leaves out, for example, violence between the children in a family, and violence by children against their parents. It also leaves out what some people call "verbal violence." One can hurt another terribly without lifting a finger. All of these, plus much else, are covered in this book. At times we felt that too much was crammed in; at other times we worried about what was left out. The end result is a compromise which hopefully indicates just how closely physical violence is woven in the fabric of family life, without at the same time burdening the reader with keeping track of so many of the threads that the pattern of the fabric cannot be seen.

This book was written to be understood by the general public. We therefore avoided technical language and kept the number of footnotes and references to a minimum. This also means that we often present the main thrust of things without sidetracking the reader with the qualifications and technical details one finds in scientific journals. From time to time, however, we do bring up some of these limitations, qualifications, alternative interpretations, and methodological details. At other times, the very ambiguity of the findings automatically indicates the tentative state of knowledge about violence in the family. The truth is, that despite all that has been written about the family and about violence, and the lesser but still considerable writings on violence in the family, our understanding of these aspects of human life remains obscure. Perhaps this is because we are all too close to the problems of the family and of violence to think clearly about what is really involved. That has been an obstacle to scientific understanding of human families since the dawn of science. We doubt that it will be rapidly overcome. Hopefully, our report on the experiences of the 2,143 families we studied is a step forward in understanding the nature of the family and especially why the hallmark of family relationships is both love and violence.

ACKNOWLEDGMENTS

This book is part of the Family Violence Research Program at the University of New Hampshire. The program was supported by grants from the National Institute of Mental Health (MH27557, MH13050, and T35 MH15161). A program bibliography and description of current projects are obtainable on request.

Richard Gelles had primary responsibility for Chapters 1, 3, 6, 8, and 10; Murray Straus for Chapters 2, 5, 7, 9, and the Appendixes; and Suzanne Steinmetz for Chapter 4.

The design of the sample, and the 2,143 interviews were done by Response Analysis Corporation of Princeton, New Jersey. It is a pleasure to acknowledge their excellent work in these crucial aspects of the study and especially the contribution of Herbert Abelson and Susan Weisbrod.

Ursula Dibble, David Finkelhor, and Cathy Greenblat each read a draft of the book and made valuable comments which, even though we could not follow all their suggestions, served to improve the book greatly.

We also wish to acknowledge and thank the many other people who made important contributions to the success of the study, including:

Lisa Belmont, Secretary
Sieglinde E. Fizz, Secretary
Shari Hagar, Data Analyst
Eileen Hargreaves, Research Assistant
Peggy Hopkins, Revision and editing of the entire book
Martha Mulligan, Research Assistant
Kersti Yllo, Research Assistant

PART I
The Issues

CHAPTER 1

Violence in the Home

Drive down any street in America. More than one household in six has been the scene of a spouse striking his or her partner last year. Three American households in five (which have children living at home), have reverberated with the sounds of parents hitting their children. Where there is more than one child in the home, three in five are the scenes of violence between siblings. Over all, every other house in America is the scene of family violence at least once a year.

As high as these figures may seem, they are only national averages. Some neighborhoods are actually more violent than this, while other neighborhoods are somewhat less violent. But whatever the case, *every* American neighborhood has violent families.

A NATIONAL SURVEY

These figures come from the first national study of violence in American homes. We have always known that America is a violent society. A war in Vietnam, a riot in Watts, a gangland slaying, a political assassination, or a rape in an alley are all types of violence familiar to Americans. What is new and surprising is that the American family and the American home are perhaps as or more violent than any other single American institution or setting (with the exception of the military, and only then in time of war). Americans run the greatest risk of assault, physical injury, and even murder in their own homes by members of their own families.

Across the country this is borne out by official crime statistics. Tales of battered babies and beaten wives are widespread enough to be identified as "child abuse" and "wife abuse." And the estimated 2 million women and children battered and beaten by family members each year are only the tip of the iceberg identified as "violence between family members."

Brothers and sisters beat, stab, and shoot each other. There are husbands who are struck and beaten by their wives, and even grandparents are battered by their own children. Violence in one generation affects and encourages violence in another generation. In many families, perhaps a majority of violent families, violence is not even considered taboo or wrong. Rather, it is an accepted and integral part of the way the family functions.

Child abuse reporting laws, research, and efforts of the feminist movement have brought on a new awareness of the high level of aggression in the modern family. But there has never been a systematic study of violence based on a representative sample of even a single state or city, much less one that is representative of the whole country.

This book reports the results of the first comprehensive national study of violence in the American family. Our purpose is to answer some fundamental and important questions about family violence.

Our first goal was to measure the extent of violence in the American family. Knowledge concerning how much violence exists, what kinds of families are violent, and what causes violence has been difficult to come by since most of the research to date is based on small, unrepresentative samples from limited geographic areas. Consequently, even the question "What proportion of American families are violent?" could not be answered with any degree of certainty.

A second goal of this study was to uncover the breadth of family violence. Wife abuse and child abuse have captured public attention because of the terms themselves and because they involve terribly violent acts with damaging consequences for the victim. However, "abuse" is only one extreme end of the continuum of violence. There are many other forms and consequences of violence in the family, which, for many reasons, never are publicly identified as "abuse." Our aim was to study a variety of forms of violence, including some which many people do not consider violent, such as spanking a child. We are concerned with the proportion of families who shoot and stab each other, as well as those who spank and shove, because we think that one cannot be understood without considering the other.

A third goal was to find out what violence meant to the participants. Is family violence uniformly condemned and viewed as wrong, or are there instances and families where violence is a normal part of family relationships? Additionally, we wanted to learn about what kinds of families were violent, and which families were not. Much of the early thinking on child and wife abuse ascribed the abuse to psychological problems of the abuser. However, further analysis of abusers and abusive families indicates that psychological factors are not sufficient explanations of the violence. Studies of child abuse and wife abuse have yielded information which indicates certain types of *families* are abuse-prone.

Finally, once we determined which families were violent, our goal was to assess what caused violence to take place. Obviously, if we ever want to reduce the human toll of family violence, including child and wife abuse, we must understand what causes violence to occur in the first place. Thus, while the study and this book are not intended to produce solutions for preventing family violence, we intend to point the way to these solutions by identifying some of the generative sources of violence between family members.

IS FAMILY VIOLENCE INCREASING?

If one were to rely on newspaper and television accounts of the battering of children and wives, and if one were to examine official reports of child abuse and wife abuse over the past ten years, one reasonable conclusion would be that families have suddenly turned violent and this violence is increasing at a massive rate. Are families more violent now than they were in 1950, 1850, 1750? Have the changes which have occurred in the society and in the composition of the average family produced a generation of violent parents and violent spouses? Is the family in danger of being destroyed by its members' unbridled violent tendencies?

These are some of the frequently asked and most important questions, which unfortunately, we still cannot answer with any certainty. There is no real way of knowng whether families have become more violent in the last decade or the last century. One reason for our uncertainty is there had been no systematic study of violence in American families until the one we report on in this book; thus, we have no data or statistics to compare with our current report.

One could use official police, hospital, and social agency statistics to assess changes in the extent of child abuse and wife abuse, but for several reasons these statistics are not suitable for estimating actual levels of violence in the family. First, official statistics compile only the cases of family violence that come to public attention. These are probably only a fraction of the total cases of family violence.

Second, official statistics are compiled by organizations and individuals who work in those organizations. These individuals and the units they work in are often influenced by publicity campaigns, public pressure, political pressure, and changes in state and federal law. It was not until 1968 that all fifty states had laws mandating reports of child abuse. Thus, official statistics compiled by the states before 1968 reflect differences in official legal attitudes toward child abuse and not the true level of abuse in each of the states. Even today, official statistics vary because each state and each compiler of the statistics in state and local agencies draw on different definitions of child abuse and child neglect. In the area of spouse abuse, few if any agencies have ever bothered to compile statistics on how many wives or husbands batter one another.

Although we cannot say definitely whether violence in the American family is on the increase, historical facts argue that family violence certainly is not new and that, probably, we are no more violent and perhaps a little less violent toward our own families than were our ancestors.

Violence Toward Children

Although parents' use of violence on children certainly is not new, the addition of the term "child abuse" to our vocabulary has come about only recently. Child abuse typically refers to acts committed by parents on their children which other members of the society view as inappropriate and harmful. Thus, child abuse depends on historically and culturally relative judgments for its meaning.

The historical record demonstrates a use of extensive and often lethal forms of violence by parents. Those who have examined the history of child abuse, such as David Bakan (1971), Samuel Radbill (1974), Eli Newberger et. al. (1977), and Lloyd De Mause (1974, 1975), document a history of violence and infanticide dating back to biblical times. The Bible itself chronicles parental violence beginning when Abraham nearly killed his son as a sacrifice. Jesus's birth coincides with Herod's "Slaughter of the Innocents." The dictum "spare the rod and spoil the child" was stated and supported in the Bible (Radbill, 1974). Infanticide, mutilation, and other forms of violence were legal parental prerogatives from ancient Rome to colonial America. Children were hit with birch rods, switches, and canes. They were whipped, castrated, and destroyed by parents, most often with the consent and mandate of the ruling religious and political forces in the society.

The history of violence toward children in America dates back to the arrival of the Puritans. Laws threatening death to the unruly hung over the children's heads, and parents supported their right to whip and punish with biblical quotations.

Religious ideology dictated that all children were born corrupted by original sin and required salvation by their parents. To "beat the devil" out of a child was not just a passing phrase for the Puritans. It was a mandate to provide salvation for their children through physical punishment.

Thus, historically we have a tradition of physical (and emotional) cruelty to children. As a society we have justified this cruelty through religious dogma, or by maintaining it is in the child's best interests. This societal mandate and tolerance of physical violence toward children may have been one factor which delayed the identification of child abuse as an important social problem.

The Society for the Prevention of Cruelty to Animals was established before a Society for the Prevention of Cruelty to Children. When New York church workers, in 1874, tried to get help for a badly abused foster child, Mary Ellen, they found they could only turn to the Society for the Prevention of Cruelty to Animals. And so, they founded the first chapter for a similar society for children (Ross, 1977).

Child abuse may have been identified as a social problem by concerned church workers, social workers, and private citizens in the nineteenth century, but it took almost 100 years after the case of Mary Ellen for violence toward children to be considered a major national social problem. In 1946, through the use of diagnostic X-ray technology, physicians began to notice patterns of healed fractures in young children that could only have resulted from repeated blows from their caretakers (Caffey, 1946).

While pediatric radiologists were able to diagnose child abuse, it was not until C. Henry Kempe and his associates published their classic work on "The Battered Child Syndrome" in the *Journal of the American Medical Association* in 1962 that battering and abuse became a focal point of public attention.

In 1968, it was estimated that more children under the age of five died from parentally inflicted injuries than from tuberculosis, whooping cough, polio, measles, diabetes, rheumatic fever, and appendicitis combined (*Newsweek*, Vol. 71 June 3, 1968).

By the end of the 1960s, all fifty states had passed and instituted laws mandating the reporting of child abuse and neglect and had begun to take steps at least to treat abused children and their families. In 1974, the federal government established the National Center on Child Abuse and Neglect in an attempt to provide a mechanism to increase knowledge about the causes of child abuse and neglect and identify steps that could be taken to prevent and treat abuse.

Thus, while Americans have probably abused their children since the first families established residence in the colonies, serious attention to the issue of abuse has only been achieved in the last twenty years. The public still asks: How many children are abused each year? What causes people to abuse their children? What can we do to prevent abuse? And most experts still shake their heads and admit they really do not know.

Violence Toward Women

As with child abuse and violence toward children, there is no evidence which can be used to estimate the incidence of "wife abuse" in America over the last 300 years. However, there are historical and legal data available which demonstrate that women have been subjected to brutal and often lethal forms of violence in their own homes. Del Martin (1976) and Terry Davidson (1978) have reviewed the history of wife abuse and report that wives in America have been raped, choked, stabbed, shot, beaten, had their jaws and limbs broken, and have been struck with horse whips, pokers, bats, and bicycle chains.

Laws and legal precedents sanctioned, to a degree, the right of a husband to use violence on his wife. The classic "rule of thumb" gave legal justification to common law that sanctioned a husband's striking his wife with a switch, provided the stick was no wider than his thumb (Calvert, 1974).

While legal records indicate that courts attended to the problems of many abused wives, wife abuse as a social problem did not receive national attention until the mid-1970s.

Since 1975, a number of American women charged with murdering their husbands have been acquitted in landmark decisions on grounds of self-defense or temporary insanity after claiming they had long been abused and battered wives.

Among these decisions is that of Francine Hughes, a Michigan woman who poured gasoline under the bed of her sleeping husband and set it ablaze, killing her husband, and destroying her home. She claimed, and the jury agreed, she had suffered temporary insanity after years of abuse.

A California woman who pumped five bullets into her husband was acquitted of murder after citing past beatings in her plea of self-defense.

And an American-Indian woman, seven months pregnant, when attacked by her husband with a broken broomstick, was acquitted of stabbing him to death, on grounds of self-defense (Boston *Globe*, December 6, 1977).

Recognition of wife abuse as a problematic aspect of family behavior was probably a consequence of two forces. The women's movement has done much to bring the issue of wife abuse into focus. Wife abuse emerged as a problem among groups of women who began to come together to discuss women's issues in the late 1960s. It was almost an "accident" that women discovered the common problem of violence in their families. This "accidental" issue swelled as more and more women, who had believed that they were the only ones being beaten and that they "deserved" or precipitated their own victimization, discovered that there were many others with similar experiences and feelings.

While the topic of wife abuse gained attention in the United States, an experiment in England establishing a center for neighborhood women to come and meet one another led to the creation of the first "shelter" or "safe house" for abused wives. Erin Pizzey, the founder of the women's center, and ultimately the founder of the world's first battered wife refuge, authored the book *Scream Quietly or the Neighbors Will Hear* (1974). She took the case to the British people in an attempt to obtain better services for the unexpected number of abused wives who came to her refuge. The political drive which Pizzey initiated in Great Britain coincided with the National Organization of Women's (NOW) decision to make battered wives a priority issue in the United States. In 1976, women's groups across the country began a political effort to establish better social services for battered wives and to force changes in legal statutes which denied women adequate legal redress from being beaten by their husbands.

By 1980, the issue of battered wives has reached the stage the child abuse issue was at in 1968: laws are being written and rewritten, and experiments with prevention and treatment programs are being initiated. However, as with child abuse, information on how many wives are abused, what causes them to be abused, and what can be done to protect and treat victims is still thin and inadequate.

Other Family Violence

As a result of political and social action, violence toward women and children, the traditional underdogs in family life, has now been termed a social problem of high priority. This should not, however, be taken to mean that there are no other types of family violence. In fact, the first biblical reference to violence was Cain killing Abel. Sibling violence may be so common in families that we fail to recognize it as violence. We do, however, have research which bears out the claim that sibling violence is extremely common. Steinmetz's study of fifty-seven randomly selected families in Delaware found that 70 per cent of the young families (average age of the children under eight years) had siblings engaging in violent fights. The lowest level of sibling violence was in the homes where the children were in their teens, and even here, nearly two of every three families had siblings using violence on one another (1977c).

Similarly, while wife abuse has captured our attention, this does not mean that husbands are not "abused." In fact, when we appear on television and radio discussing the "problem" of wife abuse, we frequently receive telephone calls from men who explain that they are victims of "husband abuse" and ask for equal time from researchers. One such caller pleaded that battered husbands fare far worse than battered wives because they do not have "men's groups" and a National Organization of Men to argue their cause. The homicide data bear out the claim that many husbands are slain by their wives—the most lethal room in the house for men is the kitchen (Wolfgang, 1958).

It is important that we should not be misdirected by "the politics of social problems," which focus attention on issues such as wife abuse and child abuse. These are indeed of major concern. But the larger problem we are facing is not one of a single class of people, sex, or age group in the family being the most victimized. As the historical data show, and as the statistics we review in the following section bear out, the problem is one of *family violence*. Fathers and mothers hitting children, children hitting one another, and spouses physically battling each other are all part of the same topic—violence in the American family.

THE VIOLENT HOME

This book documents, for the first time, the extent of violence in the American family. But even before this study, we had concluded from the available evidence that violence between family members is probably as common as love. Although the evidence is far from adequate, it persuasively argues that we live in violent homes.

Physical Punishment

The most widespread and best-documented form of violence is also the most controversially defined as "violent." Physical punishment is used by 84 to 97 per cent of all parents at some time in their child's life, according to various studies in the United States and Great Britain (Blumberg, 1964; Bronfenbrenner, 1958; Erlanger, 1974; Stark and Mc Evoy, 1970). These studies do not attempt to describe these events as violent, nor do they provide age-specific rates of the behavior. They do, however, illustrate that the individuals most likely to be struck in the family are typically the smallest, weakest members.

The violence, or physical punishment, does not end when the child begins to walk and talk. Four different studies of college and university students found that half of the parents of the students had used or threatened to use physical punishment on their children while the students were seniors in high school (Straus, 1971; Steinmetz, 1971, 1974a; Mulligan, 1977). The most recent of these studies reported that nearly 8 per cent of the students surveyed said that they had been physically injured by their parents during the last year they lived at home before entering college (Mulligan, 1977).

Child Abuse

Various techniques have been used in attempts to achieve an accurate estimate of child abuse in America. In 1967, David Gil conducted a nation-wide inventory of reported cases of child abuse. He found six thousand confirmed cases of child abuse. This is considered an extremely low estimate because it is based on reported cases only and the survey was conducted before all states had legally required reporting of abused children. His report also gives the results of an opinion survey which asked a representative sample of 1,520 individuals if they had knowledge of families where incidents of child abuse had occurred. Forty-five individuals, or 3 per cent of the sample, reported knowledge of forty-eight different incidents of abuse. Extrapolating this number to a national population of 110 million adults, Gil estimated that between 2.53 and 4.07 million children were abused the previous year, or between 13.3 and 21.4 incidents per 1,000 persons in the United States. Gil's data were analyzed by Richard Light to correct for instances where the same abuse incidents were known by more than one person. Light's refined estimate of child abuse was 500,000 abused children in the United States during the survey year—1965 (Light, 1973).

Numerous other investigators have tried estimating how many children are physically abused by their parents. Nagi surveyed community agencies who have contact with abused children. He estimated that 167,000 cases of abuse are reported annually while an additional 91,000 cases go unreported (1975). Vincent DeFrancis of the American Humane (Association) testifying before the United States Senate in 1973 projected 30,000 to 40,000 truly abused children in America each year. Vincent Fontana placed the figure as high as 1.5 million children (1973).

Because it is difficult to define what child abuse is, and because many cases of child abuse go unrecognized and unreported, it is impossible to say what the true population of abused children actually is. As Cohen and Sussman concluded when they attempted to estimate the incidence of child abuse:

> "the only conclusion which can be made fairly is that information indicating the incidence of child abuse in the United States simply does not exist (1975, p. 14).

We do not even know how many children are killed by parents and caretakers each year. Such cases are often hard to prove and many physicians and medical examiners are reluctant to get involved by suggesting foul play. One New Hampshire pediatrician, describing a case in which he suspected a child might have been battered to death, had this to say:

> "That youngster was brought into the hospital dead. It was decided there would be no investigation and the official story was that the child fell. The medical referee at that time was sufficiently satisfied with his own opinion of what happened. I think he just didn't want to spend the county's money for an autopsy" (*Foster's Daily Democrat*, Dover, N.H., March 30, 1977).

And so the matter was dropped.

Statistics vary from low estimates of a child killed each day (*Pediatric News*, 1975) to five thousand deaths each year (U. S. Senate, 1973).

Whatever the actual statistics are, and we may never know, it is evident from the projections about injury and death that violence toward children is a leading cause of injury, disablement, and death among America's children.

Murder

Murder is the one aspect of intrafamily violence on which there are reasonable data. Steinmetz and Straus (1974) suggested that this is because it is a crime which leaves physical evidence which cannot be ignored in the same way that we can overlook other forms of intrafamily violence. A graphic indicator of the extent of intrafamily homicide can be gleaned from the fact that each year about as many people are murdered by relatives in New York City as have been killed in all the disturbances in Northern Ireland from 1969 to date. Although deaths in Northern Ireland made national headlines, intrafamily murder in New York City barely rates a ten-line item on the inside pages of the New York *Times*. This illustrates how we overlook the fact that the family is a major institution of violence in our society.

Other data point to the same deadly pattern in families. In Atlanta, 31 per cent of the 255 homicides in 1972 were the result of domestic quarrels (Boston *Globe*, February 6, 1973, p. 12). Atlanta is typical of the nation at large as well as numerous other countries of the world (Curtis, 1974). Paul Bohannan's research in Africa uncovered ranges varying from 22 to 63 per cent intrafamilial homicides (1960). The highest rate in his world-wide sampling came from Denmark, where two out of every three murders are intrafamily. Bell and Benjamin's data on Canada report that from 1961 to 1974 39 per cent of all murders were within families (1977).

Assault

Data on assault are more difficult to interpret because family members rarely file charges against one another. However, indirect data on the extent of physical assault in families provide yet more evidence to support the claim that the family is society's pre-eminent violent institution. One legal researcher (Parnas, 1967) estimates that police answer more calls involving family conflicts than all calls for criminal incidents combined—including murders, rapes, robberies, non-family assaults, and muggings. In fact, more police officers die answering family disturbance calls (22 per cent of all police fatalities) than die answering any other single type of call (Parnas, 1967).

Said one New York City patrolman, shot through the ribs while breaking up a fight between a father and his sons, "Family quarrels . . . at least with a robbery you're prepared. But walk into somebody's house—man you don't know what you're in for. . . . The worst thing you can do is take sides, even if one party is dead wrong. You don't help by screaming. You can't solve their problems. You just try to calm them down. If you don't get another complaint that night, you figure you did your job" (New York *Times,* January 26, 1973, p. 37).

Aggravated assaults between husbands and wives made up 11 per cent of all reported aggravated assaults in St. Louis (Pittman and Handy, 1964), and 52 per cent in Detroit (Boudouris, 1971).

These figures almost certainly underestimate the true level of domestic assaults between husbands and wives due to the fact that many wives (and husbands) do not see being hit or even being beaten up by a mate as a case of legal assault. Even if they do, and call the police, most police officers discourage family members from filing assault charges. "Of every hundred altercations that we get, 99 per cent don't prosecute anyway," said one Michigan official. "Arrest just makes more paperwork for us" (Gingold, 1976).

Applicants for Divorce

Studies of couples in the process of obtaining a divorce also bear witness to the violent American family. Levinger (1966) interviewed couples on their reasons for divorce and found 22 per cent of the middle class and 40 per cent of the working class couples discussed "physical abuse" as a major complaint. O'Brien reported that 17 per cent of the couples he interviewed spontaneously mentioned violent behavior in their marriage (1971).

Other Research on Family Violence

The closest thing to data on a cross section of the population can be found in a survey conducted for the U. S. National Commission on the Causes and Prevention of Violence which deals with approval of violence (Stark and Mc Evoy, 1970). One out of four men in this survey, and one out of six women, approve of a husband slapping a wife under certain conditions. As for a wife slapping a husband, 26 per cent of the men and 19 per cent of the women approved. Of course, some people who approve of slapping will never do it and some who disapprove *will* slap—or worse. Probably the latter group is larger. If so, we know that husband-wife violence at this minimal level occurs in at least one quarter of American families.

Finally, our own pilot studies give some indication of the frequency of violence in the family. The first of these pilot studies (Gelles, 1974) is based on in-depth interviews with eighty families. This revealed that 54 per cent of the couples had used physical force on each other at some time. However, since this study is based on a small non-random sample of small-town New Hampshire families, the representativeness of the data is unknown.

Generalizations from the second group of exploratory studies are limited by the fact that they are studies of the families of university students (Steinmetz, 1974a; Straus, 1974a, b). These students responded to a series of questions about conflicts which occurred in their families during their senior year in high school, and to further questions about how these conflicts were dealt with. Included in the conflict resolution section were questions on whether or not the parties to the disputes had ever hit, pushed, shoved, or thrown things at each other in the course of one of the disputes.

The results show that during that one year 16 per cent of the students knew at least one situation where parents had used physical force on each other. These are figures for incidents known to the child, and only for a single year. The percentage who used violence in that year or had used violence is probably much greater. How much greater is difficult to estimate.

A third study, which did employ a probability sampling technique, is limited by the fact that it investigated only families in one community in Delaware. The research found that 12 per cent of those surveyed reported hitting a spouse with a hard object, while 22 per cent of the couples reported that one partner had hit another with his or her hand during the course of the marriage. Furthermore, more than 60 per cent of the couples reported at least one act of violence in their marriage (Steinmetz, 1977a).

The figures just presented should make clear the basis for asserting that violence between family members is by far the most common type of violence a typical person is likely to experience. But even accepting the correctness of this assertion, the limitations of the studies on which it is based do not allow us to know exactly how frequently each type of violence occurs in the typical American family.

Each of the studies we reviewed has major limitations. For example, divorced couples may well differ from other couples in their use of violence; reports of whether "physical abuse" was one of the reasons for divorce may not adequately describe the extent to which husband-wife violence occurs; and university students are not likely to know about all such fights between their parents. Also, their parents are probably not representative of the general population, especially the lower socioeconomic status groups. Finally, studies limited to one geographic area may not accurately reflect nation-wide patterns of family violence.

All of these limitations suggest the need for data on a representative sample of the population—especially data obtained by methods that minimize the problems of measurement just noted. Getting this more accurate and representative data was one of the reasons for our study.

STUDYING FAMILY VIOLENCE

It is one thing to state that there is a need to study violence in the home, it is quite another thing actually to conduct such a study. In order to learn how much violence is occurring in the American family, what families are violent, and why they are violent, we first had to define violence. And this proved difficult indeed.

What We Mean by "Violence"

One of the earliest and stickiest problems in proceeding with a study of family violence was to develop a useful, clear, and acceptable definition of "violence." No matter what definition we opted for there seemed to be hundreds of reasons for not using the definition.

At first we had hoped to distinguish "force" from "violence" by viewing the former as "acceptable hitting," and the latter as "unacceptable hitting." This would have allowed us to separate such things as slaps and spankings from forms of hitting which leave the victim vulnerable to severe physical injury. The distinction proved unworkable. Pilot studies of family violence showed that it was impossible to determine if the hitting was "acceptable" or "unacceptable." Whose definition of "acceptable" would we use—our own, the victim's, the offender's, the police's, the community's? We found that almost any kind of hitting could be considered acceptable by the hitter—some husbands and fathers were quite adamant that a punch in the mouth was an appropriate way to calm a wife or child. On the other hand, some families indicated that a spanking was outside the normal boundaries of legitimate behavior.

Ultimately, we chose to focus on two types of family violence. The first was "normal violence" while the second we called "abusive violence."

Normal Violence. Normal violence was defined as an "act carried out with the intention, or perceived intention, of causing physical pain or injury to another person." The "physical pain" can range from slight pain, as in a slap, to murder. The basis for the "intent to hurt" may range from a concern with a child's safety (as when a child is spanked for running into the street) to hostility so intense that the death of the other is desired.

Obviously, this definition is not going to be satisfactory to everyone (perhaps a majority of the readers of this book will disagree with at least part of the definition). The strongest disagreement will probably come from those who believe that slaps and spankings are not violent. While this book was being written we received letters from people who, having read about our work, argued that spanking a child is not violent because it is for the child's own good. Many people backed up their arguments for spanking with quotations from the Bible, which they felt sanctioned and even mandated the use of physical punishment.

The taken-for-granted utility of spankings and slappings of children is a deeply rooted part of many parents' child rearing repertoire. For instance, one parent explained:

> ". . . my little one would be dead by now if I hadn't spanked him and let him know he shouldn't drink or eat certain things . . . before he realized what no meant he had to learn what no meant . . . if I hadn't disciplined his temper and crying, it would have had him out of control and like a crazy person."

Because there is likely to be a great deal of disagreement over what is and is not "violent," we could have opted for another term, such as "aggression" or "physical aggression" to use in conjunction with our definition. In the end, we chose to use the word "violence" and to employ a broad definition that includes acts which are not normally thought to be violent because we wanted to draw attention to the issue of people hitting one another in their own families. We call this hitting "violence" because we would like to have people begin to question the acts which traditionally they have taken for granted as necessary, useful, inevitable, or instinctive.

Abusive Violence. The second type of violence we examined in our study, and which we will discuss in this book, is "abusive violence." We defined this type of violence as "an act which has the high potential for injuring the person being hit." Included as part of the working definition of the term "abusive violence" were acts where people punched, kicked, or bit a family member, hit the person with a hard object, "beat up" another person, or shot, or tried to shoot, stabbed, or tried to stab, another family member.

The controversial aspect of this definition of violence is that it does not take into consideration what actually happened to the person. In other words, an act where a person was punched but not hurt and an act where someone was punched and received a fractured jaw are both considered "abusive violence." Many people may argue that these certainly are not the same things, and that the former act is not abuse. We counter by saying that the things which differentiate the former from the latter, or which influence whether someone who is punched is injured or not, are typically random phenomena such as aim or luck. The research on the difference between an assault and a homicide tends to bear out our position by arguing that a random phenomenon such as aim often determines if a violent act ends up as a non-lethal assault or a homicide (Pittman and Handy, 1964; Pokony, 1965).

One caveat: Random events are not the only things which influence whether someone is injured. The physical size and strength of the attacker also play a major role in determining if the victim is injured. This is obvious when one considers husband to wife as opposed to wife to husband violence. A six-foot, two-hundred-and-forty-pound man punching his five-foot, ninety-seven-pound wife is probably going to do more harm than if she punches him. This will come up again in the next chapter when we examine violence between spouses.

The Study

Any social scientist who attempts to examine a sensitive topic of long-standing taboos—such as sexual behavior, drug usage, homosexuality, suicide—confronts three major hurdles which must be cleared if the research is to be successful.

First, the researcher has to find the people involved in the behavior or phenomenon in question. Second, once they are located, the researcher needs to get them to talk about the taboo topic. Finally, even if one can get people to talk, the investigator needs to satisfy himself and the consumers of the research that the truth was told.

In numerous studies of taboo topics, investigators have cleared all three hurdles. The classic study was Kinsey and his associates' examination of sexual behavior (1948). Since the famous Kinsey study, other researchers have gone on to do more detailed investigations, such as those of Masters and Johnson and the recent *Hite Report* on female sexuality. Others have been able to examine homosexuality (Laud Humphreys' book *Tearoom Trade*, 1970), organized crime (Francis Ianni's study *A Family Business*, 1972), and other types of deviant and illegal behavior.

Our problem in studying family violence was that we faced the not so enjoyable task of asking people questions which amounted to "have you stopped beating your wife?" We knew that it would be difficult to get people to talk about their family lives. The fact that the family is the most private and intimate institution in our society means that it is often difficult to study family behavior accurately.

Prior to beginning the plan for the research reported in this book, we had conducted a number of studies of family violence employing a variety of techniques. These studies were all done using limited populations in limited geographic areas, but they convinced us that it was possible to get people to talk about and report family violence. Straus and Steinmetz found that college students could and would accurately report on violence in their family. Gelles not only encountered people willing to talk about violence, he also found it difficult to get them to stop talking about violence once they began. Steinmetz discovered that family members were able to record detailed accounts of their violent conflicts and that these reports were consistent with information obtained during the interview and from questionnaires completed by parents and their children. Although these studies indicated that underreporting of violence would be a problem, they all pointed to the need for, and the feasibility of, a national sample survey on violence in the family.

The Families Studied

Our goal was to select families which were representative of the approximately 46 million American families in the United States in 1976. The "Response Analysis National Probability Sample" was used to locate potential families to be interviewed. The procedure is described in Appendix A.

Eligibility. For the purposes of our study we chose to interview one adult member of each of the families we selected (individuals between eighteen to sixty-five years of age). Our definition of "family" was any couple who indicated that they were married or living together as a couple. A formal marriage license was not considered a criterion. We attempted to conduct an equal number of interviews with adult males and females. The final sample yielded 2,143 completed interviews. Interviews were conducted with 960 men and 1,183 women. Of the 2,143 families studied, 1,146 had children between the ages of three and seventeen living at home.

Representativeness of the Families. The technique which was employed to select families for the study is regularly used by social scientists in national studies of public opinion, attitudes, and behavior. The same sampling procedure has been employed to assess preference for candidates for the presidency of the United States, consumer behavior, and public opinion. In the three decades that "area" or "cluster" sampling has been used, the technique has been refined to the point of yielding quite accurate samples of the national population. The characteristics of this sample of 2,143 families (such as per cent with children living at home, per cent living in urban areas, age distribution of children) are very similar to the census data for the population of the United States.

Drawbacks of the Sample. As a national probability sample, our 2,143 families were an adequate group to interview and then generalize to families in the United States. There were, however, some drawbacks to this particular sample. The most important disadvantage is that it is a sample of intact families. Because we wanted to study spousal violence, we needed to select families where both husband and wife lived together. Thus, we have no information on the levels or causes of violence in single-parent families. Since many experts on child abuse believe that single-parent families are more prone to use violence, this is an unfortunate drawback to our sample and one which might result in an underestimate of the level of parents' use of violence in our society.

A second drawback is that we did not include in our study parent-child relations with children under the age of three. Research and common sense tell us that children under three years of age present constant and unique stress for their parents and, in many ways, are likely to be frequent targets of parental hostility, aggression, and violence.

Another aspect of the sample which needs to be discussed is the completion rate. Interviews were completed with nearly two thirds (65 per cent) of individual family members identified and approached as eligible for this study. This completion rate is somewhat lower than we hoped for despite the fact that a great effort was made to interview every eligible family. Our interviewers made up to four visits to each household, we wrote each family letters, and offered monetary incentives. Given the topic of this study, a two-thirds completion rate is a remarkable achievement. But it also means that we know nothing about the family life and level of violence in the 35 per cent of the potential sample we could not talk to. Perhaps non-respondents are more violent than people who completed interviews, perhaps they are less violent. Ultimately, we cannot know for sure what went on in families who would not talk to an interviewer or who could not be reached by an interviewer.

Measuring Violence

We measured the level and incidence of violence in American families by using a series of questions called the "Conflict Tactics Scales" (CTS). The CTS were first developed at the University of New Hampshire in 1971 and they have been used and modified over the next five years in numerous studies of family violence in the United States and in other countries such as Canada, Israel, Japan, Finland, Great Britain, and British Honduras.

The Conflict Tactics Scales (see Appendix B for the questions) are designed to measure violence in the family by asking about the means used to resolve conflicts of interest among family members. The people interviewed were to consider the various ways in which they resolved conflicts between themselves and their spouses, children, or how the children resolved conflicts among themselves.

The eighteen items in the Scales can be grouped into three distinct methods of resolving conflicts: (1) the use of rational discussion and argument; (2) the use of verbal and non-verbal expressions of hostility—for example insults or acts which symbolically hurt other family members such as smashing or kicking an object; and (3) the use of physical force or violence. Of the eighteen items in the Scales, eight involve the use of force and violence. The eight violence questions range from pushing or shoving someone to the use of potentially lethal weapons such as guns or knives.

We asked subjects to consider two time frames in which conflicts occurred. First, we asked them to consider conflicts which took place in the previous twelve months. Then we asked them to think back over the duration of the marriage or the lifetime of their children. Thus, we are able to report on violence for the previous twelve months—which, because we interviewed our subjects from January to April 1976 can be thought of as 1975. There is also information on what kinds of violence occurred over the entire marriage or the duration of the parent-child relationship.

How Reliable and Valid Are These Scales? We examined this problem for five years while the questions were developed and modified. The Scales have been employed in eight different studies in which over 1,000 college students provided data on themselves and their parents. The results provide evidence that the questions produce consistent reports of violence in the home. In addition, the results of these pilot studies indicate that the Scales are valid, in that the results agree with findings from research on violence and aggression done by other researchers. Additional information on validity and reliability is given in a technical paper (Straus, 1979).

A main advantage of the Conflict Tactics Scales is that the order in which the questions are asked increases the likelihood of the interviewer establishing rapport with the subject. The force and violence items come at the end of the list. Presumably, this enhances the likelihood that subjects will become committed to the interview and continue answering questions. When we analyzed the responses to the items as the questions moved from the least to most aggressive acts (and by inference from the least to the most sensitive questions), we found no noticeable drop in the completion rate. People did not systematically resist answering the violence questions.

Two disadvantages of the Scales are: (1) they focus on conflict situations and do not allow us to measure the use of violence in non-conflict-of-interest situations. (2) The items deal with acts only. We have no idea of what the consequences of those acts were. Thus, there is only a limited basis on which to project rates of child and spouse abuse, since these acts are normally considered acts where some harm is done to the victim. While we may learn that a family member kicked or used a gun or a knife on another, and we can presume that this in and of itself had negative consequences for the victim even if he or she was not injured, we do not know what the actual consequences were.

Despite the drawbacks and disadvantages of some of our samplings, Scales, and definitions, the facts of violence and aggression remain. The acts of violence, from hitting to threats with a lethal weapon, which parents, siblings, and spouses maintain as necessary with each other, would be considered chargeable assault if administered outside the family.

We will see this time and time again in the following chapters. Our methods therefore seem to have been effective in securing the information needed to study violence in a representative sample of American families.

PART II

The Violent Family

CHAPTER 2

The Marriage License as a Hitting License

Wife-beating is found in every class, at every income level. The wife of the president of a midwestern state university recently asked one of us what she could do about the beatings without putting her husband's career in danger. Japan's former Prime Minister Sato, a winner of the Nobel Peace Prize, was accused publicly by his wife of many beatings in their early married life. Ingeborg Dedichen, a former mistress of Aristotle Onassis, describes his beating her till he was forced to quit from exhaustion. "It is what every Greek husband does, it's good for the wife," he told her.

What is at the root of such violent attacks? Proverbs such as "A man's home is his castle," go a long way in giving insights into human nature and society. The home belongs to the man. It is the woman who finds herself homeless if she refuses further abuse.

The image of the "castle" implies freedom from interference from outsiders. What goes on within the walls of the castle is shielded from prying eyes. And a modern home, like a medieval castle, can contain its own brand of torture chamber. Take the case of Carol, a Boston woman who called the police to complain that her husband had beaten her and then pushed her down the stairs. The policeman on duty answered, "Listen, lady, he pays the bills, doesn't he? What he does inside of his own house is his business" (*The Real Paper*, February 11, 1976).

The evidence we documented in Chapter 1 suggested that, aside from war and riots, physical violence occurs between family members more often than it occurs between any other individuals. At the same time we also pointed out the limitations of the data. In particular, no research up to now gives information on how often each of the different forms of family violence occurs in a representative sample of American families.

THE OVER-ALL LEVEL
OF HUSBAND-WIFE VIOLENCE

Violence Rates. A first approach to getting a picture of the amount of violence between the 2,143 husbands and wives in this study is to find out how many had engaged in any of the eight violent acts we asked about. For the year we studied this works out to be 16 per cent. In other words, every year about one out of every six couples in the United States commits at least one violent act against his or her partner.

If the period considered is the entire length of the marriage (rather than just the previous year), the result is 28 per cent, or between one out of four and one out of three American couples. In short, if you are married, the chances are almost one out of three that your husband or wife will hit you.

When we began our study of violence in the family, we would have considered such a rate of husbands and wives hitting each other very high. In terms of our values—and probably the values of most other Americans—it is still very high. But in terms of what we have come to expect on the basis of the pilot studies, this is a low figure. *It is very likely a substantial underestimate.*

Later in this chapter we will give the reasons for thinking it is an underestimate. But for now, let us examine the violent acts one by one. This is important if we are to get a realistic picture of the meaning of the over-all rate of 28 per cent. One needs to know how much of the violence was slaps and how much was kicking and beating up. This information is given in Chart 1.

CHART 1
Rate at Which Violent Acts Occcurred in the Previous Year and Ever in the Marriage

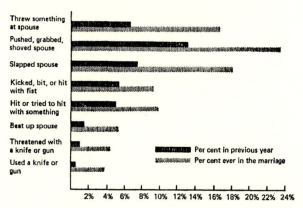

Slaps, Beatings, and Guns. Chart 1 shows that in almost seven of every hundred couples either the husband or the wife had thrown something at the other in the previous year, and about one out of six (16 per cent) had done this at some point in their marriage.

The statistics for *slapping* a spouse are about the same: 7 per cent in the previous year and 18 per cent at some time.

The figures for pushing, shoving, or grabbing during an argument are the highest of any of the eight things we asked about: 13 per cent had done this during the year, and almost one out of four at some time in the marriage.

At the other extreme, "only" one or two out of every hundred couples (1.5 per cent) experienced a *beating-up* incident in the previous year.[1] But a "beating up" had occurred at some time in the marriages of one out of every twenty of the couples we interviewed.

The rates for actually *using a knife or gun* on one's spouse are one out of every two hundred couples in the previous year, and almost one out of twenty-seven couples at some point in the marriage.[2]

We were surprised that there was not a bigger difference between the rate of occurrence for "mild" violent acts (such as pushing and slapping) and the severe acts of violence (such as beating up and using a knife or gun). This is partly because the rates for the more violent acts turned out to be greater than we expected, and partly because the rates for the "ordinary" acts of husband-wife violence were less than expected. Whatever the reasons, it seems that couples are using more than slaps and shoves when violence occurs.

Indeed, the statistics on the number of husbands and wives who had ever "beaten up" their spouses or actually used a knife or gun are astoundingly high. The human meaning of these most extreme forms of violence in the family can be understood better if we translate the percentages into the total number of marriages affected. Since there were about 47 million couples living together in the United States in 1975, the rates just given mean that *over 1.7 million Americans had at some time faced a husband or wife wielding a knife or gun, and well over 2 million had been beaten up* by his or her spouse.

How Accurate Are the Statistics? It is difficult to know how much confidence to put in these statistics because several different kinds of error are possible. First, these are estimates based on a sample. But the sample is reasonably large and was chosen by methods which should make it quite representative of the U.S. population. Comparisons with characteristics reported in the U.S. census show that this in fact is the case.

Still, there is the possibility of sampling error. So we computed what is known as the "standard error" for each of the rates in Chart 1. The largest standard error is for the over-all violence index (see Appendix B). Even that is low: there is a 95 per cent chance that the true percentage of couples *admitting to* ever having physically assaulted one another is somewhere between 26.8 and 28.8 per cent of all couples.[3]

"Admitting to" was italicized to highlight a much more serious and more likely source of error, that of an underestimate. The 26.8 to 28.8 per cent figure assumes that everyone "told all." But that is very unlikely. Three of the reasons are:

(1) There is one group of people who are likely to "underreport" the amount of violence. For this group a slap, push, or shove (and sometimes even more severe violence) is so much a normal part of the family that it is simply not a noteworthy or dramatic enough event always to be remembered. Such omissions are especially likely when we asked about things which had happened during the entire length of the marriage.

(2) At the opposite end of the violence continuum, there is another group who fail to admit or report such acts because of the shame involved if one is the victim, or the guilt if one is the attacker. Such violent attacks as being hit with objects, bitten, beaten up, or attacked with a knife or gun go beyond the "normal violence" of family life and are often unreported.

(3) A final reason for thinking these figures are drastic underestimates lies in the nature of the sample. We included only couples currently living together. Divorced people were asked only about their present marriage. Since "excessive" violence is often a cause of divorce, the sample probably omits many of the high violence cases.

The sample was selected in this way because a major purpose of the study was to investigate the extent to which violence is related to other aspects of husband-wife interaction. Questions were limited to current marriages because of interview time limits and limits on what people could be expected to remember.

The figures therefore could easily be twice as large as those revealed by the survey. In fact, based on the pilot studies and

informal evidence (where some of the factors leading to underreporting were not present), it seems likely that *the true
rate is closer to 50 or 60 per cent of all couples than it is to
the 28 per cent who were willing to describe violent acts to
our interviewers.*

MEN AND WOMEN

Traditionally, men have been considered more aggressive
and violent than women. Like other stereotypes, there is no
doubt a kernel of truth to this. But it is far from the clear-cut
difference which exists in the thinking of most people (Maccoby and Jacklin, 1974; Frodi, Macaulay, and Thorne, 1977).
This is also the case with our survey. About one out of eight
husbands had carried out at least one violent act during the
course of a conflict in the year covered by the survey, *and*
about the same number of wives had attacked their husbands
(12.1 per cent of the husbands versus 11.6 per cent of the
wives).

Mutual Violence. One way of looking at this issue is to ask
what percentage of the sample are couples in which the husband was the only one to use violence? What per cent were
couples in which the only violence was by the wife? And in
what percentage did both use violence?

The most common situation was that in which both had
used violence.

One man who found himself in the middle of a family battle,
reported it this way:

> "It started sort of slowly . . . so I couldn't tell for sure if
> they were even serious. . . . In the beginning they'd push at
> each other, or shove, like kids—little kids who want to fight
> but they don't know how. Then, this one time, while I'm stand-
> ing there not sure whether to stay or go, and them treating me
> like I didn't even exist, she begins yelling at him like she did.
>
> "'You're a bust, you're a failure, I want you out of here, I
> can always get men who'll work, good men, not scum like you.'

And they're pushing and poking with their hands, like they were dancing. She pushes him, he pushes her, only she's doing all the talking. He isn't saying a word.

"Then all of a sudden, she must have triggered off the right nerve because he lets fly with a right cross that I mean stuns. I mean she goes down like a rock! And he's swearing at her, calling her every name in the book. Jesus, I didn't know what the hell to do.

"What I wanted to do was call the police. But I figured, how can I call the police and add to this guy's misery, because she was pushing him. . . . She was really pushing him. I'd have done something to her myself" (Thomas Cottle in Boston *Sunday Globe*, November 6, 1977).

Of those couples reporting any violence, 49 per cent were situations of this type, where both were violent. For the year previous to our study, a comparison of the number of couples in which only the husband was violent with those in which only the wife was violent shows the figures to be very close: 27 per cent violent husbands and 24 per cent violent wives. So, as in the case of the violence rates, there is little difference between the husbands and wives in this study.

CHART 2
Comparison of Husband and Wife Violence in Previous Year

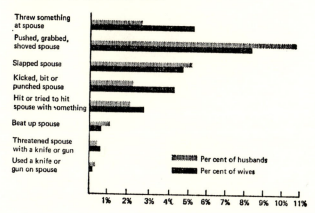

Specific Violent Acts. Chart 2 compares the men and women in our study on each of the eight violent acts. Again, there is an over-all similarity. But there are also some interesting differences, somewhat along the lines of the stereotype of the pot- and pan-throwing wife.

> "I got him good the last time! He punched me in the face and I fell back on the stove. He was walking out of the kitchen and I grabbed that frying pan and landed it square on his head. Man, he didn't know what hit him." (Case reported by the Greater Egypt [Illinois] Regional Planning and Development Commission.)

The number of wives who threw things at their husbands is almost twice as large as the number of husbands who threw things at their wives. The rate for kicking and hitting with an object is also higher for wives than for husbands. The husbands on the other hand had higher rates for pushing, shoving, slapping, beating up, and actually using a knife or gun.

WIFE-BEATING—AND HUSBAND-BEATING

Wife-beating has become a focus of increasing public concern in the last few years. In part this reflects the national anguish over all aspects of violence, ranging from the Vietnam war to the upward surge of assault and murder. Another major element accounting for the recent public concern with wife-beating is the feminist movement. Behind that are the factors which have given rise to the rebirth of the feminist movement in the late 1960s and early 1970s.[4]

What Is Wife-beating? To find out how much wife-beating there is, one must be able to define it in a way which can be objectively measured. When this is tried, it becomes clear that "wife-beating" is a political rather than a scientific term. For some people wife-beating refers only to those instances in which severe damage is inflicted. Less severe violence is not considered violence or it is laughed off. A joke one of us heard while driving across northern England in 1974 is no doubt familiar to many readers of this book. It goes like this in the BBC version: One woman asks another why she feels her husband doesn't love her any more. The answer: "He hasn't bashed me in a fortnight." Or take the following letter to Ann Landers:

> Dear Ann Landers: Come out of the clouds, for Lord's sake, and get down here with us humans. I am sick to death of your holier-than-thou attitude toward women whose husbands give them a well deserved belt in the mouth.
>
> Don't you know that a man can be pushed to the brink and something's got to give? A crack in the teeth can be a wonderful tension-breaker. It's also a lot healthier than keeping all that anger bottled up.
>
> My husband hauls off and slugs me every few months and I don't mind. He feels better and so do I because he never hits me unless I deserve it. So why don't you come off it?—REAL HAPPY.
>
> Dear Real Happy: If you don't mind a crack in the teeth every few months, it's all right with me. I hope you have a good dentist.

So a certain amount of violence in the family is "normal violence." In fact, most of the violent acts which occur in the family are so much a part of the way family members relate to each other that they are not even thought of as violence.

At what point does one exceed the bounds of "normal" family violence? When does it become "wife-beating"? To answer this question, we gathered data on a series of violent acts, ranging from a slap to using a knife or gun. This allows anyone reading this book to draw the line at whatever place seems most appropriate for his or her purpose.

Measuring Wife-beating. This "solution," however, can also be a means of avoiding the issue. So in addition to data on each violent act, we also combined the most severe of these into what can be called a Severe Violence Index. (See Appendix B for definition of Severe Violence Index.) If these are things done by the husband, then it is a "Wife-beating Index." The Wife-beating Index consists of the extent to which the husband went beyond throwing things, pushing or grabbing, and slapping and attacked his wife by kicking, biting, or punching; hitting with some object; beating her up; threatening her with a gun or knife; or using a knife or gun (the last five behaviors in Chart 1).

Why limit the Wife-beating Index to "only" the situations where the husband went beyond throwing things, pushing, grabbing, and slapping? Certainly we don't want to imply that this reflects our conception of what is permissible violence. None of these are acceptable for relationships between husband and wife—just as they are unacceptable between student and teacher, minister and parishioner, or colleagues in a department. In short, we follow the maxim coined by John Valusek: "People are not for hitting."

What then is the basis for choosing kicking, biting, or punching; hitting with an object; beating up; threatening with a knife or gun; and using a knife or gun for the Wife-beating Index? It is simply the fact that these are all acts which carry with them a high risk of serious physical injury.

What Percentage Are Beaten? How many husbands and wives experience the kind of attack which is serious enough to be included in the Wife-beating and Husband-beating Indexes? A remarkably large number. In fact, since our survey produced a rate of 3.8 per cent, this means that about one out of twenty-six American wives get beaten by their husbands every year, or a total of almost 1.8 million per year.

Staggering as are these figures, the real surprise lies in the statistics on husband-beating. These rates are slightly higher than those for wife-beating! Although such cases rarely come to the attention of the police or the press, they exist at all social levels. Here is an example of one we came across:

A wealthy, elderly New York banker was finally granted a separation from his second wife, 31 years his junior, after 14 years of marriage and physical abuse. According to the presiding judge, the wife had bullied him with hysteria, screaming tantrums and vicious physical violence.

The husband wore constant scars and bruises. His ear had once been shredded by his wife with her teeth. She had blackened his eyes, and on one occasion injured one of his eyes so badly that doctors feared it might be lost (Wilmington *Evening Journal*, April 21, 1976, p. 2).

Some 4.6 per cent of the wives in the sample admitted to or were reported by their husbands as having engaged in an act which is included in the Husband-beating Index. That works to be about one out of twenty-two wives who attacked their husbands severely enough to be included in this Husband-beating Index. That is over 2 million very violent wives. Since three other studies of this issue also found high rates of husband-beating (Gelles, 1974; Steinmetz, 1977b, c; Straus, 1974a), some revision of the traditional view about female violence seems to be needed.

How Often Do Beatings Happen? Let us look at just the couples for which a violent incident occurred during the year previous to our study. Was it an isolated incident? If not, how often did attacks of this kind occur?

It was an isolated incident (in the sense that there was only one such attack during the year) for only about a third of the violent couples. This applies to both wife-beating and husband-beating. Almost one out of five of the violent husbands and one out of eight wives attacked their partner this severely twice during the year. Forty-seven per cent of the husbands who beat their wives did so three or more times during the year, and 53 per cent of the husband-beaters did so three or more times. So, for about half the couples the pattern is that if there is one beating, there are likely to be others—at least three per year! In short, violence between husbands and wives, when it occurs, tends to be a recurrent feature of the marriage.

Was There Ever a Beating? A final question about how many beatings took place can be answered by looking at what happened over the entire length of the marriage. Did something that can be called a beating *ever* happen in the marriage?

There are several reasons why even a single beating is important. First, even one such event debases human life. Second, there is the physical danger involved. Third is the fact that many, if not most, such beatings are part of a struggle for power in the family. It often takes only one such event to fix the balance of power for many years—or perhaps for a lifetime.

Physical force is the ultimate resource which most of us learn as children to rely on if all else fails and the issue is crucial. As a husband in one of the families interviewed by LaRossa (1977) said when asked why he hit his wife during an argument:

> . . . She more or less tried to run me and I said no, and she got hysterical and said, "I could kill you!" And I got rather angry and slapped her in the face three or four times and I said "Don't you ever say that to me again!" And we haven't had any problem since.

Later in the interview, the husband evaluated his use of physical force as follows:

> You don't use it until you are forced to it. At that point I felt I had to do something physical to stop the bad progression of events. I took my chances with that and it worked. In those circumstances my judgement was correct and it worked.

Since greater size and strength give the advantage to men in such situations, the single beating may be an extremely important factor in maintaining male dominance in the family system.

We found that one out of eight couples (12.6 per cent) experienced at least one beating incident in the course of marriage. That is approximately a total of 6 million beatings. However, as high as that figure is, the actual statistics are probably higher. This is because things are forgotten over the years, and also because (as was pointed out earlier) the violent acts in question are only about the current marriage. They leave out the many marriages which ended in divorce, a large part of which were marked by beatings.[5]

Wives and Husbands as Victims. This study shows a high rate of violence by *wives* as well as husbands. But it would be a great mistake if that fact distracted us from giving first attention to wives *as victims* as the focus of social policy. There are a number of reasons for this:

(1) The data in Chart 2 show that husbands have higher rates of the most dangerous and injurious forms of violence (beating up and using a knife or gun).

(2) Steinmetz (1977c) found that abuse by husbands does more damage. She suggests that the greater physical strength of men makes it more likely that a woman will be seriously injured when beaten up by her husband.

(3) When violent acts are committed by a husband, they are repeated more often than is the case for wives.

(4) The data do not tell us what proportion of the violent acts by wives were in self-defense or a response to blows initiated by husbands. Wolfgang's study of husband-wife homicides (1957) suggests that this is an important factor.

(5) A large number of attacks by husbands seem to occur when the wife is pregnant (Gelles, 1975b), thus posing a danger to the as yet unborn child. This isn't something that happens only on Tobacco Road:

> The first time Hortense Barber's husband beat her was the day she told him she was pregnant with their first child. "He

knocked out my two front teeth and split open my upper lip,"
the 32 year old honors graduate told a New York Senate Task
Force on Women. Later Mrs. Barber's husband regularly
blacked her eyes during her pregnancy and threw a knife at
her "in jest," cutting her knee (New York *Times,* April 10,
1977, p. 16).

(6) Women are locked into marriage to a much greater extent than men. Women are bound by many economic and social constraints, and they often have no alternative to putting
up with beatings by their husbands (Gelles, 1976; Martin,
1976; Straus, 1976, 1977b). The situation is similar to being
married to an alcoholic. Nine out of ten men leave an alcoholic
wife, but only one out of ten women leave an alcoholic husband (*Good Housekeeping,* September 1977).

Most people feel that social policy should be aimed at helping those who are in the weakest position. Even though wives
are also violent, they are in the weaker, more vulnerable position in respect to violence in the family. This applies to both
the physical, psychological, and economic aspects of things.
That is the reason we give first priority to aiding wives who are
the victims of beatings by their husbands.[6]

At the same time, the violence *by* wives uncovered in this
study suggests that a fundamental solution to the problem of
wife-beating has to go beyond a concern with how to control
assaulting husbands. It seems that violence is built into the
very structure of the society and the family system itself. In
Chapters 5 and 9 we will show that wife-beating is related to
other aspects of violence in the family. It is only one aspect
of the general pattern of family violence, which includes parent-child violence, child-to-child violence, and wife-to-husband
violence. To eliminate the particularly brutal form of violence
known as wife-beating will require changes in the cultural
norms and in the organization of the family and society which
underlie the system of violence on which so much of American society is based.

NORMS AND MEANINGS

Just as we need to know the extent to which violent *acts* occur between husbands and wives, parents and children, and brothers and sisters, it is also important to know how family members feel about intrafamily violence. Just how strongly do they approve or disapprove of a parent slapping a child or a husband slapping a wife? To what extent do people see violence in the family as one of those undesirable but necessary parts of life?

It is hard to find out about these aspects of the way people think about family violence. One difficulty is there are contradictory rules or "norms." At one level there are norms strongly opposed to husbands and wives hitting each other. But at the same time, there also seem to be implicit but powerful norms which permit and even encourage such acts. Sometimes people are thinking of one of these principles and sometimes of the other.

Another thing is that violence is often such a "taken for granted" part of life that most people don't even realize there are socially defined rules or norms about the use of violence in the family.

The existence of these implicit norms is illustrated by the case of a husband who hit his wife on several occasions. Each time he felt that it was wrong. He apologized—very genuinely. But still he did it again. The husband explained that he and his wife got so worked up in their arguments that he "lost control." In his mind, it was almost involuntary, and certainly not something he did according to a rule or norm which gives one the right to hit his wife.

But the marriage counselor in the case brought out the rules which permitted him to hit his wife. He asked the husband why, if he had "lost control," he didn't stab his wife! This possibility (and the fact that the husband did not stab the wife despite "losing control") shows that hitting the wife was not just a bubbling over of a primitive level of behavior. Although this husband did not realize it, he was following a behavioral rule or norm. It seems that the unrecognized but operating norm for this husband—and for millions of other husbands—is that it is okay to hit one's wife, but not to stab her.

There is other evidence which tends to support the idea that the marriage license is also a hitting license. For example, "Alice, you're going to the moon," was one of the standard punch lines on the old Jackie Gleason "Honeymooners" skits which delighted TV audiences during the 1950s, and which are currently enjoying a revival. Jokes, plays, such as those of George Bernard Shaw, and experiments which show that people take less severe actions if they think the man attacking a woman is her husband (Shotland and Straw, 1976; Straus, 1976) are other signs.

It has been suggested that one of the reasons neighbors who saw the attack didn't come to the aid of Kitty Genovese in the 1964 Queens murder case was because they thought it was a man beating his wife!

Or take the following incident:

. . . Roy Butler came over to help his bride-to-be in preparations for their wedding, which is why the wedding is off.

Roy, 24, made the mistake of going to a stag party first.

On the way to fiancée Anthea Higson's home, he dropped the wedding cake in the front garden.

In the shouting match that followed, he dropped Anthea's mother with a right cross to the jaw.

Anthea, 21, promptly dropped Roy. She said the wedding was off and she never wanted to see him again.

"If he had hit me instead of my mother, I probably would have married him all the same," [italics added] she said yesterday after a court fined Butler $135 for assaulting Mrs. Brenda Higson.

"But I'm not having any man hitting my mum," Anthea said (Providence *Journal*, September 21, 1976).

Interesting as are these examples, none of them provide the kind of systematic and broadly representative evidence which is needed. That is what we attempted to get in this study.

Measuring the Meaning of Violence. To find out how our sample felt about violence in the family, we used the "semantic differential" method (Osgood, Suci, and Tannenbaum, 1957). For husband-wife violence, we asked subjects to rate the phrase "Couples slapping each other." They were asked to make three ratings: unnecessary . . . necessary; not normal . . . normal; and good . . . bad.

How many of the husbands and wives rated "Couples slapping each other" as "necessary," "normal," or "good"? Over all just under one out of four wives and one out of three husbands (31.3 and 24.6 per cent) saw this type of physical force between spouses as at least somewhat necessary, normal, or good.

These statistics are remarkably close to those from a national sample studied by the U. S. Violence Commission. The Violence Commission found that about one quarter of the persons interviewed said they could think of circumstances in which it would be all right for a husband to hit his wife or a wife to hit her husband (Stark and Mc Evoy, 1970). This is slightly lower than the percentages for our sample. But if the Violence Commission survey data had been analyzed in the way we examined our data, the results could well have been almost identical.

CHART 3
Per Cent of Husbands and Wives Who Rated "A Couple Slapping Each Other" as at Least Somewhat Necessary, Good, or Normal

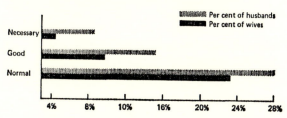

The separate ratings for violence being necessary, normal, or good are interesting in the contrast they provide with each other and in the way men and women think about violence. On the one hand, there are big differences in the percentage of husbands as compared to wives who could see some situations in which it is necessary for a husband or wife to slap the other (see Chart 3). There is also a larger percentage of husbands who could see some situations in which this would not be a bad thing to do. In fact, for both these ratings, twice as many husbands as wives felt this way.

On the other hand, the percentages for the not normal . . . normal rating are particularly interesting because they are larger and because there is little difference between the men and the women. The figures in the chart show that a large proportion of American husbands and wives see violence as a normal part of married life. It may not be good, and it may not be necessary, but it is something which is going to happen under normal circumstances. The marriage license is a hitting license for a large part of the population, and probably for a much greater part than could bring themselves to rate it as "normal" in the context of this survey.

SUMMING UP

We are reasonably confident that the couples in the study are representative of American couples in general. But we suspect that not everyone told us about all the violence in his or her family. In fact, the pilot studies and informal evidence suggest that the true figures may be double those based on what people were willing to admit in a mass survey such as this. If this is the case, then about a third of all American couples experience a violent incident every year, and about two thirds have experienced such an incident at least once in the marriage.

Of course, a large part of these "violent incidents" are

pushes and slaps, but far from all of them. A large portion are also actions which could cause serious injury or even death. We know from the fact that so many murderers and their victims are husband and wife that this is not just speculation. For the couples in this sample, in fact, almost one out of every twenty-five had faced an angry partner with a knife or gun in hand.

If the "dangerous violence" is not limited solely to use of a knife or gun, and includes everything *more serious* than pushing, grabbing, shoving, slapping, and throwing things, the rate is three times as high. In short, almost one out of every eight couples admitted that at some point in the marriage there had been an act of violence which could cause serious injury.

Another way of grasping this is to compare the rates for wife-beating and husband-beating in our survey with assaults which are reported in official statistics. The Uniform Crime Reports on "aggravated assault" are given in rate per 100,000. But the rates in this chapter are percentages, i.e., rates per 100, not per 100,000.

We can translate the rates for this survey into rates per 100,000 per year. They are 3,800 per 100,000 for assaults on wives, 4,600 for assaults on husbands, and a combined rate of 6,100 per 100,000 couples. Compare this with the roughly 190 per 100,000 aggravated assaults of all kinds known to the police each year.

Of course, many crimes are not reported to the police So there have been surveys asking people if they were the victims of a crime. The rate of aggravated assault coming out of the National Crime Panel survey is very high: 2,597 per 100,000. But our rate for wife-beating and husband-beating of 6,100 per 100,000 is almost two and a half times higher. Also, since the Uniform Crime Reports, and especially the National Crime Panel data, include many within-family assaults, the amount by which husband-wife assault exceeds any other type of assault is much greater than these rates suggest.

Leaving aside the fact that our figures on husband-wife violence are probably underestimates, and even leaving aside the psychological damage that such violence can produce, just the danger to physical health implied by these rates is staggering. If any other crime or risk to physical well-being involved almost 2 million wives and 2 million husbands per year, plus a much larger number at some point in the marriage, a national emergency would probably be declared.

CHAPTER 3

Spare the Rod?

"What that kid needs is a good crack in the teeth."

How literally do parents take such phrases? For centuries our society has provided parents with the right and even the mandate to use hitting, slapping, spanking, and other physical force against children.

Parents have been "beating the devil" out of junior since colonial times. Jokes about being taken behind the woodshed or having one's backside warmed by father's razor strap have been around almost as long.

Early colonists, in fact, developed a most effective method of dealing with the unruly child. Many communities enacted "stubborn child laws," which gave parents the right to kill children who were beyond their ability to control.

Our culture is full of reminders of the right of parents to employ violence against their children. Fairy tales, folklore, and nursery rhymes are full of violence against children. Hansel and Gretel's parents, for instance, abandoned their offspring to starve in the forest when money got scarce. The wicked queen told her huntsman to take Snow White into the forest and cut out her heart because the young stepdaughter was so beautiful. Mother Goose's "Old Woman in the Shoe" whipped her children soundly and sent them to bed without any bread.

Today, most parents hit their children at one time or another. Few deny it. And if not proud of it, many honestly believe the slap on the bottom is a just and necessary tool of discipline.

The previous chapter illustrated the fact that there are contradictory rules and attitudes about violence between marriage partners. On the one hand, there are norms which define this kind of violence as wrong. On the other hand, there is a set of attitudes, values, cues, and signals that makes the marriage license a hitting license. This chapter on parental violence reveals an equally contradictory set of rules.

The fact that parents receive the message that using physical force is good, necessary, and beneficial (to them and their children) does not mean that parents have unlimited freedom in their use of physical force. Tradition and now child abuse laws limit parents from inflicting severe or lethal harm. By the end of the 1960s all fifty states enacted legislation which attempted to define illegal acts of physical violence as child abuse and mandated that certain individuals would have to report families in which these acts took place. Presently, American parents have the right to use violence, up to the point of abusing their children.

Unfortunately, the concept of child abuse establishes no precise guide lines to settle what is or is not illegitimate force in the eyes of the law, parents, or communities.

Despite the fact that child abuse has been viewed as a major social problem for the last two decades, a single accepted and acceptable definition simply does not exist. The mother who hits her child with a belt may be praised as a good parent in one community; while in another, the mother who slaps her child's face may risk being reported as an abusive parent.

ARE SLAPS AND SPANKINGS VIOLENT?

Let us assume for the moment that, as a society, we take for granted the fact that parents spank their children. Evidence to support this assumption can be drawn from a variety of sources. For example, how many people intervene when an adult spanks or slaps a child in a supermarket?

There is also the tacit and legal approval of corporal punishment in schools, which is based on the belief that schools function as surrogate parents while children are in class. Take, for example, a school district in Oklahoma. There, a rule stating that anyone late for school five times must either submit to a spanking by the principal or be dismissed from school with failing marks had appeared in the student handbook for years. No one ever questioned its use until two parents who didn't believe in spanking threatened to take the school board to court (Boston *Globe*, November 16, 1977, p. 2). Hitting children is so taken for granted that almost all parents view a spanking or a slap as an inevitable part of raising a child.

Given that spankings and slaps are taken for granted, are they violent acts? According to the definition of violence which we presented in the first chapter, our answer is yes. Although violence is a pejorative word and the current thinking about slaps and spankings of children is that they are legitimate parenting tools, our view is that slaps and spankings are simply one end of a continuum of violent acts. When pressed, parents will admit that they slap or spank a child hard enough to get the child to stop doing something the parent does not want done. In one of our early studies we discussed this point with a parent:

Interviewer: When do you slap or spank your child?
Parent: When I want her to stop something . . . like when I want her to get away from the stove.
Interviewer: How hard do you hit her?
Parent: Hard enough to get her to stop.

Interviewer: You mean if the first slap doesn't get her to
   stop . . .
Parent: I hit her again, a little harder.

We interpret this dialogue to mean that parents will slap their
child hard enough to stop the offensive behavior—in other
words, the child gets hit hard enough so the "hurt" outweighs
the desire to continue the forbidden act.

Over the years our discussions with parents concerning their
use of slaps and spankings revealed that most parents do not
see these acts as violent, but they do admit that they will
spank or slap a child hard enough for the child to be "hurt"
and get the message that the parent is angry and wants the
child either to change his or her behavior or to learn a lesson.
Although parents and the society at large can explain away the
hurt by stating that the slaps or spankings were in the best interest of the child, the fact remains that these actions are consistent with the phenomenon we refer to as "violence."

THE IDEOLOGY OF SPARING THE ROD

"Spare the rod and spoil the child," "kids need to be hit,"
"the bamboo stick makes a good child" (message in a fortune
cookie)—these phrases all have the same thing in common—
they argue that hitting a child is necessary, normal, and good.
One question we wanted to answer in our national study of
family violence was what proportion of American parents accept the wisdom that spankings and slaps are necessary, normal, and good ways to bring up their children?

We employed the semantic differential technique to measure parents' attitudes toward spanking or slapping a child. We
faced a particular problem in creating the exact question
which we wanted people to react to. At first we thought of asking a question similar to the one we asked about marital
violence—"Couples slapping each other." However, the general

question about couples could not be used with children since the term "child" could mean many things to a respondent, ranging from a newborn baby to an eighteen-year-old, six-foot four-inch, two-hundred-pound son. We could have asked numerous questions about spanking and slapping children of various ages, but there simply was not the time in the interview to allow for more than one question. We ultimately decided to ask a specific question about one age group. But what would it be?

Slapping a three-year-old is thought to be different in motivation and consequence than slapping an eighteen-year-old. There were numerous debates over what age child we should select for this question—especially since one of the authors had a "terrible" two-year-old; one had children covering the range from "mouthy" preteen to a "never wrong" teen-ager; and one had children in their late teens, approaching the total independence of adulthood. All could find persuasive reasons for arguing that each child was uniquely "hittable." We settled on twelve-year-old children because, althought a difficult age, it is also an age when a parent has alternatives to spankings or slappings (e.g., "grounding," cutting off a child's allowance, early curfew, etc.).

Our results illustrate that most Americans view spanking and slapping a twelve-year-old as necessary, normal, and good. Seventy per cent viewed slapping or spanking a twelve-year-old as somehow necessary; 77 per cent felt this was normal; and 71 per cent viewed these acts as good. The only comparable national statistics come from the study conducted for the National Commission on the Causes and Prevention of Violence in 1968. In this study 86 per cent of a national sample agreed that young people needed "strong" discipline by their parents. While not the same as our question, this question lends support to our hypothesis that spankings and slappings are viewed as normal, necessary, and acceptable means of raising children.

How normal is it to slap or spank a twelve-year-old? We did

not find a wide distribution of feelings among the people we questioned. Their responses were measured by the average scores reported by the respondents in answering each of the three semantic differential items. The items were measured using a scale that ranged from 1 to 7 (1 = unnecessary, not normal, and bad; 7 = necessary, normal, or good). The average ranking of the necessity of slaps or spankings was 3.5, normality was 4.0, and goodness was 3.6.

Men and Women

Men were found to be slightly more inclined to view slapping and spanking a twelve-year-old as necessary and good, while men and women equally viewed these forms of punishment as normal. Combining all three adjectives, men ranked higher than women in their agreement as to the necessity, normality, and goodness of violence.

Our findings are consistent with most studies on violence and aggression, which indicate that men approve of the use of physical force more than women.

Although there was not a great deal of variation in the perceptions of slaps and spankings, the profile of those most likely to view these acts as necessary, normal, and good, is male, without children, under thirty, and non-white.

Parents and Non-parents

Does having children affect a person's views on whether or not slaps and spankings are normal, necessary, and good? Childless individuals were more likely than parents to view slapping and spanking a twelve-year-old as necessary, normal, and good. The differences were much larger than the differences between men and women.

It is interesting that having a child seems to make people less likely to see slaps and spankings as normal, good, and necessary. Perhaps this is because parents have learned that slaps and spankings do not always get the desired results and other means of training or disciplining children are more effective. Moreover, some parents who spank their children and then see the children turn around and "spank" the family pet or a brother or sister might change their convictions about the "goodness" of a spanking.

Age

One of the clearest and most pronounced differences in people's attitudes toward the use of slaps and spankings appears when we compare people of different ages. Younger Americans are much more likely to view slaps and spankings as necessary, normal, and good. The most agreement with these forms of violence being necessary, normal, and good came from those under thirty. On the other hand, less than two thirds of the people we interviewed who were over fifty years of age saw slaps and spankings of twelve-year-olds as being necessary, normal, and good.

Why were there such pronounced age differences and why is support for slaps and spankings greater among younger Americans? We must state that we really do not know whether the age differences are a result of the different experiences each generation faces or if they indicate that people change their views on slaps and spankings as they grow older. Since we did not study our respondents over a period of time, we cannot answer this point. There are, however, some possible explanations for the age-related perceptions of slaps and spankings.

For one, it may be that as parents grow older they see less necessity, normality, and goodness in using physical punishment. Our comparison of parents and non-parents seems to bear this out, in that parents are less supportive of these forms of violence than non-parents.

Second, the younger respondents may be less likely to have children, and we have seen in the preceding section that not having children is related to approving slaps and spankings.

Another explanation is that the older respondents were more likely to have older children and therefore had less recent experience with actually using slaps and spankings. The farther people are removed from using a behavior, the less they may approve of it. This explanation, however, is less supportable. If true, it would mean that non-parents would be less approving of slaps and spankings—and we found just the opposite.

We think the differences between age groups point to a general cultural ideology which approves of slapping and spanking children. We found that more than 80 per cent of the individuals under thirty viewed the two forms of hitting as necessary, normal, and good. Most of these individuals would not be old enough to have twelve-year-old children. Thus, their approval of slapping or spanking a preteen could be derived from a general societal support for these acts rather than actual experience.

All the explanations just offered suggest that as people grow older and have children, they experience changes in attitude. But the greater approval of violence in child rearing by the younger people in the sample could reflect differences in the learning experiences and beliefs of different generations. Wars tend to produce an increase in killing one's fellow citizens as well as in killing the enemy (Archer and Gartner, 1976). People in their fifties were born after World War I and grew up in the Depression, whereas those in the younger age groups were born after the Second World War and grew up during the Korean and Vietnam wars. Moreover, those under thirty were the first generation to grow up with high and continuous exposures to TV violence. The under-thirty generation has seen violence on both television programming and television news. They were the first generation to see a war reported on television (Vietnam), and to see someone killed on television (Lee Harvey Oswald in 1963).

So the older groups may always have been less favorable to violence because they grew up in a less violent context, and the younger group may continue to be more favorable to violence even when they are in their fifties.

Finally, we may be witnessing a change in the younger generation. New parents in the 1970s may be resorting to an older, more strict style of child rearing as a reaction to the turmoil, permissiveness, and "instability" of the 1960s. Today's parents, facing children going out into a world of drugs, delinquency, and disorder, might be using standards and views that their grandparents held. Certainly there is rising evidence of a "new conservatism" emerging in our society. *Newsweek* magazine headlines America's "turn to the right" while the percentage of Americans supporting capital punishment is higher today than any time in the last thirty years. Schools are under pressure to abandon "enrichment" and return to the three R's, while traditional and fundamental religions are enjoying a new revival. The high proportion of those under thirty supporting spankings and slappings of children may be one outcropping of a new era of fundamental and conservative attitudes.

The most important thing we learn from the analysis of people's attitudes toward using slaps and spankings is that these acts are generally seen as useful, normal, and acceptable parenting techniques. In fact, it is almost certain that the figures which are presented in this section underestimate just how much support for the necessity, normality, and goodness of slaps and spankings there is in America. Had we chosen to substitute "two-year-old" for "twelve-year-old" we might have seen proportions close to 100 per cent of the population

VIOLENCE TOWARD CHILDREN

"Ordinary" physical punishment and "child abuse" are but two ends of a single continuum of violence toward children. In between are millions of parents whose use of physical force goes beyond mild punishment, but which, for various reasons, does not get identified and labeled as "child abuse." The responses to the questions which asked if slapping or spanking a twelve-year-old was necessary, normal, and good provide us with information on American attitudes about hitting children. But attitudes are not the same as behavior. One could view a slap or a spanking as useful and not slap or spank a twelve-year-old, while, on the other hand, an individual could condemn all hitting, but still slap a child. What one parent may regard as "spanking" may well be considered a brutal beating by others.

We examined the extent, level, and kinds of violence that took place in the homes of 1,146 American couples who had children between the ages of three and seventeen living at home. It would have been too time consuming to ask each respondent about the use of violence on each of the children who were at home (in families with six or more children the interview might have gone on for hours). Instead, we randomly selected one "referent" child in each family. The child was the focal point for the discussion of physical punishment and violence. Thus, our examination of parental violence is not a study of all the violence each parent engaged in, but rather, all the violence a selected child in each family experienced from *one parent*. By using this procedure, we can generalize to how much violence children in the United States experience in one year and over a period of time.

Violence Rates

Seventy-three per cent of the respondents report that at some time in their child's life they used some form of violence on the child. Sixty-three per cent of the respondents who had children between the ages of three and seventeen living at home mentioned at least one violent episode occurring in 1975.

As might be expected, the milder forms of violence were the most common. Slaps or spankings were mentioned by 58 per cent of the parents as occurring in the previous year and by 71 per cent as having ever taken place. Forty-one per cent of American families report pushing or shoving the referent child in 1975; while 46 per cent said pushes or shoves had occurred at some time in the child's life. Hitting with an object was reported by 13 per cent of the parents in the previous year and by 20 per cent for the years up to the survey year. Throwing an object was less common; approximately 5 per cent of the parents did this during the survey year while more than 9 per cent admitted that they had thrown something at their child prior to the survey year.

The more dangerous types of violence were the least likely to occur. But even the figures for these extreme forms of violence yield an astoundingly high number of American children who were kicked, punched, bitten, beaten up, threatened with a gun or a knife, or had a gun or a knife used on them in 1975. Let us look first at the number of parents who admitted to having engaged in each type of violence.

Approximately 3 parents in 100 *kicked, bit, or punched* their child in 1975.

Nearly 8 in 100 stated that they had done these things to the referent child prior to the survey year.

Slightly more than 1 per cent of the respondents reported beating up the referent child in the previous twelve months, and 4 per cent said that they had done this at some point in the child's life. While the term "beat up" was not specifically defined in the course of the interview, the item followed the question on kicking, punching, and biting. Thus, we assume that beating up a child implies more than a single blow.

One child in 1,000 faced a parent who *threatened to use a gun or knife* on him or her in 1975, while nearly 3 children in 100 have grown up facing a parent who at least once threatened them with a gun or knife. The same proportions hold for children who had *guns and knives actually used* on them. Thus, 1 in 1,000 children in 1975 had a parent who shot or tried to shoot him, or stabbed or tried to stab him.

There were nearly 46 million children between the ages of three and seventeen who lived with both parents in 1975 (Bureau of Census, 1975). Extrapolating our findings to these children we estimate that between 3.1 and 4 million children have been kicked, bitten, or punched by a parent at some time in their lives; while between 1 and 1.9 million were kicked, bitten, or punched in 1975. Between 1.4 and 2.3 million children have been "beaten up" while growing up, and between 275,000 and 750,000 American children were "beaten up" in 1975. Finally, our data mean that between 900,000 and 1.8 million children between the ages of three and seventeen have had a parent use a gun or a knife on them at some time. Our figures do not allow for a reliable extrapolation of how many children had guns and knives used on them in 1975, but our estimate (based on an incidence of 1 in 1,000) would be something close to 46,000.

Frequency of Violence

With the exception of being threatened with a knife or gun or having a knife or gun used on them, children who experienced violence in 1975 experienced it more than once. Children who had something thrown at them had it happen an average 4.5 times that one year. Children who were pushed or grabbed or shoved experienced that 6.6 times over a twelve-month period. As we would expect, spankings and slappings were the most frequent—happening 9.6 times. The average for kicks, bites, and punches was 8.9 times in 1975, while children were hit with objects 8.6 times. Beatings occurred less than once every two months—an average of 5.9 times over the year. If a gun or knife was used, it happened "only" once in the survey year.

The figures on how often a form of violence was used must be interpreted with care. For some items these frequencies seem to be low. Most people would expect that if a child is spanked by a parent, this would occur more frequently than once a month. But our data are based on children aged three to seventeen. Thus, the frequencies are the average for all children, three to seventeen, who are spanked by their parents. Obviously, older children might be spanked less often than once a month, while some younger children might be spanked weekly, daily, or in some families, hourly.

We did not expect the more extreme forms of parental violence to be used so frequently. For a child to be kicked, bitten, punched, and beaten up every other month came as a surprise. This finding indicates that the extreme forms of parental violence are not rare, one-shot events. They occur periodically and even regularly in the families where these types of violence are used. If a beating is considered an element of child abuse, then our findings point to the conclusion that child abuse may be a chronic condition for many children, not a once in a lifetime experience for a rare few.

X-ray examinations of suspected child abuse victims have borne this out in recent years. Doctors often find evidence of healed or partially healed broken bones from previous beatings. Physicians were suspicious, for example, when one four-year-old girl told them that "Mama kept hitting me with a big black stick." The little girl, unconscious when brought to the hospital, was suffering from a fractured skull and lacerations of the back, face, arms, and legs. Although her mother indicated there had been an accident, X-rays showed this was not the first time the child had received such injuries (Flato, 1962).

Children at Risk

Our data on parental violence describe what parents did, not the results of these actions. Consequently, we cannot accurately estimate how many children were harmed by their parents while they were growing up, or in 1975. We do not know exactly what respondents meant when they admitted that they "beat up" their child, we do not know what objects they used when they hit a child (a pipe or a paddle?), and we do not know whether children who had guns and knives used on them were wounded. Nevertheless, we can attempt to estimate how many American children were "at risk" of being physically injured. The Child Abuse Index (see Appendix B for details on how the index was constructed) combines all the items which have the highest probability of injuring or damaging a child (kicks, bites, punches, beatings, threats with a gun or knife, use of a gun or knife). Between 3 and 4 out of every 100 parents (3.6 per cent) admitted to using at least one of these dangerous forms of violence at least once in 1975. Assuming that any of these acts has a high probability of causing harm to a child victim, between 1.4 and 1.9 million children were vulnerable to physical injury from their parents in 1975.

Granted, being at risk of being injured is not the same as being a victim of child abuse. However, these figures may still be the best available for estimating how many children might be abused each year in the United States. This is because they are the only statistics ever generated from a nationally representative sample using sound scientific measurement procedures. If they are a reasonable estimate of child abuse, then they offer new and surprising information:

First, the estimates are 500,000 to 1 million children higher than previous estimates of the incidence of child abuse.

Second, the figures underestimate the true level of abuse for five important reasons. (1) They are based on self-reports of the parents. Underreporting is quite possible when sensitive questions such as "Did you beat up your child?" are asked. (2) The survey deals with only seven specific forms of violence. Omitted are such things as burning a child, torturing a child, sexual abuse, and other acts which are considered child abuse. (3) The data on violence toward children refer to violent acts of only one of the two parents. (4) The children we studied were only between the ages of three and seventeen. Previous research suggests a large amount of child abuse is directed toward children between three months and three years of age, and these children are not covered in our survey. Had they been included, our figures would certainly be higher. (5) We studied only "intact" families (husbands and wives who were living together). The literature on child abuse suggests that abuse may be more common in families where only one parent lives with the child. Had we studied single-parent families, we might also have uncovered a higher rate of extreme violence toward children. The actual violence children experience is probably much higher than the figures we report here. Thus, while our figures are accurate (in terms of the parent-child relations we investigated) they only hint at a much more extensive incidence of the abuse of children in the United States.

MOTHERS, FATHERS, AND VIOLENCE

During the survey year, mothers were more likely to have used violence at least once on the referent child and they were more likely than fathers to have used violence on the child in previous years. Sixty-eight per cent of the mothers and 58 per cent of the fathers engaged in at least one violent exchange with the referent child during the survey year, while 76 per cent of the mothers and 71 per cent of the fathers had been violent toward the child at another time.

We also found that mothers were more likely to use severe or abusive violence on their children than were fathers.

The finding that mothers are more prone to use severe violence on their children is consistent with the scientific and popular thinking on violence toward children. Research on child abuse often finds mothers to be at least as violent if not more violent than fathers (Bennie and Sclare, 1969; Steele and Pollock, 1974; Gil, 1970).

A simple explanation of mothers' violence is that they spend more time with children than do fathers. The actual explanation of mothers' greater use of violence is probably more complex. In our society, mothers, irrespective of how much time they actually spend with their children, are typically held more responsible for the actions, behavior, and development of their children than are fathers. Thus, frustrations created by children tend to affect the mother more than the father. A problem with the child reflects on her competence as a parent more than the father's.

One woman wrote to Ann Landers stating:

> Last night I did something that really frightened me. I was helping our son with his homework and he refused to try to solve the math problem—just kept saying, "I can't get it."
>
> I became so infuriated I started to slap his face as hard as I could and I couldn't stop. Today the little guy was black and blue marked on his cheeks. I was so ashamed I didn't let him go to school.

A second aspect of the explanation is that children interfere with mothers' plans and self-concepts more than fathers'. When a child is born, if a parent has to quit a job or change personal plans and goals, the parent is usually the mother. If a child is sick, the parent who stays home from work is usually the mother. Thus, again, mothers experience more than simply temporal frustration from their children; children affect the total range of their mothers' plans, goals, and expectations.

Carol, a Boston housewife trying to overcome her tendencies toward child abuse, described her feelings this way:

> "I can feel it coming. More or less I think it's depression. I get so damned fed up with the house and knowing that I've gotta watch the kids. I've gotta feed them. I've gotta do dishes. Like you get up in the morning, you cook breakfast, you do dishes, you clean the house. Next thing you know, it's lunchtime. While you're fixing lunch, they're out there messing up two or three rooms. You feed 'em, you do dishes, you clean the rooms, it's suppertime. It's the *same* thing" (*The Real Paper*, February 5, 1975, p. 18).

Undoubtedly, even more factors need to be considered to explain the greater likelihood of mothers using force and violence.

Mothers are more likely than fathers to throw objects at their children, slap or spank them, or hit their children with objects. There is no difference between mothers and fathers for pushing or grabbing; kicking, biting, or punching; or, lastly, beating.

It is interesting to note that mothers are at least as likely as fathers to use even the more serious forms of violence, such as kicks, bites, punches, and beatings. This is important because family violence is probably the only situation where women are as or more violent than are men. If men have a genetic predisposition to be violent, one would expect them to be more violent at home than their wives. Yet, an examination of violence between couples and violence by parents toward children reveals that women are as violent or more violent in the home than are men. This casts a shadow of doubt on the pure genetic theories of violence and points to a need to investigate social and psychological factors associated with family violence.

How Often?

With the exception of using or threatening to use guns and knives (which was admitted only by fathers in the survey), mothers use each type of violence as much or more frequently than their husbands. Children who are kicked, bitten, or punched by their parents encounter these forms of violence twice as frequently from their mothers than from their fathers. While fathers who beat up their children do this on an average of once a year, mothers who beat up their children do it more than once every other month—an average of 7.2 times per year! Mothers and fathers were roughly equal in their frequency of pushing, grabbing, and shoving their children, while mothers more frequently threw objects and slapped and spanked the children.

The final comparison between mothers and fathers reveals that mothers were more likely to use forms of violence which placed their children at risk of physical injury than were fathers. More than 4 per cent of the mothers (4.4 per cent) compared to "only" 2.7 per cent of the fathers had kicked, bitten, punched, or beaten up their child during the survey year. This may seem like a small difference, but it amounts to a 62 per cent greater rate of child abuse by mothers than by fathers.

SONS AND DAUGHTERS AS VICTIMS OF VIOLENCE

We found male children to be the most likely victims of parental violence. Nearly two thirds of the sons (66 per cent) and 61 per cent of the daughters of the respondents were struck at least once during the year. The greater likelihood of sons becoming victims is linked to parents' use of pushing, grabbing, or shoving their sons more than their daughters. Sons were beaten up somewhat more frequently than daughters were. Also, sons were reportedly the only ones who had guns and knives threatened or used on them.

Although there are few major differences between how violent parents are toward boys and girls when each type of violence is looked at separately, these small differences add up. In addition, the difference between the treatment of boys and girls becomes greater as the seriousness of the violence increases. As a result, the number of boys who are at risk of physical injury is 61 per cent greater than for girls (4.5 per cent compared to 2.8 per cent).

A popular theory to explain boys' greater vulnerability to parental violence is that boys are more difficult to raise and commit more "punishable offenses" than girls. Another hypothesis is that our society accepts and often values boys' experiencing violence because it "toughens them up." Seven out of ten people responding to the 1968 survey conducted for the National Commission on the Causes and Prevention of Violence said that they believed it was important for a boy to have a few fist fights while he was growing up (Stark and

Mc Evoy, 1970). Many people might approve of boys being hit more than girls because boys will experience a rougher, more violent world than their sisters. Violence may be approved of and used as a "character builder" for young boys (Straus, 1971).

Age of the Child

There are various hypotheses about what age a child is more vulnerable to being struck or abused by his parents. Some researchers and clinicians propose that the most dangerous period in a child's life is from three months to three years of age (Kempe et al., 1962; Fontana, 1973; Galdston, 1965). Psychologist Urie Bronfenbrenner proposes that the highest rates of child abuse and battering occur among adolescents (1974). David Gil's research on child abuse in America revealed that half of the confirmed cases of child abuse were children over six years of age, while nearly one fifth of the confirmed reports were children in their teens (1970). A recent survey of college students at an eastern university found that 8 per cent of a sample of more than 250 students stated that they had been physically injured by their parents during the last year they (the students) lived at home (Mulligan, 1977).

Our survey indicated younger children were most likely to be victims of some kind of physical force. Since the survey did not include children under three years of age we cannot draw any conclusions about this age group. Eighty-six per cent of the three- and four-year-olds had some mode of violence used on them, 82 per cent of the children from five years old to nine had been hit, 54 per cent of the preteens and early teen-age children (ten to fourteen years old) were struck, and "only" one third of the children fifteen to seventeen years old were hit by their parents.

Younger children were vulnerable to a wide range of forceful and violent acts. Preschoolers and children under nine years old were more likely to be pushed, grabbed, shoved, slapped, spanked, kicked, bitten, hit with a fist, and hit with an object. Teen-age children were more vulnerable to having a gun or a knife used on them, although the differences were not significant.

Younger children are not only more likely to be struck by their parents, they are more likely to be hit frequently. The youngest children in our survey were pushed, grabbed, shoved, slapped, spanked, and hit with an object more frequently than older children. For these modes of violence, each older age group experienced violence less frequently than the younger group. The exceptions to this pattern were beatings, kickings, punches, bitings, and having an object thrown at the child. Children five to nine years of age were kicked, bitten, or punched and had objects thrown at them more frequently than other age groups of children. Older teens were beaten up more frequently than younger children (although this figure is influenced by the fact that one fifteen- to seventeen-year-old was reported beaten up twenty times).

Children under 5 and older teen-age children were the most likely to experience violence that held a high chance of causing physical injury. More than 6 per cent (6.7) of children three and four, 2.5 per cent of children five to nine, 3 per cent of children ten to fourteen, and 4.3 per cent of the oldest group of children (fifteen to seventeen) had parents use dangerous forms of violence on them during one year.

The results of our national study of violence toward children tend to confirm both previous theories concerning physical punishment and the abuse of children. Younger children are more likely to be struck by their parents and to be struck more frequently than older children. However, older children, even those in their late teens, experience a wide range of violence (including spankings) and experience it more than once a year. Our data tend to resolve the seeming contradiction which argues that younger children are more vulnerable. If we go by the parents' reports of what they do to their children, we find that preschoolers and children in their late teens are both vulnerable to physical abuse.

The fact that preschoolers and older teen-age children share in the risk of being abused is very important. Many parents and social scientists have felt that the abuse of young children was the result of their parents frustration in dealing with them. The "terrible two's," toilet training accidents, touching hot stoves, and getting into mischief are all cited as reasons why younger children are spanked and often beaten. But if, as our data suggest, both preschoolers and older teen-agers are vulnerable to being injured by their parents, then we cannot accept the explanation that many children are abused because they are too young to be reasoned with. Of course, one often hears parents of older teen-agers using the same lament as parents of preschoolers. Many parents of children in their late teens bemoan the fact that their children "no longer *listen* to reason." Thus, we find that children too young to reason with and older teen-agers, who refuse to be reasoned with, are both vulnerable to the same resolution of the conflict— violence.

Fathers, Mothers, Sons, and Daughters

We found mothers to be the most frequent users of violence in families and sons the most common victims. We also examined violence toward children by focusing on mothers' and fathers' use of violence on sons and daughters. In no instance were fathers more likely than mothers to strike their children. The general trend of mothers being the more frequent users of violence and sons being the more usual targets persisted.

Fathers were twice as prone to push, grab, shove, slap, or spank their daughters. There was no significant difference in the frequency of mothers and fathers pushing, grabbing, shoving, slapping, or spanking their male children, but mothers were much more likely to do these things to their daughters than were fathers. Mothers also tended to throw things more at their daughters than did fathers.

Sex and Age of Children

Discussions with parents who used violence on their children indicated that perhaps the age of the child influenced which sex child was hit more often or more severely. Some of our early pilot studies (Gelles, 1974) hinted that there was no difference between sons and daughters being struck when they were younger; but, as children got older, boys were the most common victims of frequent and severe parental violence. We did find that for younger children (under nine years old) there were no statistically significant differences between sons and daughters being pushed, grabbed, shoved, slapped, or spanked. However, boys over ten years of age were more likely to experience these forms of violence. In fact, sons fifteen to seventeen were twice as likely as girls to be pushed, grabbed, or shoved.

SUMMING UP

Most American parents approve of spanking and slapping their children, and almost two out of three American parents slap or spank their children in any given year. Nearly all parents slap or spank their children at least once in their lifetimes.

The total package of information presented in this chapter on attitudes toward violence and violent behavior suggests that children are injured and abused because we as a society are committed to norms which approve of and legitimize using violence as a frequent form of training and punishing children. Given the general attitudes of the society toward using violence and the extent and frequency of parental violence, we should not be surprised to find millions of parents going beyond the "normal violence" permitted to parents and placing children of all ages at risk of being physically injured.

One important point we make in this chapter is that we have demonstrated for the first time, with reliable scientific data on a nationally representative sample, that violence toward children goes well beyond ordinary physical punishment. Millions of children each year face parents who are using forms of violence that could grievously injure, maim, or kill them. In many families these episodes of violence are not merely one-shot outbursts. They are regular patterned ways which parents use to deal with conflict with their offspring. We do not mean to imply that the majority of parent-child exchanges are violent; rather we mean that many children periodically experience severe beatings, kicks, and punches in their homes.

A second point concerns the level of severe violence in families. Our figures do offer some solace since they demonstrate that relatively few parents do use beatings and guns and knives on their children. Nevertheless, although the actual percentage of parents who physically beat their children is small, when you extrapolate the figures to the national population it means that millions of children are involved. Consider how we would react if we found that millions of children faced guns and knives and experienced beatings in schools. If we were talking about smallpox, mumps, or flu, these figures could be interpreted to mean that there is an epidemic of these diseases in the United States. Somehow, people tend to focus on the more dramatic instances of child abuse and exhibit less concern over the mundane and undramatic forms of violence children experience. But violence of any kind is important. The consequences are potentially dramatic, since children who experience violence in their home experience it from those who claim love and affection for them.

One wonders why, when so many have expressed concern about violence in television, no one has ever voiced concern about the consequences of children seeing or being victims of violence in their own homes. The conventional theory is that the more violence a child sees on television, the more he or she tends to be violent, or is at least tolerant of violence. If this is the case, imagine the consequences of millions of children growing up seeing their parents using violence on each other, and on their children.

Researchers who have studied child abuse continue to find that children who were abused often grow up to be abusing parents (Bakan, 1971; Kempe, et al., 1962; Gil, 1970; Steele and Pollock, 1974). Research on murderers finds that killers experienced more frequent and severe violence as children than their brothers who did not go on to commit a homicide (Palmer, 1962; Gillen, 1946). Examinations of presidential assassins or would-be assassins also find these individuals sharing common histories of violent upbringing. In his diary, Arthur Bremer, Governor George Wallace's would-be assassin, wrote, "My mother must have thought I was a canoe, she paddled me so much." Lee Harvey Oswald, Sirhan Sirhan, and Charles Manson all experienced violent childhoods (Button, 1973).

A study of violent inmates in San Quentin prison found that 100 per cent of them experienced extreme violence between the ages of one and ten (Maurer, 1976). Psychologist Ralph Welsh (1976) claims that he has never examined or talked with a violent juvenile delinquent who did not come from an extremely violent background. Moreover, Welsh claims that even if the extreme violence ceases before the child is four years old, the child still is likely to exhibit violent tendencies as a juvenile.

Violence in the streets, violence in the schools, assassinations, murders, assaults, wife abuse, child abuse—are they caused by violence on television, violence in the movies, permissive upbringings? These probably contribute something. But the evidence appears to support the notion that our homes and how we raise our children are the main sources of our violent society.

Surely the pattern is not as simple as "being beaten causes one to beat." A society in which millions of children are kicked, beaten, punished, bitten, shot, and stabbed by their parents has a bigger problem than mere child abuse. Millions of our children are "time bombs" of violence which can explode at home, at school, or in the streets.

CHAPTER 4

Kids Will Be Kids: Violence Between Brothers and Sisters

Imagine a typical hospital emergency room. A young boy, perhaps seven or eight years old, is escorted from the waiting room into the examining area. His face is covered with blood from a gash above the eye, and his lip is swollen.

A nurse returns from the examining area to talk to the mother. The nurse's demeanor—her disgust—coupled with stage-whispered comments from other attending staff suggest they suspect this is a case of child abuse. Other patients exchange looks of shock and revulsion, clearly indicating the contempt they feel toward this mother.

Consider the same scene—the same child, the same mother, the same injuries. What if the information given to the attending staff and conveyed to those in the waiting room is that the injured child was fighting with his brother and some misplaced blows caused the injury? The atmosphere in the waiting room would change. Patients would now nod their heads in agreement, noting that "boys will be boys," "all kids fight," and convey similar messages of condolence to the mother, whose distress they would now try to relieve.

ACCEPTANCE OF SIBLING RIVALRY

Scenes like this are played out regularly in hospital emergency rooms, school nurses' offices, and family homes. Somehow we assume that as children grow, it is normal to learn to stick up for oneself and use one's fists if necessary. When brothers and sisters fight, parents often view the fights as practice for skills which will be required in order to deal with their friends and schoolmates. There is widespread acceptance of the desirability of learning how to use physical violence effectively. In Chapter 3 we reported on a survey which found that seven out of ten Americans agree with the statement "When a boy is growing up it is very important for him to have a few fist fights" (Stark and Mc Evoy, 1970).

The way society defines an act often tells us how important, serious, or disruptive that act is considered to be. Violence between siblings is the most prevalent form of family violence. It also portends much for the future. In the next chapter we will show that the methods children use to resolve conflicts are very likely to be similar to those they observed their parents using to resolve marital conflicts, and those which the child has personally experienced when disciplined by the parents. Fights between brothers and sisters are a child's first opportunity to attempt to resolve conflicts by physical force.

THE HISTORY OF SIBLING VIOLENCE

During the last fifty years there has been a tremendous amount of research on children and their relations with their parents, peers, and siblings. But none of this seems to have looked at physical fighting between children in a family. There is no previous study we can use as a base line to compare with our survey. However, historical documents, diaries, and court records provide some insights.

Perhaps the earliest and best-known account of sibling violence is the biblical story of Cain killing his brother Abel:

> And Cain talked with Abel his brother: and it came to pass, when they were in the field, that Cain rose up against Abel his brother, and slew him (Gen. 4:8).

In the traditional Arab world, a brother, father, or other relative *must* murder a girl who brings dishonor on the family. The effects of this tradition can still be seen today, even in a sophisticated city such as Beirut. As recently as the 1978 civil war in Lebanon, a mother who had seen her daughter raped and killed said, "She's better off dead. No one would have married her and she would have lived in shame the rest of her life" (Toronto *Globe and Mail*, August 29, 1978, p. 4; see also Safilios-Rothschild, 1969).

Insight on life in colonial America can be gained from the diary of Philip Fithian, a tutor for the Carter family at the dawn of the American Revolution. Fithian's observation of the fights between the Carter children will seem remarkably familiar. He recorded the following fight between two adolescents:

> Bob called Nancy a Lyar: Nancy unbraided Bob, on the other hand, with being often flog'd by their pappa; often by the Masters in College; that he had stol'n Rum and had got drunk; & that he used to run away. These reproaches when they were set off with Miss Nancys truely feminine address, so violently exasperated Bob that he struck her in his rage. (1945, p. 66)

About a month later Fithian described the following incident between Nancy and her younger sister:

> Before Breakfast Nancy and Fanny had a fight about a shoe brush which they both wanted. Fanny pull'd off her shoe and

threw it at Nancy, which missed her and broke a pane of glass of our school room. They then enter's upon close scratching which methods seem instinctive in women (1945, p. 85).

CURRENT EXAMPLES OF SIBLING VIOLENCE

There is contemporary evidence illustrating the prevalence of violence between brothers and sisters. Steinmetz's survey of fifty-seven randomly selected families (1977c) found a high level of physical violence between siblings. These families' comments (both during interviews and in the diaries they kept for one week) suggest that fights between brothers and sisters are very similar to those attributed to the Carter children two hundred years earlier. Furthermore, while families were reluctant to talk about wife-beating and child abuse, they readily acknowledged sibling violence as a normal aspect of family relationships. The scope and extent of sibling violence are illustrated in the following examples:

One mother, who recorded only two conflicts in her diary during a two-day period, followed by a conflict-free day, predicted:

> Next week will probably be hell on wheels around here. This can't be a lasting peace—war must be at hand!

Another said:

> It's a wonder they're not all bruised and bloody. They must get tired of yelling at each other.

When asked how her children got along, one parent reported:

> Terrible. They fight all the time. Anything can be a problem, it's just constant, but I understand that this is normal. I talk to other people, and their kids are the same way.

A TV commercial touting the advantages of long distance phone calls features two brothers reminiscing about their childhood. The older brother remembers that

> When we were little we fought like cats and dogs just like normal kids, but I wouldn't let anyone hit him but me.

The attitude expressed in the telephone commercial signifies a generally tolerant attitude toward family violence. If the same act of physical violence took place between non-related adults or children, it might well be considered a criminal offense. When it occurs between brothers and sisters, it becomes acceptable or at least tolerable.

The list of things leading to sibling fights is almost infinite. One family noted the following sources of conflicts during the one-week period:

use of the glider
sharing the truck
sharing the tricycle
knocking down one child's blocks and taking them
taking one child's toy sticks from the play "fire"

HOW MUCH SIBLING VIOLENCE?

Of the 2,143 families interviewed for this book, 733 had two or more children between three and seventeen years of age who were living at home.[1] We asked the parents our standard series of questions about conflicts. Highlighting our discoveries are the following findings:

> Sibling violence occurs more frequently than parent-child or husband-wife violence.
> The older the child, the lower the rate of sibling violence.
> Boys in every age group are more violent toward their siblings than are girls.
> The highest level of violence occurs when a boy has only brothers.

Some of the specific details of what we discovered are summarized in Chart 4. These figures confirm and document the impression from historical sources and from our earlier small sample studies that almost all American children are violent toward their brothers and sisters.

CHART 4
Per Cent of Children Who Were
Violent to a Sibling in Previous Year

VIOLENT ACT	PER CENT
Any violence	82
Pushed or shoved	74
Slapped	48
Threw things	43
Kicked, bit, punched	42
Hit with an object	40
Beat up	16
Threatened with a knife or gun	0.8
Used a knife or gun	0.3

Four out of every five American children between the ages of three and seventeen who have a brother or sister at home carry out at least one violent act toward a sibling during a typical year. Of course, the percentage hitting a brother or sister is greater for the very youngest children. But, as we will see later in this chapter, the rates are very high even for children as old as the late teen ages.

The violence rates may be more meaningful when applied to the nation's estimated 36.3 million children between three and seventeen with siblings at home during the year of our survey. Over 29 million American children engage in one or more acts of physical violence toward a sibling in a single year.

It might be claimed that this overstates the case because so much of the "violence" is pushing, slapping, shoving, and throwing things. But kicking, biting, punching, hitting with objects, and "beating up" are also very common. In fact, fifty-three out of every hundred children per year attack a brother or sister this severely. That means well over 19 million attacks which would be considered an assault if they occurred outside the family.

When it was asked if "beating up" a sibling had *ever happened*, rather than just during the survey year, we found that 20 per cent had beaten up a brother or sister. In other words, over 7 million children in the United States have been "beaten up" by a sibling.

Although "only" 3 children in 1,000 used a knife or gun on a brother or sister, when one applies this rate to the country's 36 million children between 3 and 17 it suggests that about 109,000 had actually used a knife or gun on a brother or sister during the survey year.

Of course, it is hazardous to derive estimates like this from the 3 per 1,000 rate in our survey. Of those we questioned, we found only three children who actually produced a knife or gun during a conflict with a brother or sister. However, we also asked if this had *ever happened*. This revealed 32 cases! That makes a rate of 4.7 per 100 children. Translating that into actual numbers, over 1.5 million American children have at some point faced an angry brother or sister wielding a knife or gun.

How accurate are these estimates of violence between children in American families? There are several reasons to think that they are underestimates (and also one factor which might lower the true rates).

First, parents probably do not know about every physical fight their children have.

Second, since such fights are a taken-for-granted part of family life, many of the less severe acts of violence are likely to have been forgotten.

Third, we studied only two-parent households. The amount of sibling violence in one-parent households might well be greater than in two-parent families.[2]

Fourth, we only studied violence used by one child. The total level of sibling violence in the families we talked to is probably higher when all children are considered.

SIBLING VIOLENCE IS THE MOST FREQUENT TYPE OF FAMILY VIOLENCE

Obviously, a large number of children are perpetrators and victims of violence between siblings. In fact, as we said before, sibling violence occurs more often than violence by parents on children or violence by spouses on each other. For example, each year three out of every hundred children are kicked, bitten, or punched by a parent, and two out of every hundred spouses kick, bite, or punch each other. But a whopping forty-two out of every hundred children age three to seventeen kick, bite, or punch a brother or sister each year. Likewise, during the year of our study, while 15 per cent of parents hit their children with an object and 10 per cent of the spouses hit each other with an object, 40 per cent of the children hit a brother or sister. The pattern is continued when we consider "beating up." Although 1 per cent of the children were "beaten up" by their parents and 1 per cent of their parents "beat up" each other, 16 per cent of the children "beat up" a brother or sister. The only act of severe violence to occur *less* frequently among siblings was the use of a gun or knife, and that is probably the only reason why there are more husband-wife and parent-child homicides than siblings who kill each other.

THE MORE THE MERRIER?

The families in this study represent the spectrum of family size in the United States. Twenty-one per cent of the families were single-child families; 43 per cent had two children; 22 per cent had three children; 9 per cent had four children; 4 per cent had five children; and 1 per cent had six or more children.

What is the effect of the size of the family on sibling violence? Is there less violence in families with two or three children than when there are many children? Obviously, if there are fewer children, then each child has fewer siblings to fight with. Furthermore, there is probably less conflict over scarce resources such as toys, television, radio, and stereo sets, and bathroom facilities—a major source of conflict among teen-agers. Finally, fewer siblings may mean that there is less com-petition for parental attention. However, larger families, fol-lowing the theme expressed in "The Waltons" or *Cheaper by the Dozen,* may have fewer conflicts since each child has a specific role and the older children look after the younger, rather than competing with them.

It turns out that there is not a very clear answer to the ques-tion about number of children and violence between the chil-dren. If the criterion is whether any violence occurred during the year, the two-child families have slightly higher rates than those with three, four, or five or more children. The same applies if the measure used is severe violence (see Appendix B for distinction between violence and severe violence). The rate goes from 55 per cent for two-child families to 53 per cent for three-child families, 50 per cent for four-child families, and 51 per cent for families consisting of five or more children. On the other hand, if we consider how often violence occurred, then the more children, the more violent incidents there were. However, the differences are not large enough to be statis-tically reliable.

AGE AND SEX DIFFERENCES

Parents often ask, "When will my kids stop squabbling?" To many parents it seems that while the subjects of fights may change, the battles don't stop until the children leave home. One parent we talked to, when asked if her kids were fighting less now that they were older said:

> I don't think there has been any change. Now that they're older, they can verbalize more, and say more hateful things. When they were tiny they could throw a handful of sand in

each other's eyes or something. The type of fighting may have changed and they have become more sophisticated.

How typical is this mother's experience? Does age influence the type and degree of physical violence used by siblings? Since younger children may have trouble resolving conflicts verbally, they might resort to physical violence more frequently than older children. One mother of four closely spaced children reported that small children: ". . . do have a lot more hitting . . . bopping each other on the head with toys." On the other hand, it seems that teen-agers might rely on their greater physical size and strength to intimidate, if not actually beat up a brother or sister.

A father we interviewed, discussing his seventeen-year-old son and thirteen-year-old daughter said his daughter was always complaining about her brother hitting her:

> Not the vicious hitting. Some of the taps are exaggerated. His sister will scream. "Man he hauled off and whaled the day-lights out of me!" I'll ask, "Well let me see the bruises." She'll come back with "Well, he didn't really hit that hard."

Our earlier studies, as well as everyday observations, suggest that early adolescence is a period of high confrontation of all kinds—whining, yelling, and hitting. Typical of this apparently constant bickering is our interview with one parent who described sibling fights:

> They fuss. They say "He's sitting in my seat." Or "He has got an inch of his pants on the line where I am supposed to be." Or "He's got his seat moved right in the middle so I can't see the television." Or "He has a dirty pair of pants on my bed." It is just nonsense and silliness.

There also is evidence to suggest that this violence may continue into the early twenties. One of the secretaries typing this chapter said that she and her brother fought quite a bit. When asked "When did it stop?" She replied:

I was twenty-two, my brother was twenty-four. My brother had borrowed some of my husband's records. He lived with my mother and we were visiting them. I asked him to get my husband's records and he kept putting it off. So I said I'd get them. I was going through the records and he said, "Get the hell away from there, I'll do it," and pushed me away and threw me on the floor. I waited till he got down to look through the records. I never attacked my brother unless his back was turned. I jumped on his back, got hold of his ears, and shook his head. I kept yelling, "I'm sick and tired of you throwing me around." My brother yelled to my husband, who finally pulled me off of him.

Of course these are only impressions. They might represent extreme, rather than typical families. To find out, we compared the violence rates for children of different ages in the national sample.

As expected, the violence rates go down steadily from 90 per cent for children ages three and four, to 87 per cent for the five- to nine-year-olds, 76 per cent for the ten- to fourteen-year-olds, and 64 per cent of the fifteen- to seventeen-year-olds. But more important than the steady decline is the fact that even at age fifteen to seventeen, almost two out of three American children hit a brother or sister at least once during the year. Moreover, for many it is not just an isolated incident. In fact, among those fifteen- to seventeen-year-olds who have been violent to a sibling, it tends to happen on the average of nineteen times a year. So the twenty-two-year-old woman and her twenty-four-year-old brother engaging in a pitched battle over records may not be as unusual as we would like to think.

BOYS AND GIRLS

Although boys and girls may argue and fight with others in the family just about as much, it is widely believed that girls do more of their fighting verbally, whereas boys tend toward physical fights. Our data support this view—but just barely. Although the expected difference between boys and girls is certainly there, the difference is much smaller than we expected. Eighty-three per cent of the boys attacked a brother or sister during the survey year, but so did 74 per cent of the girls. Perhaps the small difference is due to the presence of so many young children in the sample. To check on this we compared boys and girls at four ages (three to four, five to nine, ten to fourteen, and fifteen to seventeen). At all ages, the girls were less violent than the boys, but only slightly so. So the nearly equal rates of violence which we found for husbands and wives (see Chapter 2) seem to be a continuation of a pattern which exists in the families children grow up in.

THE MIX OF BROTHERS OR SISTERS?

Can the above differences or lack of differences be attributed entirely to the sex of the child? Couldn't some of these differences be the result of whether boys had only brothers or girls had only sisters? Parents of boys tend to think that brothers fight more than sisters. Parents of girls could respond, "Oh no, girls bicker constantly." Parents who have boys and girls might insist that the combination is more violent since they have nothing in common. Thus we felt it was important to look at the sex of the child and the sex of the other children.

We found girls use less violence than do boys, irrespective of whether the girls had only sisters, only brothers, or both brothers and sisters. Another interesting finding was the apparent effect of girls on reducing the violence of their brothers. The violence of boys who only have sisters is lower than for boys with brothers or with both brothers and sisters. The effect of the sex mixture is most dramatic for things which go beyond the ordinary punching, slapping, and shoving violence, which, as is clear by now, is just about universal between children in American families. For violence that is severe enough to go into the Sibling Abuse Index (see Appendix B), the rates are 67 per cent in all-boy families, 52 per cent in mixed-sex families, and "only" 40 per cent in all-girl families.

This finding is consistent with Orville Brim's classic study of the effect of the sex of one's siblings (1958). His data is on families with two children. Brim found that boys with a sister were more "feminine" in their behavior than boys with a brother, and that girls with a brother were more "masculine" than girls with a sister. It seems that siblings provide a role model influencing behavior in the direction typical of the sex of that sibling; in this case girls influence their brothers toward the less violent ways of girls (and boys influence girls to be more violent than is expected of females).

AGE AND SEX COMBINATIONS

Boys and girls mature at different rates. Interests and activities which at one age may make the children close companions may reduce them to bickering rivals at another age. Thus, the lucky high school freshman girl with an older brother may be the envy of her crowd, while the high school senior girl who has a freshman brother may live in perpetual fear of being humiliated by his clumsy, socially inept, immature behavior. In one of our early studies this problem was frequently mentioned by teen-agers. It may be that the unique combination of age and sex of siblings can raise or lower the level of violence. Thus, we must consider not only whether the family has just boys or girls or both sexes, but the age of these children. What we found is that the sex of the sibling *group* makes a big difference in the level of violence. This is in contrast to the relatively small difference between *individual* children of each sex.

CHART 5
Sibling Abuse by Sex Mix of Children and
Age of Children

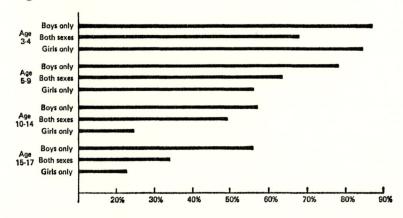

Families with only male children have consistently more sibling violence than a family composed only of girls. Furthermore, the difference between the all-boy and all-girl families increases markedly as the children grow older. There are only small differences between all-girl and all-boy families when the children are three or four. A greater difference is found at age five to nine. The rate of violence for ten- to fourteen-year-old boys in all-boy families is more than double the rate for girls. For the oldest age group (fifteen through seventeen), the rate for all-boy families is roughly twice as great as that for all-girl families.

DANGEROUS ASSAULTS

Up to this point we have compared boys and girls and children of different ages using an over-all measure of violence. Most of this is "petty violence." Perhaps that is why there is not much difference in the over-all violence rates for boys and girls. Would the differences be greater if we consider "serious violence" like punching and beating up a brother or sister?

As for age differences, we found that younger children are more often violent. But what about the severity of their violence? Perhaps the violence of the younger children is confined to pushing, shoving, and slapping? Are older brothers and sisters the perpetrators of "beating up" or using a gun or knife on a brother or sister? Differences like these are what we might expect for children of different ages.

However, we found that virtually all acts of violence *decreased* as the children grew up. Even "beating up" showed a consistent decrease for each older age group. The only exception to the decrease in violence with age is in the use of a knife or gun. This went from 2.6 per cent of preschoolers to 6.5 per cent of high schoolers.

We hasten to point out that we have gathered a sample of children at one point in time and divided the sample into age groups. There is always the possibility (though we think it is unlikely) that the fifteen- to seventeen-year-olds, who have the lowest rates, might have been relatively non-violent when they were younger. Likewise, the three- and four-year-olds, who have the highest rates, might maintain this high level of violence until adulthood.

When we were considering husband-wife violence and parent-child violence, it was useful to combine the more severe acts of violence into Child Abuse and Spouse Abuse Indexes (see Appendix B for details). We can do the same thing for sibling violence. The Sibling Abuse Index (see Appendix B) consists of all acts of violence that are more serious than pushing, slapping, shoving, and throwing things.

More than half (53 per cent) of the children in the sample had attacked a brother or sister this severely during the year we asked about. As with the over-all violence index, more boys are severely violent than girls (59 per cent compared to 46 per cent). But even for serious violence, the difference is not as great as stereotypes about girls and boys might suggest.

As for age differences, the Sibling Abuse Index rates decline sharply with age (the percentage using a knife or gun is too small to influence importantly the Sibling Abuse Index). But even at age fifteen through seventeen, over a third (35.5 per cent) of the children had severely assaulted a sibling during the survey year.

Do these high rates of sibling abuse portend an even more violent society when these children are adults? That is doubtful. We think the main reason these figures seem so high is that no one has gathered such data before. The cases we cited at the beginning of the chapter suggest that similar assaults by children on their brothers and sisters have been common since earliest history.

The following examples of sibling murder illustrate, all too clearly, the ease with which even young children can inflict fatal injuries.

> Freddie, age 9, smothered his six-month-old half brother, Jack, when the baby's crying distracted him from watching a television murder story. Freddie had been left in charge of Jack and another half brother, George, age 2, when their parents went out one evening. In accordance with his mother's instructions Freddie gave Jack a bottle. When it failed to quiet him, Freddie held a pillow over Jack's face until he was dead, then lay down in his parents' bed beside the body and fell asleep. He was still sleeping when his parents returned (Sargent, 1972, p. 107).

> Gertrude, age 7, decapitated her 6-year-old sister, Helen, with a single blast of her step father's shotgun, which he had left loaded behind the headboard of his bed. While Gertrude later admitted she was angry at her sister, she was "only playing," and had no intention of killing her (Sargent, 1972, p. 109).

Although the violence exhibited by these two cases had a more extreme outcome than that represented by our families, it does illustrate that lethal violence can be perpetrated by very young children. It also should be remembered that based on parents' reports, at some time in their lives nearly 2 million children used a gun or knife on a sibling.

Many readers will know about at least one such incident. One of us, for example, knows a person who at age ten, and with a brother who was twelve, experienced the following: Her mother was at work and her brother had chores to do after school. Her brother would make her do his work by threatening to "beat her up."

> I refused one day and he hit me. I began chasing him around the dining room, kitchen, and living room but I couldn't catch him. He kept taunting me, making faces and saying, "You can't catch me." I decided I couldn't. A butcher knife was on the dining room table next to a cake. He was in the kitchen by the stove. I was in the dining room by the cake. I picked up the knife and heaved it at him. I missed him but hit the stove handle and broke it off. He was shocked and yelled, "It could have hit me or killed me." That stopped the argument for then. Later that afternoon he had two of his boy friends come in and hold me up against the wall while he kept going at me with an ice pick, pretending he was going to stab me.

MUST KIDS FIGHT?

Conflicts and disputes between children in a family are an inevitable part of life, just as they are in all other human groups. But the use of physical force as a tactic for resolving these conflicts is by no means inevitable.

A student in one of our classes related the following interaction between the children when baby-sitting:

> I recently spent a week with two children (seven-year-old girl, six-year-old boy) whose parents use no physical restraints or force in their control. In one week of continuous contact with them, without their parents, I did not once see one strike the other. Furthermore, their vocabulary did not include threats of impending violence. I witnessed occasional response to frustration by crying and one outburst of "I hate you." I also

witnessed frequent verbalizations or arguments dealing with problem circumstances which were mostly in the form of the older child "explaining why" to the younger. When questioned, she indicated her mommy usually would tell them a few times to do certain things and if they did not obey then she would scold them or send them to their rooms. Interestingly, I watched her *imitate* her mother's behavior throughout the week. This isolated situation seems the optimum in family behavior.

Many Americans are likely to think that parents who do not use physical punishment will end up with uncontrollable children. Why not in this case? The student who did the baby-sitting felt it was because the mother was educated and taught child development. It would be reassuring if that were the reason, but we are skeptical. First, the advice in child development books is tremendously variable. It includes some books which take the view that aggression is a drive or instinct which, if suppressed, can cause psychological problems for the child. Another school of thought among professionals giving child care advice to parents is typified by the following advice a pediatrician gave to a friend of ours:

> Don't stop a fight until there is bloodshed. Let the kids figure it out themselves. Kids are smart enough to do this.

Our conclusion from this study and from other research is just the opposite. It is based on the idea that human beings learn to be violent. It is possible to provide children with an environment in which non-violent methods of solving conflicts are learned. The mother described above was doing just that.

SUMMING UP

While public attention has been focused on child abuse and wife-beating, we found that the over-all level of violence between siblings far outstrips that which occurs between parent and child, or between spouses.

As for steps which might reduce the high level of violence between children in American families, part of the answer is suggested by what will be reported in the next chapter. Violence between siblings often reflects what children see their parents doing to each other, as well as what the child experiences in the form of discipline. Children of non-violent parents also tend to use non-violent methods to deal with their siblings and later with their spouses and children. If violence, like charity, begins at home, so does non-violence.

PART III

Social Patterns in Family Violence

CHAPTER 5

The Social Heredity of Family Violence

He began hitting her even before they were married. The first time was on a warm evening after they had returned from a walk.

Craig doesn't remember now why he did it. He only knows he hit Patsy with the cane, the cane he had just bought. . . . He stood over her in a bedroom of her mother's house in the Bronx, raised the cane over his head and let it come down on her arms and hands. She suffered contusions on both hands; he turned and ran out of the house.

"I can remember hitting her on the hand with it. I cannot remember what motivated me, what the actual reason was. We had an argument about something. I remember leaving the house and sitting by myself at the bus stop. I can remember being upset after I had done it. It's really hard to remember. I'm sure I don't want to."

The next time was three months after they married. Craig was stationed out west and Patsy came to live with him in a trailer camp near the Army base. "We were fighting about the music. I felt like I wasn't being allowed to listen to the music, and she went out to the car and she wrecked my tapes." Craig said.

He went roaring back into the trailer, knocking over Patsy's record player and grabbing a rubber hose. "I hit her on the arms and legs. We were shouting a lot, we were screaming at each other." With the hose he whipped at his bride's arms and legs until she gained enough self-control to run to a neighbor's.

The same scene was still being played seven years later. But now they had two daughters, a modest ranch-style house in central Suffolk and a small sheet-metal shop, which Craig owned and worked in. Patsy was the housewife-next-door, if you didn't notice the welts and black-and-blue marks (Goldstein, 1977, p. 9).

How could a couple inflict such a situation upon one another? A clue turned up when Craig and Patsy finally consulted a marriage counselor. Craig said:

"I was a product of seeing my mother being beaten up. I also was beaten up, whipped with a belt. I thought once that maybe my mother died to get out of that relationship with my father. I mean, I know she died of cancer, but . . . That's the ironic part: I remember wanting to dial the police when they were arguing to protect her, and yet it's funny how I did the same thing as my father" (Goldstein, 1977, p. 10).

The family—the fountainhead of both love and violence—that paradox confronted us time and again in this study. And Craig's case seems to be a typical example. People imitate what they saw and experienced as children, thus re-enacting in adult life their family experiences as children.

To test this theory we needed answers to a number of questions:

Do sons of wife-beaters become wife-beaters?
Do daughters of beaten wives tend to marry wife-beaters?
Do daughters of beaten wives grow up to be violent?

Do children who are slapped and spanked, in turn, visit similar punishment on their own children or spouses?

Each of these questions will be considered in this chapter.[1]

TWO GENERATIONS OF HUSBAND-WIFE VIOLENCE

In this first part of the chapter we will examine violence by the parents of the people we interviewed. Since these people had to be old enough to have children at least eighteen years old, they themselves would probably be no younger than thirty-five, with the average age around sixty. We will call them the "grandparent generation," since most of their children (the people we interviewed) had children of their own.

Were Grandparents' Marriages Less Violent? In remembering their teen-age years, the people interviewed were asked if there ". . . were occasions when your father [or stepfather] hit your mother [or stepmother] or threw something at her." About one out of seven of our respondents (13.1 per cent) remembered at least one such incident within a given year. That figure is very close to the annual rate of violence by the husbands in the current generation (see Chapter 2).

When it comes to violence by the grand*mothers*, the situation is a little different. "Only" one out of twelve of the grandmothers (8.5 per cent) were remembered as having hit the grandfathers. A high rate of violence, to be sure, but it is *less* than the one out of eight or nine of their daughters who admitted to hitting their husbands in the survey year.

This does not mean, necessarily, that the current generation of married women are more violent than their mothers. We think the difference is due to the way the data were gathered.[2] There has probably been little change in the amount of violence between couples from the grandparent generation to the current generation.

Do Violent Grandparents Produce Violent Men and Women? Of course not all the grandparents and not all the current generation of parents are violent. Why are some violent and some not? The theory behind this chapter is that the majority of today's violent couples are those who were brought up by parents violent toward each other.

To test this theory we compared the husbands whose parents had not been violent toward each other with the husbands who reported at least one instance of violence between their parents. A clear pattern was evident. Men who had seen parents physically attack each other were almost three times more likely to have hit their own wives during the year of the study. In fact, about one out of three had done so (35 per cent) compared with one out of ten (10.7 per cent) of the sons of non-violent parents. We found roughly the same statistics for women. Women whose parents were violent had a much higher rate of hitting their own husbands (26.7 per cent) as compared to the daughters of non-violent parents (8.9 per cent).

Although the violence rate is lower in the group whose parents were not violent, the group includes many people who hit their partners during the year we asked them about.

Some of these people commited extremely violent acts. People whose parents were violent, on the average, continued in the same vein, but *not always*. Although we saw a clear tendency for the children of violent couples to be violent toward their own spouses, there were many exceptions.

If seeing your parents hit one another increases your chances of hitting your spouse, does it also increase the likelihood that you will abuse your husband or wife?

Using the Wife- *and* Husband-beating Indexes described in Appendix B, we found that people whose parents were never violent to each other experience the lowest rates of wife- and husband-beating—about 2 per cent.

Of course, the "high" and "low" rates we speak of are relative. If one belonged to a church or worked in an office where "only" one or two out of a hundred members or employees severely assaulted another every year, it would not be considered a low rate of assault. However, when compared to the rates for those who grew up in violent homes, these rates are low. In fact, *the sons of the most violent parents have a rate of wife-beating 1,000 per cent greater than that of the sons of non-violent parents (20 per cent).*[3] The daughters of violent parents have a husband-beating rate that is 600 per cent greater than the daughters who grew up in non-violent households (13.3 per cent). The scale of violence toward spouses seems to rise fairly steadily with the violence these people observed as children between their own parents. Quite clearly, the more violence that took place between the parents of our couples, the more the couples tend to be extremely violent to each other.

Violent Grandfathers Versus Violent Grandmothers. Does it matter who was violent—the grandfather or the grandmother? Does growing up in a violent home have different effects on boys and girls? We looked into these questions and found that over all, the effect of violence by the father was slightly greater than the effect of violence by the mother. However, violence by the father did not affect sons more than daughters, and violence by the mother did not affect daughters more than sons.

Generally, those who grew up in homes in which parents were violent to each other tended to be violent in their own marriages. It made no difference whether it was the father or mother who was violent, or whether the child was a boy or a girl.

PHYSICAL PUNISHMENT
AND LEARNING TO BE VIOLENT

The first part of this chapter clearly shows that children who observe their parents being violent to each other tend to be violent when they themselves marry. This is probably because children imitate the models of behavior acted out by adults who are important in their lives. But other learning processes are probably also part of the story. We look now at *the effect of physical punishment* as a learning process.

We set out to test the theory that violence in the family is commonplace because the family is the setting in which most people first experience violence. More importantly, it is the setting in which most people learn the emotional and moral meaning of violence. Almost everyone's first experience with violence comes as physical punishment—usually being slapped as a child. Numerous surveys show that this is almost universal, i.e., over 90 per cent of all American parents hit their children.

Parents justify these slaps as being in the child's best welfare. They slap a child, for example, to prevent him from picking up and eating dirty or dangerous things. At a slightly later age the slaps are for things like running into the street. That the parent does this to protect the child blinds us to the fact that these slaps and spankings are violent acts. Even though done for the good of the child, these acts still fit the definition of violence given in Chapter 1: an act carried out with the intent of causing physical pain or injury.

The issue, however, is far more important than classifying what is or is not violent. The fact that the parent is doing the hitting is profoundly important because of its long-lasting effects on the child's personality and view of the world. These effects are felt long beyond the time it takes to learn that playing in the street is dangerous. Indelibly stamped on the child's mind, such punishment can have, as we explain below, significant effects on actions in adult life.

Lesson One. The first of these unintended lessons teaches that *those who love you the most are also those who hit you.* It is an easy step from there to the opposite side of the coin: those you love are those you hit. We believe that here lies the basis for the link between love and violence which is so much a part of the human experience. Seen in its extreme form, there are people who can enjoy sex only when it is accompanied by violence or violent fantasies. In less extreme form it tinges the lives of a vast number of people.

One social worker explained it this way: "There are battered women whose fathers knocked their mothers around and who knocked them around when they were kids . . . the beatings were how they got their strokes. My opinion is that you tend to repeat the feeling that you had as a child . . . not just the behavior patterns, but you repeat experiencing a familiar feeling. Even if it's unpleasant . . . it's familiar" (Maine *Times*, October 14, 1977).

Nursery schools are often the first place society comes to grips with children who hit other people. Just as each classroom has its "class clown," each preschool has its class "hitter" or "bully." As one nursery school teacher remarked, "The thing I never understand about the children who hit out is that they seem to hit their friends. When we ask them, 'Why did you hit so and so?' they say, 'Cause I like him.' I just never understand that."

From our vantage point, the nursery school teacher should not be perplexed. She should expect aggressive children to be hitting those they like. By and large, these children have spent the first three years of their lives growing up in homes where love, liking, and hitting coexisted and were taken for granted. Many of the nursery school hitters may have difficulty separating hitting from love or friendship.

Lesson Two. The second of the unintended things learned through physical punishment is the idea that violence can be and should be used to secure good ends—the moral rightness of violence. This applies most directly within the family. Since violence is used to train the child in morally correct behavior or to teach the child to avoid injury, it *establishes the moral rightness of hitting other members of the same family.* We think it goes even beyond that. We believe it teaches that violence is okay even in non-family situations, provided it is for a socially worthy purpose. However, our data limited us to the family part of the theory.

Lesson Three. A third unintended principle learned through physical punishment is the idea that *violence is permissible when other things don't work.* Almost every reader of this book knows the ending to: "Johnny, I've told you ten times . . ." When other things don't work, the use of physical force is justified. This carries over into adult life. Many are the adults who find themselves using almost the identical phrases to spouses that were heard as children. And many are the husbands or wives who now follow through with the threat.

Children also learn this at a young age. Beaten wives we interviewed told us that their children began threatening them after seeing their fathers become violent. A child who sees his mother hit by his father comes to view hitting as "the thing to do"—a means of getting what he wants. Some mothers of young children report that when they refuse to give their child candy or cookies, the child will indignantly retort: "You better give me some candy, or I'll get Daddy to hit you!" Later on, the child takes matters into his own hands. Our survey uncovered many women battered by both their husbands and their teen-age children.

TWO GENERATIONS OF PHYSICAL PUNISHMENT

Not everyone will find the ideas just outlined convincing. To get a definitive answer, we would have had to observe the people we surveyed when they were children. That way we would know for sure how often their parents hit them. Since that was not possible we asked the husbands and wives how often they had been physically punished when they were thirteen or older. Then we compared people who were physically punished with those who were not to see if the pattern of violence was being repeated.

Did Grandparents Hit Less? There is a widespread belief

that child abuse is on the increase. The vast amount of abusive violence described in Chapter 3 might be taken as a sign that this is true. Our survey, however, did not indicate that this is the case.

We obtained information from our respondents about how often their parents (the people we refer to as grandparents) hit them as teen-agers. We asked whether the respondents had been physically punished as teen-agers and how often. We did not gather information on the kinds of punishment our respondents experienced, so we do not know how severely they were hit or whether they were victims of child abuse as teen-agers.

Three hundred and six of the couples we interviewed had a teen-aged child between thirteen and seventeen, living at home, who happened to be the child selected for the study. Over a third of these parents had used physical punishment on these teen-aged children during the year of the survey. We asked these parents if *their* parents had used physical punishment on them when they were teen-agers.[4] The results show an *almost identical rate of hitting teen-agers by the grandparent generation:* 37.3 per cent. Although a lot may be forgotten in the years since our respondents were teen-agers, the evidence from this study does not indicate either an increase or a decrease in the use of physical punishment from one generation to the next.

This and other studies suggest little difference in the "normal" use of force by parents, thus bearing on the much discussed question of whether child abuse is increasing. Also relevant is the fact that infanticide and abandoned children are now rare when compared to previous historical periods (Radbill, 1974). All of this suggests that *there is probably no more, or even less, child abuse now than in previous generations.* The seeming increase in child abuse is probably the result of greater public awareness, less public toleration of cruelty to children, and the uncovering of cases through new laws that require doctors and others to report cases of child abuse.

Do Punishing Parents Produce Punishing Parents? The question of whether the use of physical punishment has gone up or down over the last few generations is important because most people assume that this method of dealing with children has important consequences. Those who subscribe to the "Spare the rod and spoil the child" philosophy believe it builds moral character. Those who subscribe to the "violence begets violence" point of view believe it builds a new generation of violent people.

As a first attempt to answer this question, we compared the amount of physical punishment used by the respondents' parents to the physical force used by the respondents on their own children. This revealed only a slight tendency for the mothers and fathers who had experienced the most violence to be more likely to hit their own children.

We think the reason we found no strong relationship between being physically punished as a child and using physical punishment on one's own children is because, in cases of major disobedience or actions that endanger the child, *almost everyone in our society hits his or her children.* Parents seem to feel it is morally right to do so—even required in some circumstances. Differences between parents based on their experiences as children are overshadowed by the norm permitting or requiring parents to use physical punishment. Parents don't need to learn to use physical punishment by following the example of their own parents. They see it every day in the behavior of others and in the mass media, and perhaps even more in the stories they all read as children (Huggins and Straus, 1979).

Aunt Polly in Mark Twain's *The Adventures of Tom Sawyer,* having, for once, let Tom off without a beating, expresses the beliefs that have been long part of our tradition: "I ain't doing my duty by that boy, and that's the Lord's truth, goodness knows. Spare the rod and spile the child, as the Good Book says. I'm a-laying up sin and suffering for us both, *I* know."

Young children start out early learning about "Tom the Piper's Son," who was "beat and sent crying down the street." Books for older children, such as *David Copperfield* and the *Prince and the Pauper* continue in the vein of cruelty, brutality, and abandonment of children.

Do Punishing Grandparents Produce Abusing Parents? We have seen that it is not necessary to have been treated violently for one to use physical punishment. Therefore, "ordinary" physical punishment cannot be used as a yardstick in testing our theory that "violence begets violence." We do have, however, data which partly get around the problem. This is the index of abusive parental violence. This Child Abuse Index (see Appendix B) leaves out the ordinary slapping, pushing, and shoving by parents and includes only those acts which are severe enough to put the child at risk of physical injury. Our survey found that about one out of eight American parents were this violent toward their children in the year under study.

The relationship between punishment as a child and child abuse as an adult is clear for the mothers: the more they were punished physically as teen-agers, the higher the rate of violent acts which could cause serious injury they inflicted on their own child. In fact, over one out of four of the mothers who were punished the most did things to their own children which many would consider child abuse. This compares with one out of ten of the mothers who were not hit as teen-agers.

One mother, anguished over her own capacity for child abuse, explained her plight:

> When I was a child, my step-father beat me. He beat me often enough to prompt me to swear that when I had kids I wouldn't lay a hand on them.
>
> It didn't work that way. The first couple of years everything went fine, then Bob (her husband) started making frequent and lengthy trips out of town. After he was gone a few days, I started taking it out on the kids.
>
> When Bob would ask me why the kids were black and blue,

I would pass it off by saying they fell while playing or bumped into a door.

As time passed, I would work out elaborately detailed stories to answer his questions of the injuries or bandages. . . . I would never take the kids to the same doctor or hospital twice. I would never use the same name. I even paid all the bills in cash so I wouldn't have to give anyone my address (New Hampshire *Times,* February 12, 1975, p. 4).

As in the case of mothers, fathers hit most by their parents have the same truly astounding rates of abusive violence toward their own children, namely one out of four.

Grandfathers Versus Grandmothers. Taking this one step further, we wanted to determine if physical punishment inflicted by one's father had any different effect than from one's mother. Generally, we found it didn't.

On the other hand, when we also took into account the sex of the child, something really interesting showed up: being punished frequently by *a father* has a much greater tendency to be associated with being an abusive parent *for boys* than it did for girls. The reverse also seems to be true. Physical punishment by *the mother* is much more strongly related to *the daughters* rate of abusive punishment than it is for sons. Assuming that children tend to pattern their behavior most closely after the behavior of the parent of the same sex, this finding supports the role model theory of why some people are violent and others are not. Apparently we learn violence best from parents of the same sex.

Returning to the original question—do punishing parents produce violent children? The answer is "yes." But this is not just a simple matter of "violence begetting violence." For one thing, the tendency to follow society's rules, which virtually require parents to spank their children, masks the effects of having experienced violence as a child. The effects of a violent childhood, however, come out when we look at violence which verges on or is child abuse. Parents who were subjected to a great deal of physical punishment have the highest rates of abusive violence toward their own children.

PHYSICAL PUNISHMENT
AND HUSBAND-WIFE VIOLENCE
IN THE NEXT GENERATION

We have seen that parents who were frequently punished physically as children tend to do the same with their own children. But perhaps that is as far as it goes. Perhaps being on the receiving end of frequent punishment from one's parents does not tend to make people violent in general—only when it comes to dealing with their own *children*. Does it also carry over to being violent toward one's husband or wife?

We found a clear tendency for the effects of being hit as a teen-ager to go beyond being only a model for physical punishment of one's children. People whose parents did not hit them as teen-agers have the lowest rate of violent *marriages* (one out of sixteen). The more punishment one experienced as a child, the greater the rate of violence in marriages fifteen or more years later. One out of four or five of those who were punished the most hit his or her spouse during the year of this survey. Physical punishment received as a child does increase the likelihood of domestic violence when people marry. If this is true, then it provides even stronger evidence for the "violence begets violence" theory.

Physical Punishment and Wife-beating. We know that children who experienced physical punishment as teen-agers have higher rates of violence toward their spouses. Typically this is of the pushing, shoving, slapping variety. But does being hit as a teen-ager make people more prone to wife- or husband-beating? The answer is a clear yes. The wife-beating rate for men who were *not* physically punished in their teens was about two out of a hundred. The same "low" rates apply to husband-beating by women who had not been hit as teen-agers. As the amount of physical punishment experienced as a child goes up, the rates of wife-beating and husband-beating also go up. *The people who experienced the most punishment as teen-agers have a rate of wife-beating and husband-beating that is four times greater than those whose parents did not hit them.*

Again, one has to be careful about these conclusions. It is true that people who were the victims of high levels of physical punishment as teen-agers have much higher rates of later beating their own husbands or wives. That does not mean that all children who have been beaten will be beaters. Nor does it mean that none of those whose parents did not hit them as teen-agers will be wife- or husband-beaters. In fact, about 2 per cent of the people who were *never* hit as teen-agers grew up to assault their husbands or wives severely during the survey year. But this is still only a quarter of the rate of wife- and husband-beating for those who were often punished physically.

Does Punishment By Itself Make a Difference? There are several qualifications which must be added to our conclusion that physical punishment tends to produce children who grow up to be violent husbands and wives. For one thing, the results might just reflect the way different people view the world. Violent people may tend to see others—including their own parents—as violent, even though their parents were not any more violent than other parents. Or it could be that people who were beaten by parents as teen-agers were aggressive anti-social types whose parents were trying to control them. Both the spouse-beating and the fact they themselves were punished may evidence the fact that these are aggressive types. We have no way of checking on these two alternatives to the social learning explanation. However, we do have information on another alternative explanation.

This alternative occurs because people who are violent toward their children also tend to be violent toward their husbands or wives. Over a third (36 per cent) of the most punishing grandparents had also attacked each other. This is six times the rate we found for the non-punishing grandparents. Thus, violence in marriage may be attributable to the violence witnessed between one's own parents rather than the physical punishment personally received at their hands.

To answer the question, we divided the sample into two groups: people whose parents were violent toward each other, and those whose parents never hit each other. We looked to see if being physically punished was associated with later violence toward one's spouse. Even for men whose parents were *not* violent to each other, those who had been physically punished as teen-agers had twice the rate of violence toward their wives as the sons who had not been hit as teen-agers. Women who were hit as teen-agers also tended to be more violent toward their husbands, even those who grew up without seeing their parents hit each other. However, the link between being hit as a teen-ager and hitting a marriage partner is not as close for women as it is for men.

Grandfathers Versus Grandmothers. What we have just reported shows that the more physical punishment by one's parents, the more an individual grows up to be violent in his or her marriage. But combining punishment by the father with that by the mother may cover up important aspects of things. Being physically punished by one's father as compared to one's mother may have a different impact on violence in the marriages of boys and girls.

We discovered that there is a stronger relationship between being punished as a child and later being violent toward a spouse when the punishment is done by the father. This applies to boys as well as to girls. *Physical punishment received as a teen-ager seems to lay the groundwork for both child abuse and spouse abuse—most often when it is done by the father.* Perhaps this is because violence by men is more acceptable in our culture than is violence by women and therefore is more appropriate as a model for the child's own behavior. Perhaps it is because fathers tend to hit harder. Or perhaps it is because the father is often called in only as a last resort—as the "or else!"

THE DOUBLE WHAMMY

Physical punishment seems to train people in family violence. So does growing up in a house where the mother and father hit each other. Each seems to make its own contribution to training the next generation in violence. Does it follow that children who experienced *both* kinds of violence when they were growing up would be the most violent of all? The case of Craig and Patsy at the beginning of this chapter is such an example. As a child Craig was beaten by his parents and also saw his mother being beaten up. How typical are Craig and Patsy?

CHART 6
Marital Violence in Survey Year
by Amount of Family Violence
Experienced as a Teenager

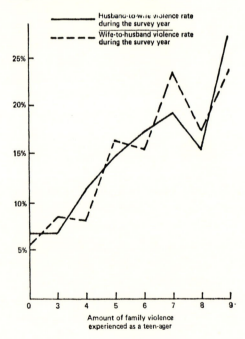

The chart we drew up to answer this question provides striking evidence for the idea of social heredity in violence—

that violence by parents begets violence in the next generation. The scale along the bottom of Chart 6 combines the four aspects of violence in the homes our respondents grew up in. Those with scores of zero are the people whose parents did not hit them *and* did not hit each other. At the other extreme are the people with scores of 9. They are the people whose parents frequently hit them when they were teen-agers *and* whose parents frequently were violent to each other.[8]

A score of 9 on this scale means having been brought up with a double dose of violence. If our theory is right, these should be the most violent people in our sample. And, in fact, they are. First, they have the highest rate of violence in their own marriages. About one out of four of them had used physical force on their partners in the survey year.

Even that is an understatement because marriages are not just made up of individual acts. There may be an unconscious selectivity in who one marries. Some sixth sense may bring together people with tendencies toward assuming the role of victim and aggressor. For this reason it is valuable to calculate the violence rate for *couples* as well as for husbands and wives. When one member of a couple had experienced the double whammy of being hit as a child *and* observing his or her parents hitting each other, there was a one in three chance that at least one act of violence had occurred during the year of the study!

Wife-beating and Husband-beating. To round out the picture, let's consider only violence that is severe enough to be in the category of wife-beating and husband-beating. One out of every ten husbands who experienced this much violence at home as a child turned out to be a wife-beater. This is a 600 per cent greater rate of wife-beating than we found for the husbands who came from non-violent homes. The same thing applies to the wives; in fact, even slightly more strongly. About one of eight wives (13.2 per cent) from the most violent homes had severely assaulted their husbands in the year covered by our study. That is almost nine times the rate for wives from non-violent homes. Taking the couples, irrespective of who did the beating, if *either* the husband or the wife was in the highest childhood violence group, the rate of serious assault jumps to 15 per cent during the survey year, and 18 per cent at some time in the marriage.

Obviously, not everyone who grew up in a violent home will be a wife-beater or a husband-beater. But a marriage involving a person who did is much more likely to be the scene of violent battles than are other marriages. In fact, depending on which sex and which measure of violence is used, these marriages are *from five to nine times more likely to be violent* than when one of the partners experienced neither physical punishment nor parents assaulting each other. The double dose of violence seems to be a double whammy.

Child Abuse. Finally, there is the question of the extent to which growing up in a home with both kinds of violence produces people who turn out to be child abusers. The answer is a great deal. The rate of abusive violence by fathers who grew up in the most violent homes (16 per cent) is about double the rate for those who grew up in non-violent homes. For mothers who had the double dose of violence in their own childhoods, the rate of abusive violence climbs to a staggering 30 per cent.

A THIRD GENERATION OF VIOLENCE

The last set of questions we will try to answer in this chapter concerns the relationship of violence between husbands and wives to the amount of violence they inflict upon their children. In addition, what are the effects upon the children—are they as violent as their parents, perhaps more so, or less?

Spouse Abuse and Child Abuse. In a previous section of this chapter we found that grandparents who hit each other also tended to hit their teen-age children. We did not have the data to determine how much of the hitting by grandparents was the kind most people consider ordinary physical punishment and how much was severe enough possibly to cause serious injury to the child. For the couples who actually participated in the study, we do have the information to answer this question, and the answer is all too clear.

CHART 7
Abusive Parent-to-Child Violence by Amount of Violence Between Husband and Wife

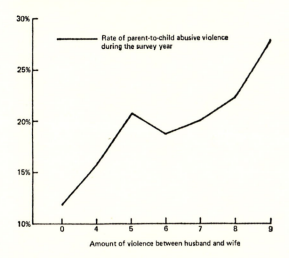

Amount of violence between husband and wife

The couples who did not hit each other had the lowest rate of abusive violence toward their children. They are the zero group at the left side of Chart 7. From there, the rates for child abuse go up fairly steadily until we reach group 9 on the right side of the chart. In fact, 28 per cent of the children of these high violence couples had been abused during the year. If we use the figures showing whether the child had *ever* been abused, the figure rises to an astounding 77 per cent. Clearly, *violent husbands and wives are also likely to be child abusing parents.* Cases such as the following are typical.

Jane met Larry at the hospital where they both worked—he a doctor, she a lab technician. After about a year they got married.

"When the kids were about two years old, a faculty position opened up at the medical school. Larry had always wanted to teach and decided to consider it. . . . He knew the competition would be stiff but I encouraged him to try for it.

"After he made the formal application his attitude towards me changed. He became very irritable and the littlest things would set him off. . . . One night he came home from the hospital in a really bad mood. When I asked him what was wrong, he slapped me and said, 'Why don't you just mind your own business? You can't understand what I'm going through.'

"The more I thought about it, the more convinced I became that Larry worked under incredible pressure. . . . Eventually he had to let it out somewhere, and the most logical or acceptable place was to do it at home. . . . In this way I was able to rationalize the first couple of times he hit me. . . .

"As the weeks went by, things didn't improve. . . . There were several terrible beatings. . . . Then Larry got the teaching appointment. . . . He apologized for acting so crazy and said that sometimes men reach a point in their careers where their egos are really on the line. At those times the thing they need most is a supportive, compassionate wife who's willing to stick by them.

"That spring a big medical convention was scheduled in California. . . . Larry wanted to go. . . . The day he found out . . . someone else was chosen, he was livid. He stormed into the kitchen at lunchtime while the kids were eating. When Jenny asked him why he was so mad he smacked her across the face with such force that she fell off her chair.

"In that instant I realized things would never change. Larry was a very competitive person, used to getting what he wanted. And when he didn't he couldn't handle it. It became very clear to me that if he could lash out at his own daughter simply because she asked him a question at the wrong time, then he could do almost anything if he felt angry enough" (*The Real Paper*, February 11, 1976, p. 13).

Child Abuse and Sibling Abuse. How does child abuse affect the children? Are they also violent? In a previous section we found that the people who had been hit as teen-agers tended to be the most violent to their own husbands or wives and to their own children. Now we can find out if this is repeated in a third generation; that is, with the children of the couples interviewed in our study. We have information on one child for each couple with children between the ages of three and seventeen. We asked about the fights these children had with their brothers and sisters, and whether or not they had ever hit their parents.

Chart 8 shows that the more often the parents in our study had hit their children, the more likely the child was to have *severely* attacked a brother or sister during the survey year. In fact, almost all the children who were on the receiving end of the most severe abuse from a parent also engaged in intensely violent acts. Had these acts occurred between two strangers rather than between two children in the same family, they would have been considered chargeable assault. Taking the most dangerous of the situations we asked about—a child actually grabbing for a knife or gun in an argument with another child—.03 per cent had done this in the survey year, and 5 per cent at some time. The .03 figure comes to a national rate of 138,000 children a year; while the 5 per cent figure means that about 2.3 million children in the United States have at some time used a knife or gun on a brother or sister. It is no wonder that our murder rate is one of the highest in the world.

Thus it appears that the more violent parents are to a child, the more violent the child is to brothers and sisters. Chart 8 shows that this applies to children whose parents were in addition violent to their spouses (broken line in chart); as well as

CHART 8
Per Cent of Children Who Severely
Assaulted a Sibling During the Year by
Parent-to-Child and Marital Violence.

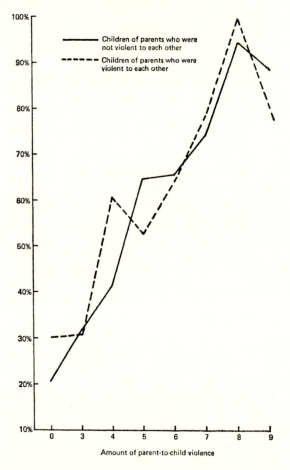

Amount of parent-to-child violence

to children whose parents were not violent toward each other (solid line in chart).

The very close relationship between having been hit by one's parents and being severely violent toward a brother or sister supports the theory about the effect of physical punishment put forward earlier in this chapter. It does indeed seem that physical punishment is one of the main means by which children learn one of the covert rules of American family life. This rule says that in a conflict with another family member, physical force is permissible. Indeed, in cases of severe transgression, force not only may be used, it should be used.

Do as I Say and Not as I Do. By this time, readers may be overwhelmed by charts and statistics. But at the risk of overdoing things, we need to consider one more set of figures. We need to know how many of the parents interviewed had been hit by their children.

Very little data are available concerning children who hit their parents. It is a topic more taboo than wife- or husband-beating. The only study we could find which dealt with it at all indicated that the most frequent reason that parents give for slapping a young child is that the child has hit, kicked, or somehow attacked the parent (Sears, Maccoby, and Levin, 1959). That shows just how taboo it is for children to hit parents. Granted it is taboo. We still suspect it is very common. Perhaps one does not hear about it (and researchers do not study it) because of the need to preserve the myth that all children love and respect their parents.

Almost one out of five of the children in this study (18 per cent) had hit the parent we interviewed in the year we asked about. Since we interviewed mothers in half of the families, and fathers in the other half of the families, the number of children who had hit a parent during the year might actually be double. This means *one out of three children between the ages of three and seventeen hit their parents each year.*

These are sobering figures. However, in the context of this chapter, the more important issue is whether the level of violence *by children* to their parents is related to violence level of the parents to the child. Chart 9 shows that the two are very closely related. The more often parents have hit the child, the higher the probability that the child has hit the parent. This is true both for parents who were not violent toward each other

CHART 9
Child-to-Parent Violence by Parent-
to-Child and Marital Violence

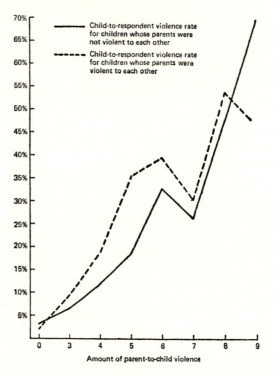

Amount of parent-to-child violence

(solid line in Chart 9) as well as for the couples whose marriages were violent (broken line).

Less than one out of four hundred of the children whose
parents did *not* hit them were violent to the parent we interviewed. This is in striking contrast to the children who had
been hit the most by their parents (those with scores of 8 and
9 on the bottom of Chart 9). About half of these children had
hit their parents in the year we asked about. A great deal of
this was violence that would legally be aggravated assault if
not within the privacy of the home.

Children brought up in violence have a whole different perspective of its acceptance and uses in society. A thirty-three-

year-old convict, imprisoned much of his adult life for violent assaults, told a psychiatrist:

> Violence is in a way like bad language—something that a person like me's been brought up with, something I got used to very early on as a part of the daily scene of childhood, you might say. I don't at all recoil from the idea, I don't have a sort of inborn dislike of the thing like you do. As long as I can remember I've seen violence in use all around me—my mother hitting the children; my brothers and sisters all whacking our mother or other children; the man downstairs bashing his wife and so on (Steele, 1977).

No doubt many of the instances of violence by children toward their parents are in direct retaliation at the time the parent hits the child. In fact, parents of older children often say they don't hit them any more because "they're too big now." This is often said in the sense of retaliation being dangerous, rather than because they think it is wrong to hit children of that age.

Although direct retaliation is part of the explanation, it is not the whole story. The correlation between parents hitting children and children hitting parents also comes about because children tend to model their behavior after that of their parents. When a parent hits a child, it is a powerful learning experience, teaching the moral rightness of the use of force between family members.

"VIOLENCE BEGETS VIOLENCE"

Over and over again, the statistics in this chapter suggest the same conclusion. *Each generation learns to be violent by being a participant in a violent family.*

We traced this learning process through three generations. The more violent the grandparents, the more violent the couples in our study are as husbands and wives, and the more abusive they are to their children. The children of these couples, in turn, tend to follow the pattern of their parents. The more violent the couple we interviewed, the more violent their children are to each other, and to their parents. "Violence begets violence," not only against people who are violent to you (in this case, parents), but also against others (brothers and sisters, husband and wives).

Some of the learning about violence in the family occurs by example: Children see their parents hitting each other.

Some of the learning occurs as a result of being the victim of violence: The more children are hit by their parents, the more likely they are to hit others.

When a child grows up in a home where parents use lots of physical punishment and also hit each other, the chances of becoming a violent husband, wife, or parent are greatest of all: About one out of every four people who grew up in these most violent households use at least some physical force on their spouses in any one year. Some of this is an occasional slap or shove. But one out of ten of the husbands who grew up in violent families are wife-beaters in the sense of serious assault. This is over three times the rate for husbands who did not grow up in such violent homes. The same thing applies to assaults by wives on husbands.

The effect of growing up in a violent home is even more predictive of child abuse: Over one out of every four parents who grew up in a violent household were violent enough to risk seriously injuring a child.

At the same time, it would be a mistake to put the whole burden of violence on what is learned in the family. To see this one needs only to look at the violence rates for the children of the non-violent parents in each chart (the zero group). This shows that there is lots of violence by people whose parents are *not* particularly violent to them and not violent to each other, even though the rates are a fraction of the rates for those who came from violent homes. The family may be the main training ground for violence, but in a violent society like ours, this role is shared with others.

CHAPTER 6

Who Are the Violent Americans?

Do social factors have a bearing on violence in the family?

Who most likely beats his wife—a man with an eighth-grade education or one who finished college? Do Catholic mothers abuse their children more than Jewish mothers? Is there apt to be more violence in a black welfare family in Georgia than in a white middle class family in Michigan?

The possibility that social factors such as race, income, education, and regional differences are related to violence in the family was often overlooked in early studies of the problem. People tended to view family violence as a rare occurrence.

When social factors were considered, most people looked on family violence as a lower class problem. There was, in fact, evidence to support the claim that domestic violence was an exclusive problem of poor people. The research on child and wife abuse carried out in the 1960s and early 1970s was based primarily on clinical cases of family violence which came almost exclusively from police or medical records. As in most instances of illegal behavior, the poor, powerless, and defenseless are more likely to get caught and labeled for their illegal acts, and therefore, theirs were the cases recorded.

Middle class families, with the privacy of separate houses and larger house lots of suburbia, are far more insulated from prosecution for illegal behavior than the lower class city dwellers in their three-room tenements. Moreover, middle class families rely most often on private medical and legal agencies for help with their problems. We know, for example, that injured children seen by private physicians are less likely to be reported as victims of child abuse than are children treated in public clinics or emergency rooms.

Most early research on family violence was generated by social workers, psychiatrists, and physicians who drew on their own professional contacts with violent individuals. These investigators recognized that violence and abuse were not confined to one type of person or one area of the country. Children were slain by their parents in New York and Denver, in rural communities, and in crowded city ghettos. Some abusers were unemployed; others were truck drivers, construction workers, police officers; still others were doctors, lawyers, and business executives.

Researchers in the sixties and early seventies either argued that social factors were not related to family violence because cases of abusive violence could be found in all social classes, or they argued that only poor people were violent. The first argument, that people from all social classes are violent, overlooks the possibility that, while all portions of society are represented in acts of family violence, some people and places are overrepresented. In other words, although people from all income levels abuse their children and spouses, it may be that people from one income group are more likely to be abusive, while those from another group are less likely. The second argument overlooks the fact that our society is more likely to label poor people deviant, no matter what the actual distribution of illegal acts is.

A second reason for overlooking social factors as reasons for family violence was the deep conviction on the part of many professionals and laymen that only mentally disturbed people could possibly be violent toward those they love. The notion that abusers and violent people are mentally ill gains credence when one hears about some of the things family members do to one another:

> Mr. Timmons grew angry at his son for constantly knocking into things around the house and breaking valuable objects like lamps and ashtrays. One evening, his son banged into a table and broke yet another lamp. Mr. Timmons, enraged, dragged his four-year-old into the basement and held him down while putting the whirling bit of a power drill through the boy's chest. His son died instantly.

> Mrs. King had long tried to teach her daughter not to touch hot objects. When the little girl wandered near the stove and tried to play with the knobs on the front of the stove, Mrs. King grabbed her hand and held it down on the gas burner until the hand was burned beyond recognition.

> Mr. and Mrs. Pall routinely used a bicycle chain to whip their eight-year-old foster son. His body bore new and old scars from these beatings.

A reader of these accounts might be convinced that only a parent who had totally lost grip on reality could do such things to a defenseless child. And yet, these parents were "normal" in the psychological sense of the word. In fact, one would have difficulty identifying these parents as abusers if one met them at a party or if one worked along side them every day.

Granted, in some instances of physical abuse, the offender is so mentally disturbed that he or she cannot comprehend reality. But in the vast majority of cases of violence in the family, the participants possess none of the symptoms or problems which we normally associate with those who are mentally ill or suffering from personality disorders. If violent family members are not "ill" or "sick," what is the matter? Who are these people? Where are they likely to live? How much education do they have? How much money do they make? How old are they? Do any of these factors make a difference in terms of a family's likelihood of being violent?

We will answer each of these questions by focusing only on abusive violence between families. Although we have defined a violent act as anything ranging from a push to a shooting, we will concentrate here only on serious injurious abuse. Among our reasons are that people who study domestic violence and are interested in reducing its terrible toll need to discover the factors which cause the most injury. A second reason for focusing on only abusive violence is that the job of presenting the findings would become extremely complicated if we were to include the rates of "normal" violence in the following sections.

REGION

Research on violence in the United States now indicates that some regions are more violent than others. There are important differences in the homicide rates and in citizen attitudes toward violence. As far back as 1925, Frederick Hoffman, in his book *The Homicide Problem*, reported that Memphis, Tennessee, had an extremely high homicide rate of 88 murders per 100,000 population. Data on homicides in 1960 (Gastil, 1971) also illustrate a predisposition of Southerners toward lethal violence. Georgia, Alabama, South Carolina, and Virginia had the highest rates of homicide in 1960. Georgia, South Carolina, and Florida reported the highest rates of homicide and nonnegligent manslaughter in 1968 (Bureau of Census, 1970). On the basis of such data, Gastil concluded that the southern states have, and have always had, higher rates of lethal violence than other regions of the country. Rates of homicide in the South, for example, are much higher than in the northeast.

New England reports fewer homicides and violent crimes than any of the other places in the United States.

The South also has a high *potential* for violence. Half of the respondents interviewed in the South for the 1968 survey for the National Commission on the Causes and Prevention of Violence (Stark and Mc Evoy, 1970) reported that they owned firearms. This figure is twice as high as the proportion of respondents in the East who owned guns.

However, when noting such statistics, we must not forget southern traditions and the rural nature of the land. The southern gun owner for generations has kept a shotgun about because of his fondness for, or the necessity of, providing meat for the family table. In continuing to own guns, he may be exhibiting a fondness for squirrel stew or roast quail rather than a predisposition for interpersonal violence. Nevertheless, the mere presence of a gun in the home increases the likelihood that a lethal weapon will be used in a family conflict.

In spite of the predisposition of Southerners to engage in lethal violence and to own guns, our survey of 2,143 American families reveals that Southerners are not more prone to engage in abusive domestic violence.

The most fascinating and unexpected finding when we examine the regional rates of family violence is that the rates are so evenly distributed across the United States. Although we anticipated that there would be family violence in each region of America, we did not expect to find so *little* variation between regions. Homicide, aggravated assault, rape, and other forms of violence occur with different frequencies depending on whether one is in the North, South, East, or West. Behavior in families also varies depending on what part of the country you examine—the West has traditionally had the highest rate of divorce in America. But family violence varies very little.

Where there are differences, they are slight. We found:

Southerners have the lowest rates of abusive violence toward their children. (The exact figures are in Chart 10.)

CHART 10

Abusive Family Violence in 1975

SOCIAL FACTOR	CHILD TO CHILD	PARENT TO CHILD	COUPLE	HUSBAND TO WIFE	WIFE TO HUSBAND
Region					
East	50%	13%	6%	3%	5%
Midwest	44	19	7	4	6
South	50	10	6	4	3
West	51	17	7	4	5
Residence					
Large City	50%	19%	8%	5%	7%
Small City	45	12	6	4	3
Suburban	47	13	5	3	4
Rural	51	14	6	5	3
Race					
White	50%	14%	5%	3%	4%
Black	41	15	11	11	8
Other	56	18	8	5	10
Husband's Religion					
Catholic	48%	15%	7%	4%	6%
Protestant	48	14	5	3	3
Jewish	48	6	3	1	4
Other	51	19	10	6	8
None	49	14	13	9	6
Wife's Religion					
Catholic	49%	15%	6%	3%	5%
Protestant	49	14	5	4	3
Jewish	45	7	6	2	7
Other	51	19	11	8	9
None	42	13	14	9	9

Age of Respondent					
30 and under	54%	21%	15%	9%	11%
31 to 50	48	13	4	3	3
51 through 65	25	4	1	0	0
66 and older	100	0	0	0	0
Education of Husband					
8th grade or less	46%	11%	4%	3%	4%
Some high school	46	15	9	6	7
High school graduate	50	18	7	4	4
College	49	11	6	3	5
Education of Wife					
8th grade or less	47%	12%	5%	4%	5%
Some high school	52	14	9	7	6
High school graduate	46	17	6	4	4
College	51	11	5	2	4
Family Income					
$5,999 and under	53%	22%	15%	11%	11%
$6,000 to $11,999	52	16	9	6	7
$12,000 to $19,999	51	15	4	2	3
$20,000 and over	41	11	3	2	2
Occupation of Husband					
Blue Collar	49%	16%	8%	5%	6%
White Collar	47	11	4	2	3
Occupation of Wife					
Blue Collar	45%	16%	8%	4%	7%
White Collar	50	10	5	2	4
Employment Status of Husband					
Full time	49%	14%	6%	4%	4%
Part time	62	27	18	12	13
Unemployed	49	22	15	8	14
Retired	44	9	1	1	0
Disabled	40	14	9	4	7

The Midwest, and to a lesser extent, the West, have the highest rates of violence toward children.

The rate of abusive violence by wives toward their husbands is twice as high in the Midwest as it is in the South.

The most interesting finding is that the South is not the leader in family violence. In fact, in the case of child abuse and husband abuse, Southerners are the least violent. The "violent culture" which has been attributed to the South by social scientists may well be modified by saying that the South possesses a "selectively violent culture." The attitudes and values that produce a high rate of killing and lead half of the adults living in the South to purchase at least one firearm do not spill over into violence in their homes. Perhaps this is because Southerners, while they may be more prone to violence on the streets, hold different values about behavior in the home. The image of the chivalrous southern gentleman and the gracious southern lady may be one reason why southern homes are less violent.

Perhaps owning a gun means different things in different parts of the country. The firearms owned in the South are often the shotgun or long gun hung on a wall or a rack in a pickup truck. A gun owned in New York or Los Angeles is more probably a handgun kept in the home, or worse still, a pistol carried on one's person.

While we can perhaps explain why the South is less violent than expected, we cannot explain why the Midwest has a rate of child abuse which is 100 per cent higher than the rate in the South. Do people in Illinois, Indiana, Minnesota, and other midwestern states dislike their children more? Are they under more stress? Is it more acceptable to use abusive violence in the Midwest than the South? We do not know. While we cannot explain why the rate of midwestern violence toward children is higher than the rates for the rest of the country, we can certainly argue that, based on this data, the need for services for child abuse is greater in the Midwest than in other areas of the country.

CITY AND COUNTRY

Many people view family violence as a mostly urban problem. More cases of child abuse and wife abuse come to the attention of urban police departments than rural police. City hospitals, such as Children's Hospital in Boston or Children's Hospital in Los Angeles, see more cases of abused children than do country hospitals. Most services for child abuse and wife abuse are provided in cities, under the assumption that this is where the largest number of people in need of services live. The assumption that urban areas have more family violence is reasonable. More cases of family violence are uncovered in cities because:

1. More people live in the cities—actually over three quarters of our population now live in metropolitan areas.
2. The resources to detect abuse are more abundant in the city. Services for violent families are more common in cities because social services of all kinds tend to be concentrated in urban areas (along with large universities and medical centers).

However, the key question is are the *rates* of family violence higher in cities than in country settings? In other words, are a larger *proportion* of city families prone to family violence? We found that:

Families in large cities (population 1 million or more) have higher rates of abusive violence toward children and higher rates of abusive violence between husbands and wives.

The rate of wife abuse in the suburbs is half the rate of wife abuse in cities larger than 1 million.

Sibling abuse and wife abuse are as common in rural areas as in large cities.

It comes as no surprise that America's largest cities have the highest rates of violence. Why cities are so violent is another question. Most research efforts on homicide, assault, rape, and violence tend to find cities more violent than suburban or rural communities. But no one has ever definitely explained why. There are many plausible explanations; but no confirmed theories.

A common explanation for urban violence is crowding. Research conducted with rats and other animals (Calhoun, 1962; Christian, 1960, 1963; Galle, et al., 1972; Southwick 1955; Tinbergen, 1952) finds that as living space becomes more confined, animals become more aggressive. Applying the same logic to humans we would expect to find that the denser the population, both in terms of how many people inhabit a square mile and how many people share a room, the more likely violence is to occur. In other words, city dwellers, packed into high-rise apartments or ghetto tenements, would be more predisposed to violence than people with more room.

Recently, however, sociologist Alan Booth studied the effects of crowding on human beings. Booth's investigation, carried out in Toronto, Canada, contradicts the animal research. Booth examined physical, social, and psychological adaptations to crowding and concluded that crowding into a city block or tenement apartment does not increase the level of violence in families. Booth's explanation for the lack of a relationship was that either humans are probably more adaptable to crowding or they are never as compacted as are the rats and dogs in the animal experiments (Booth and Edwards, 1976).

A second plausible explanation for city violence is the high degree of social isolation that characterizes city life. Although people may be packed into high-rise buildings and dense neighborhoods, they may often know less about their neighbors than do rural dwellers who live miles from their nearest neighbor. Family violence may be a reaction to the social isolation that people feel in cities.

A third explanation may be the fast pace and high level of stress found in the city as opposed in the country. Cities are hotter, noisier, dirtier, and function at a faster pace than suburban or rural communities. The stress and fever pitch of city life may provide the blasting cap for violence in many families.

RACE, RELIGION, AND AGE

We know where in America families are the most violent. Our concern in this and the remaining sections of the chapter is to identify in which families violence is most likely to occur.

Race

To discuss family violence with emphasis on race can be misleading. Factors beyond one's color may well cause differences in rates of violence. Which contributes more to violence in the family, simply belonging to a racial minority or being unemployed or existing on a low income? To state flatly that blacks are more violent than whites fails to take into consideration lack of income or education.

However, racial differences can also be due to differences in cultural expectations and values concerning violence. The macho male, for example, is more highly valued among Spanish-speaking black groups than among white Anglo-Saxons (Brown, 1965). Thus race, as a cultural property, may produce different rates of violence.

We chose to present the rates of violence by racial category. To do this we "collapsed" our categories into three racial groups: black, white, and other (American Indian, Oriental, other).

Official statistics on child abuse show that blacks and other racial minorities are overrepresented as child abusers. This could be a result of income, education, and cultural values, or this could be because racial minorities are more likely to be singled out and labeled as deviants by those who compile official statistics. Surveys which ask individuals to report experiences with violence conclude that blacks are more likely to encounter violence in the streets and in the homes than whites (Stark and Mc Evoy, 1970). However, blacks own fewer firearms than whites and the same proportion of blacks and whites state that they have spanked their children (Stark and Mc Evoy, 1970). Also, studies of attitudes show that blacks are less likely to approve of violence than whites (Smith and Snow, 1975). So the picture from previous studies is mixed. What is the picture we get from focusing on the sample of 2,143 families?

Comparing the rates of family violence found in different racial groups provides some interesting contrasts and similarities:

> *Parental Violence:* Highest among American Indians, Orientals and other racial minorities. No difference between blacks and whites.
>
> *Wife Abuse:* Highest among blacks—nearly 400 per cent more common than in white families.
>
> *Husband Abuse:* Highest among racial minorities. Twice as common in black families compared to white families.
>
> *Sibling Violence:* Highest in families of racial minorities. Lowest in black families.

The varying pattern of violence among racial groups makes for a complex and difficult assessment of what the rates mean. One thing which we found was that official statistics on child abuse are misleading. Those statistics indicate that blacks are more likely to abuse their children than are whites. Our national study of family violence found very little difference between blacks and whites in terms of their reported acts of physical violence toward their children. Our study supports the research carried out by Andrew Billingsley ten years ago (1969) which found that blacks were not more violent toward their children than whites.

Our survey of American families did support the claims

made in official statistics that black men had the highest rates of wife abuse. Black males could be using acts of violence on their wives to compensate for resources such as income or prestige from which they are culturally deprived. Or, black male violence may be a reflection of the macho image of man which condones and encourages acts of physical and sexual aggression.

If we argue that minority males are violent because they are attempting to live up to a culturally prescribed model of the aggressive and dominant male, then how do we explain the fact that black men are twice as likely as white men to be abused by their wives? Moreover, other minority men, a number of whom are Spanish-speaking, have a rate of husband abuse which is nearly three times the rate for white men. Unfortunately, we cannot provide a precise answer to this question, because research and thinking about husband abuse are so new. However, it may be that attempts to dominate and achieve a macho image in the home are often responded to by equally violent acts on the part of the wives of macho men. If this is the case, then it is likely that the attempt to be a macho man sets up a chain reaction of violence, since each violent act of a wife would be responded to in kind by a man who was seeking to dominate his wife and family.

Our finding that minority racial groups tend to have the highest rates of violence (with the exception of the difference between blacks and whites for violence toward and between children) leads us to propose that the stress, discrimination, and frustration that minorities encounter, and the fact that minorities are still disenfranchised from many advantages which majority group members enjoy, can lead to higher rates of violence.

Religion

Early in our study of family violence we were interviewing a woman who had been beaten by her husband:

My husband really knocked me around last year. He got mad because I had gone out to a bar and had seen a man. This guy was a friend of ours and he had recently gotten divorced. I met him one night at a party. We got to talking. I guess I encouraged him because Larry, my husband, and I had a fight before the party. Larry had slapped me a couple of times and I was mad. Anyhow, this friend called me a few times and asked me to have a drink with him. One night I said I was going to the store and I got dressed and met this friend at a bar. When I got home Larry hit the roof. He said, "You don't get dressed like that to go to the store!" He kept after me to tell him where I went. So finally, I said, "I met Fred and we had a drink, so there!" Well, Larry really socked me. I hurt all over.

The feature of this interview that distinguished it from all the rest was not that the woman had been beaten by her husband. What was unusual was her response when we asked her what religion she was. She said, "I'd rather not answer that question." This answer was totally unexpected. She had just told a perfect stranger that her husband beat her, but she wouldn't answer a simple question about religion. We asked her again, and after a while she said, "We're Jewish." When we asked her why that was so difficult to say, she replied that "Jewish families are not supposed to have hitting."

Looking at the differences between religious groups can often help understand the way society works. French social scientist Emile Durkheim was an early pioneer in research which examined religious affiliation and its relation to human behavior. Durkheim attempted to explain suicide by focusing on social rather than psychological factors. He found that suicide rates varied by religious group and used this finding to propose that suicide was explainable if one examined the social context an individual lived in rather than the psychological make-up of the suicide victim.

Although social scientists have investigated many differences between religious groups, there really is not much in the research on child, wife, or husband abuse which examines the rates of violence by religious affiliation (Carroll, 1979).

We had some expectations based on our own personal and professional experiences. For instance, we might expect members of fundamentalist religious groups to be most likely to advocate and support certain types of family violence. On occasions when we have publicly defined spanking and slapping children as violent acts, we have received numerous letters and telephone calls from people belonging to fundamentalist religious organizations. Our callers and letter writers criticized us for terming spankings "violent." They supported their arguments with biblical quotations which said that parents have the God-given right to punish their children physically. Members of fundamentalist religious groups brought their beliefs before the South Carolina state legislature and said that the Bible gave parents the right to "bend the will of their children." The fundamentalists argued that the state should not enact child abuse legislation which interfered with parents' God-given rights.

The first aspect of religion we examined in our national survey was whether or not lack of religious preference influenced the level of violence in families.

The results of our look at religion are complicated because we assessed violence in terms of the husband's and the wife's religion. Interestingly, the relationship between religion and family violence sometimes varied when we compared men with women. For instance:

> The children of men without religious preference have the same level of sibling violence as the children of men who have a religious preference. But, when the mother has no religion, her children are less violent toward one another than the children of mothers who have a religious preference.

Abusive violence toward children is unrelated to whether or not a mother or a father has a religious preference.

Violence between husbands and wives is related to having a religious preference. Men and women without religious affiliation have the highest rate of violence between partners.

We found that women without religious preference are more likely to be abused by their husbands, and that husbands without a religious preference are more likely to use violence on their wives.

Women without religious preference have a slightly higher rate of husband abuse than do women who profess a religious preference.

But, husbands with religious preference are as likely to be struck by their wives as men who have no religious affiliation.

Thus, the pattern is mixed. Lack of religious affiliation seems to have most effect on violence between husbands and wives, especially acts of violence toward women. We know that people without religious affiliation are unconventional by virtue of the fact that they are in the distinct minority in their lack of religious preference. Moreover, these individuals often have the highest rates of divorce. Perhaps people with no religion feel less constrained by social rules which say: "people should have a religion," or "people should hold a marriage together," or "husbands should not hit their wives."

When we compared those people who had religious preferences, we again found a mixed and somewhat complicated picture.

For sibling abuse: The rate is lowest among families where the mother is Jewish. The rate is highest in families of minority religions (other than Catholic, Protestant, and Jewish).

For child abuse: The rate is lowest among Jews. The rate is highest for those families where one or both parents have minority religious affiliations.

For wife abuse: Jewish husbands have the lowest rates, minority religion husbands the highest.

For husband abuse: The rate is the lowest among Protestants and highest among minority religious groups. One interesting finding for husband abuse was that Jewish women, who normally live in the least violent homes, have a rate of abusing their husbands which is more than double the rate for Protestants and almost as high as the rate for minority religious group families.

Certainly, no religious group is immune to violence in the family. But there are differences between groups. For certain types of violence, certain religions have higher rates, for others, the rates are lower. Are the differences (and similarities) between religious groups due to some property of a religion? Do some religions involve dogma, teachings, rituals, or other components which make people violent? We would say no. The differences between religious groups probably reflect a number of things which lead to the varying rates of violence:

1. The social make-up of religious groups varies. Jews, by and large, are better educated, have higher incomes, and are more likely to be employed in a profession than people of other religious affiliations. Differences in income and occupation, rather than religion, could be causing the rates of violence to vary.

2. Being a member of any minority religion may contribute more to violence than the particular religious group one belongs to. Minorities experience more discrimination, more stress, and are the furthest from the mainstream of society. These qualities may lead them to adopt two attitudes which enhance the likelihood of family violence occurring. First, they may perceive the need to be tougher and stronger to survive as a minority. Thus, they use more physical measures to bring up their children and they are more tolerant of sibling violence. Second, they may adapt to their powerlessness outside the home by resorting to physical power within the home.

Mixed Religion Marriages

Do "mixed marriages" result in a higher degree of violence within the family? This was our final question concerning religion and violence.

We found that in families where both husband and wife were of the same religious affiliation, rates of violence were uniformly less than in those families with mixed religious marriages. This included every type and form of family violence. The differences are small, but consistent, for violence between siblings and violence by parents on their children. But in studying violence between spouses, we see that a man or a woman who marries someone of a different religion is almost twice as likely to hit or be hit by a spouse than someone married to a person of the same religion.

Why mixed marriages are more violent would seem to be related to the fragility of marriage and the fact that any additional conflict can be magnified by small differences. It is not that mixed marriages are bad, in and of themselves, or even that they should be avoided. It is simply that they cause more stress. This stress can be internal to the marriage, or it can be produced by people outside of the marriage, such as parents who oppose their children marrying people of different faiths and continue the pressure after the children marry.

How Old?

Judging from newspaper reports of family violence, one would conclude that most violence erupts in the families of younger couples. A sampling of wire service reports of violent homes over the past four years bears this out:

Kansas City, Missouri: A six-year-old boy died from what police reported as the "worst beating" they had ever investigated. Two- and three-inch strips of flesh had been torn raw from his face, arms, legs, back, buttocks, and stomach. A purple bruise covered his chest. Blood had soaked through his shirt and pants. . . . His twenty-year-old stepfather was charged with second-degree murder.

Wyandanch, Long Island: A twenty-eight-year-old housewife was charged with fatally beating her three-year-old adopted son. She had slapped and shaken the child. He slipped from her grip and struck his head on the floor.

Central Falls, Rhode Island: A thirty-three-year-old woman was stabbed outside her apartment by her forty-one-year-old husband while their ten-year-old daughter watched.

Providence, Rhode Island: A thirty-six-year-old man pleaded no-contest in court to the hatchet murder of his twenty-eight-year-old wife. The couple argued over the custody of their child on the porch of a friend's house. The man picked up a hatchet that was on the porch and struck his wife.

New York, New York: Police jailed a thirty-three-year-old man who had held his common-law wife and her four children captive for six weeks. He had also punished the woman's seven-year-old son by placing him in a lighted oven.

CHART 11
Abusive Violence by Age of Respondent

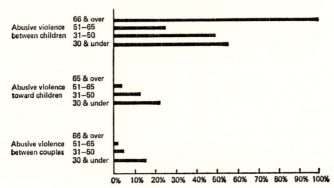

More often than not, these and other media accounts of family violence involve husbands and wives in their twenties or thirties. Only occasionally does one read about an older couple involved in an extremely violent marriage.

The public record of violent families must be measured against what we learned in our own research on family violence. Our early studies uncovered a number of violent homes where the husbands and wives were in their fifties and early sixties. We interviewed a pert sixty-five-year-old grandmother who reported the following:

> Sure I hit him. He gets me mad when he calls me a dumb Polak. When he does that I punch him in the gut . . . and it happens every once in a while.

The contrast between the newspaper accounts (which tend to describe violence between young couples) and our pilot studies (which uncovered many cases of violence between older couples) is like the controversy over social class differences. Family violence does occur at all ages, just as it occurs in all social class groups. But the statistics from this nationally representative sample of couples leave no doubt that younger couples are more violent. One can see in Chart 11 that the rates of each type of family violence are uniformly the highest in families where the respondent was under thirty years old. As the age increases, the rate of violence decreases.

Younger families are the most violent families. The obvious question is, why? Again, we must highlight the fact that since we only studied these families at one point in time, we cannot provide a definitive answer to the question. To explain adequately the differing rates of violence in each age group, we would have to follow people over twenty years of their marriage. Nevertheless, there are some logical, plausible, and disturbing possibilities to consider:

1. First, it could reflect the fact that younger people are more violence-prone. Certainly the information we have on violent crimes confirms this idea. The highest homicide rate is

for those between the ages of eighteen and twenty-four and drops off rapidly after that. Violent juvenile gangs are also evidence of a predisposition of younger people toward violent acts. Younger people have more physical energy and go through more social, physical, and psychological changes which may contribute to their high rates of violence.

2. A second possibility, not excluded by the first explanation, is that younger marriages are more violence-prone. The early years of a marriage involve two people learning to live with one another, learning to adjust to one another, and going through frequent and often drastic changes—such as the birth of a first child. The exuberance of youth coupled with the conflict and tensions of building a marriage may contribute to violent modes of conflict resolution between partners, parents and children, and even between siblings.

3. A possibility that we cannot overlook is that violent marriages are more likely to break up. Thus, by the time a person reaches his or her fiftieth birthday, he or she is unlikely to be in a family where there is violence between husbands and wives. A variety of events may cause violent families to dissolve. First, battered husbands and wives may seek divorce or separation. Second, state departments of welfare may remove children from violent parents. Third, some violent partners kill their spouses. All these factors may reduce the chance of a violent marriage enduring for more than a few years. But we must realize that only a portion of victimized spouses seek to leave a violent marriage, and that state governments are limited in terms of how many children they can remove from violent homes—the city of New York spent 250 million dollars on foster care in 1976 and that only served a portion of the children who were in need of placement due to abuse or neglect.

4. The most disturbing possibility is that our findings might be indicating that violence in the family is increasing. It is quite possible that our study has uncovered a violent generation under thirty years of age. It is also possible that this violent generation will remain violent as it grows older and be fol-

lowed by yet another generation of violent adults and violent families. The under-thirty generation is, as we said earlier in this book, a generation which grew up during the Korean War, came of age during the riots, violence, and wars of the sixties, and was the first generation to grow up in an era when the majority of all American families watched television and its nightly dose of violence.

Our study clearly illustrates that violence is much more likely to occur in younger families. Whatever the reason, this is a conclusion which bears close attention. If we are seeing the first crest of a wave of violent generations, we need to be aware of this and be prepared for future increases in the level and human toll of family violence. If this is not a generational phenomenon, but rather one which is due to younger people and newer marriages being most violence-prone, then we need to recognize that younger families require the most concentrated treatment and prevention resources if we are ever to reduce the level of family violence.

RICH MAN, POOR MAN: SOCIAL CHARACTERISTICS AND FAMILY VIOLENCE

"Violence between family members can be found in all social classes."

"Family violence is more common in lower class families."

These two statements, which at first reading seem to contradict one another, are the usual answers to the question: "In which families or social groups are child and wife abuse most common?" The first statement, that violence between family members can be found in all social groups, highlights the fact that we find people from all social groups abusing their children and their spouses. In fact, in our study of eighty families in New Hampshire, the most violent was a family with the highest annual income.

In a recent Massachusetts case, the captain of an oil super-tanker shot and killed his wife, critically wounded his three young children, killed the family dog, and then killed himself. The bodies were found strewn around the family's $80,000 house in a wealthy Boston suburb. Said a neighbor of the incident: "None of us knew of any trouble between the couple. Jim was very helpful. He was a nice guy. She was a nice lady. The kids were beautiful" (Boston *Globe*, May 30, 1978, p. 1).

Despite the fact that families from all social classes are violent, researchers and the public alike have recognized that violence may be more common in the homes of people with little education, low incomes, and among those who are either unemployed or hold menial, unskilled jobs. An examination of official records of child abuse and wife abuse, such as state and local child abuse registries and police files, bears out the claim that lower class individuals are the most common wife-, husband-, and child-beaters. But official data can be misleading. The most important bias in these data is that they represent only those individuals or families who get caught in the act of family violence. People with less education, low income, and unskilled jobs may be more likely to get caught abusing family members than college graduates or highly paid professionals. We know of one case in which a physician declined to report a family for suspected child abuse because the suspected abuser was a fellow doctor. Another physician told us that a child who is injured and seen in a public hospital emergency room is five times more likely to be reported as abused than a child with the same injury seen by a private physician. Thus, the official records of family abuse are not very accurate pictures of which families and which individuals are using violence in their homes.

Education

One of the more common views about family violence is that it is typically confined to families who have minimum education. There is a certain amount of scientific information which supports the view that the poorly educated are the most violent. First, violent criminals (at least those who get caught and jailed) are more likely to be uneducated (of course that may be why they got caught!). We also know that the less education a person has, the more likely he or she is to approve of and support violence such as capital punishment in the courts or corporal punishment in schools.

Because we expected the rates of family violence to be highest among those with the least education, our survey results produced a major surprise which challenges the conventional thinking about the relationship between education and family violence. Not only were the uneducated *not* the most violent, in some instances they were the *least!* Among husbands and fathers:

> The most violent fathers and husbands were those who had graduated from high school. The least violent were grammar school dropouts and men with some college education.
>
> Men who have not completed high school are the most likely to be victims of their wives' violence.
>
> Men with the most education have children who are most likely to use abusive violence on their siblings.

Among wives and mothers:

> The most violent mothers are those who have graduated from high school. The least violent are those who did not complete grammar school or those who had some college education.
>
> College-educated women are the least likely to be abused by their husbands. Women who have not completed high school are the most likely to be physically abused.
>
> The most violent wives are those who did not complete high school.
>
> Women who did not complete high school and women

who had some college education have the most violent children.

The expected relationship of years of education to the degree of violence in the home did not materialize in our survey. Violence was not more common among the least educated and least common among the most educated. Surprisingly, we found the least violence occurred among the well educated *and* among those who had never attended high school. The patterns we found showed violence most common among individuals with high school diplomas or at least some high school education.

Perhaps the complex relationship between education and violence may be explained in terms of a person's relative rather than absolute educational attainment. From what we know about education and violence we might argue that it is more stressful to an individual to have a moderate education than to have little education. Men and women who have been to high school, but not beyond, have achieved the average education in America (the median years of education in 1970 was eleven), but they still find themselves cut off from the high status, well-paying professional jobs. In some instances, high school graduates find themselves working beside grammar school dropouts, earning the same salary and job status as their less educated counterparts. If this is the case, it probably causes more stress for the educated worker than the uneducated worker.

Income

Just as we expected those with the least education to be the most violent, we also expected those with the smallest incomes to report the highest rates of family violence. Certainly the official statistics on child abuse and wife abuse support this claim.

We examined the total income of each family for the survey year and compared that to their reported level of family violence. The results showed that income makes an important difference in terms of how violent a household is:

There was a small relationship between income and sibling violence, with the families earning less than $5,999 a year having the most violence and the families earning over $20,000 having the least violence between children.

Income made a bigger difference in terms of parental violence. There was an indirect relationship between income and abusive violence toward children. Families earning more than $20,000 had a rate of violence which was half the rate for families earning under $5,999.

Family income makes the biggest difference in terms of violence between couples. The families living at or below the poverty line (under $5,999) had a rate of violence between husbands and wives which was 500 per cent greater than the rate of spousal violence in the most well-to-do families (incomes over $20,000).

Thus, we see that income does appear to have a direct bearing on levels of violence in the American home, just as previous investigators have often claimed. However, most past research was done, as we have explained, using only officially reported cases of family violence. And there is evidence that in such cases, poor families are far more likely to be "caught" in deviant acts.

But our survey does not look at only "caught" cases. Not all poor people are violent, of course. In fact, the majority of poor families do not use excessive violence in their family life. To be sure, some rich families are also violent. However, the likelihood of extreme violence is much greater in the home of a poor family than in the home of a wealthy family.

Occupation

In addition to education and income, a third indication of a person's position in society is occupational status. Although generally true that the more education one has, the better one's occupation, and thus, the higher one's salary and social status, such is not always the case. Some occupations not highly regarded in terms of middle and upper class standards, offer better salaries than some well-regarded professional positions. A construction worker, for example, often makes more money than a college professor. Thus, a person's occupational status could be considered a more precise indicator of position in society than either income or education alone.

The pattern of violence which we found for income held true for the relationship between family violence and the occupation of the husband (and wife, if she held a job).

> With the exception of violence between siblings, the consistent pattern was that men and women who held blue collar jobs had higher rates of family violence than people who had white collar occupations.
>
> The rate of violence between husbands and wives was twice as high in the families of blue collar workers (men and women) than for white collar workers.
>
> The rate of severe violence toward children in blue collar homes was nearly twice as large as the rate in families of white collar workers.
>
> Men who had blue collar jobs had children who had a higher rate of severe violence among themselves, but women with blue collar jobs were likely to have the least violent children.

Unemployment

If having a lower status and lower-paying job is more likely to increase the rates of family violence, then we could predict that not having a full-time job or not having a job at all would dramatically raise the likelihood of violence in the home. A stark example of this was the case of a man who had been laid off from his job as a truck driver. His response was to go home, load his shotgun, and proceed to pump shotgun blasts into every room of his house—while his wife and young daughter cowered on the floor of the kitchen.

It did not come as a surprise to us to find that households where the husband was unemployed or employed only part time (at the time of our interview) had the highest rates of violence between spouses and violence by parents toward children. We found that:

> If a man is employed part time, or unemployed, there is more severe violence in his home.
>
> Unemployed men are twice as likely to use severe violence on their wives as are men employed full time, and men employed part time have a rate of wife-beating three times the rate for full-time employed men.
>
> Unemployed men and men employed part time are three times more likely to be beaten by their wives.
>
> Children whose fathers are employed part time are nearly twice as likely to be victims of severe violence than are children whose fathers hold full-time jobs.
>
> The least family violence occurs in the homes of retired men. This would seem to be the most likely occurrence since these men are the oldest in our survey and we have already found that increased age results in less violence at home.

Our findings suggest that it would certainly not be unreasonable to expect that the rates, and deadly toll, of family violence would fluctuate with national and local rates of unemployment.

Certainly it is understandable that not being able to hold down a full-time job or not having a job at all would be a major problem for a man and his family. We recall one interview with a draftsman who had been laid off from a position with a shipbuilder. The layoff came on the very day that the man had signed a one-year lease for a new apartment. His wife was expecting a baby, and Christmas was only three months away. Although the man reported no violence between himself and his wife, we could not help but think how different the interview might be if we returned in six months and he was still out of work.

Although the relationship between education and family violence was not what we expected, we do find that social position makes a clear difference. Although violence toward children, between children, and between marital partners occurs in all income groups, all educational groups, and in the homes of doctors and truck drivers alike, we do find that some households are much more likely to be the scenes of severe family violence. Poor, unemployed, or part-time employed men more often live in violent households than men whose total family incomes exceed $20,000.

SUMMING UP

To sum up this detailed examination of the factors which were and were not related to violence in the family, we can say that social factors do indeed make a difference in a family's inclination to engage in violent behavior. The factors which had a strong bearing on family violence were age, income, having a full-time, part-time, or no job. To a lesser extent, religion, residence in a city or the country, region of the country, and race were related to violence in the home.

We encountered a surprise when we learned that the uneducated were not the most violent, and we saw that some factors were more strongly related to specific types of family violence —for instance race was more strongly related to husband-to-wife violence than the other forms of violence.

There is a very important insight to be gained from our finding that social factors do influence whether or not a child, wife, or husband is physically abused. The majority of all treatment approaches to family violence involve some kind of personal counseling for violent family member(s). The counseling is proposed because most people assume that there is something "wrong" with a person who uses abusive violence on a family member.

To be sure, our national survey of family violence cannot be used to rule out the theory that personal factors are related to violent behavior. But because we found social factors are related to violence we can argue with conviction that personal counseling will never be enough to treat or prevent violence in the home. According to our study, psychological health will not prevent family violence if a person is young, poor, and unemployed. Even if we "cured" the presumed psychological malady of violent individuals, the cure would have no effect if we send them back into the same social environment which influenced them to be violent in the first place.

PART IV

Some Immediate Causes

CHAPTER 7

Marital Conflict and Marital Violence

It's Saturday night, and from most of the houses in Ed and Sally Anderson's subdivision come sounds of television and children being put to bed. But at Ed and Sally's, angry voices can be heard rising louder and louder.

"Ed and Sally?" says a neighbor. "Oh yeah, they argue all the time. It really gets bad sometimes. Why just last week we had them over—started going at each other right at the dinner table, arguing over their kid's bike. Ed ran over it when he drove in the driveway—said Sally should teach the kid to keep his stuff out of the way. Sally said he drove like a maniac and never watched where he was going—said he never picked up his stuff either, and the kid was just copying him. Gee, it turned into a real row—embarrassing for us, you know? It's the last time we ask them here."

Like most Americans, Ed and Sally's neighbors view marital conflict—either verbal or physical—as something to be avoided. "Harmony" is the ideal. Most people agree that some marital conflict is inevitable, but it is looked on with distaste and embarrassment, something that one can and should avoid.

In this chapter we will take a look at conflict in marriage, determining its possible links with physical violence. We need to know whether conflict is good—is it necessary for a healthy marriage? Or is just the opposite true—if people assault each other verbally, do they eventually turn to physical mauling as well?

We need to know the reasons for conflict. Why do people fight with each other? Does conflict most often stem from things like money, sex, or children? How much trouble does conflict over such issues create for a couple? Are people who argue over sex more likely to batter each other than couples who fight over emptying the trash? The data we gathered help answer these questions.

THE MOST FREQUENT CONFLICTS

As a first step, we needed to know how often certain conflicts occurred among the 2,143 couples in the study. We posed the question to each person this way:

"I am going to read a list of things that couples do not always agree on. For each of them, please tell me how often you and your [husband/wife/partner] agreed *during the past year*. First, take managing the money. Did you and your [husband/wife/partner] always agree, almost always agree, usually agree, sometimes agree, or never agree about managing the money?"

This was repeated for "cooking, cleaning, or repairing the house," "social activities and entertaining," "affection and sex relations," and (if the respondent had children) "things about the children."

Sex, Money, or Children?

Which of these five issues most frequently leads to conflict: money, children, housekeeping, social activities, or sex? Chart

12 shows that the most frequent conflict is not about sex but about housekeeping, i.e., things like cooking, cleaning, and repairing the house. One out of three American couples say they *always* disagree about this!

Can people really become violent over scrubbing the kitchen floor or cooking a steak? We found again and again that the answer is yes. Women who have suffered violence from their husbands often give such reasons for the abuse. They report having plates of food broken over their heads and bowls of soup thrown in their faces by husbands unhappy with the quality of the meal.

One New Hampshire woman said she knew the honeymoon was over when:

". . . soon after we moved into our first apartment, we had an argument, a stupid argument over the Con-Tact paper I was putting up in the kitchen. He told me I was doing a sloppy job. 'Do it yourself, then,' I said. The next thing I knew he was clobbering me, first with the mop handle, and then with his fists" (New Hampshire *Times,* "Marriage and Mayhem," March 1, 1978, p. 12).

Some people may question whether or not there is any real difference in how often American couples disagree on these five issues. The percentages who always disagree really do not differ very markedly (see Chart 12).

CHART 12
Conflict about Five Aspects of Family Life

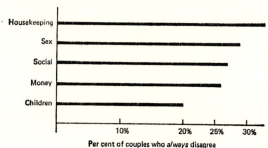

Per cent of couples who *always* disagree

There is even less difference between what husbands and wives see as conflicts in marriage. In fact, the largest difference is only 5 per cent. It concerns housekeeping: 34 per cent of the wives and 29 per cent of the husbands said they always disagreed with their partner about "cooking, cleaning, or repairing the house."

THE TRADITIONAL VIEW OF CONFLICT VERSUS "CONFLICT THEORY"

With the above survey, we documented a high level of intractable conflict within many families. Now let us turn our attention to something more subtle. What are the consequences of such conflict between husbands and wives?

The traditional view, as we said earlier, is that conflict is an evil which "healthy" marriages avoid. A good marriage is a marriage without conflict. There is, however, a school of thought in sociology known as "conflict theory," which takes the opposite point of view. Conflict theory differs from the traditional view in a number of ways.

First, instead of a lurking suspicion that a certain amount of conflict is part of life, conflict theorists assert that conflict is an *inevitable* part of the human condition, including marriage.

More importantly, conflict theorists emphasize that not only is conflict inevitable, it is a useful and necessary part of life. In fact, these theorists claim that without it, society would eventually disintegrate.

Why? Because it is through conflict that changes and adaptations take place. Whenever change or revolution is in the wind, there are some people who want the change, while others fight to maintain the status quo. A current example is the equal rights for women movement.

Conditions in modern life make the traditional system of male dominance not only morally objectionable, but also terribly inefficient. In earlier times, the traditional division of labor between men and women (i.e., "women's place is in the home") perhaps made more sense. But with changes brought about by modern technology, unequal treatment of women denies society the full contribution of the female half of the population.

Thus, we see social change is necessary to cope with the realities of modern life. Conflict over this change is therefore part of the adaptation which helps keep a group in tune with the changing realities of life.

Of course, conflict can be denied or suppressed—especially in families. Many families try to maintain a public image of tranquillity and harmony. Unfortunately, the underlying differences do not disappear by declaring that one belongs to "one big happy family." If conflict is suppressed in this way, the issues over which there are differences usually smolder beneath the surface harmony. Resentment mounts and saps the loyalty and solidarity of the group until the hostility level becomes so great that the surface harmony is finally breached, often with physical violence. By this time, things may have reached a point where people refuse to listen to reason in resolving the conflict. Instead, it becomes an all-or-nothing battle with each side out to hurt the other. The group may not survive if the members have the alternative of leaving. If there is no such alternative, the internal war may make the group so ineffective that the basic purposes of the group are no longer achieved.

Take the example of Walter and Jane. To all outward appearances they were happily married. They had five bright children and a home in the country with horses, chickens, and dogs. Unfortunately, Walter did not mind living above their income and was constantly bringing home expensive gifts for the kids, new tools for the workshop, and once, even a motorcycle, without consulting his wife or their checkbook.

Wanting to maintain peace, Jane seldom complained, but

she deeply resented having to try to make ends meet, balance their accounts, and stall creditors. Although she occasionally lost her temper, she would not have considered separation or divorce, in part, because of their religion. But also, she knew Walter could never be counted on for financial support if they separated. This situation went on festering for years.

The last straw came when Walter announced that he had bought half share in a racing car and intended to learn to race himself, all for a mere $25,000.

Jane completely lost control, accusing him of sacrificing his family's welfare by throwing away money they didn't have and possibly losing his life in a dangerous sport he knew nothing about.

She threw several dinner plates at him, and he countered by slapping her face several times. Jane ordered him out of the house, which she backed up with a court order to keep him away, and refused to speak to him again.

Walter, finally coming to his senses, tried to reason with her, and offered to give up all his schemes. She remained firm.

The family split up. Walter remarried two months later, acquiring three more stepchildren in the process. His own bright, eldest son was unable to attend college because there was no longer any money. Two more children began to get into trouble over acts of vandalism and truancy. Jane also remarried and was divorced again within a year. The children were shuffled back and forth between the parents, neither of whom could afford to support them. The family unit had virtually disintegrated.

Given problems such as this, who is right? On the one side are the average citizen, typical social scientist, and marriage counselor. They are most likely to assert that conflict undercuts marriage and should be either avoided or reduced. These people would probably say that if Jane had not blown up, or at least listened to reason when Walter apologized, the results would not have been so tragic.

On the other side, however, is a minority of social scientists and marriage counselors who view conflict as an inherent and essential part of a satisfactory and enduring marriage. These people would probably say that accepting his apology without any real change in Walter's behavior is a delusion. Jane should have been airing her complaints from the beginning—getting angry every time Walter spent money foolishly and confronting the issue from the very beginning. Rather than accept an illusory "harmony," they encourage people to face up to this inevitable part of married life.

CONFLICT AND VIOLENCE

This is too important an issue to be left as a debate. We further examined it by giving each couple a conflict score based on the number of times they disagreed on the five issues of money, children, sex, housekeeping, and social activities.[1] A couple could receive a score anywhere from 0 (they always agreed about all five of these issues) to 20 (they never agreed on any of them). The scores did actually range from 0 to 20, but only a few couples (9.4 per cent) reported no conflict at all. Even fewer—in fact, only one couple—said they never agreed about any of these five things. The average score was almost 6 (5.9).

When the non-conflict and low conflict couples are compared with the other couples there are large differences. Couples who reported no conflicts during the survey year had a very low violence rate compared to the high conflict couples. In fact, Chart 13 shows that as the amount of conflict increases, so does the rate of violence. The couples with the most conflicts had a violence rate of 43.9 per cent, which is sixteen times higher than the rate for the non-conflict couples (2.3 per cent).

CHART 13
Husband / Wife Violence by Amount of
Family Conflict

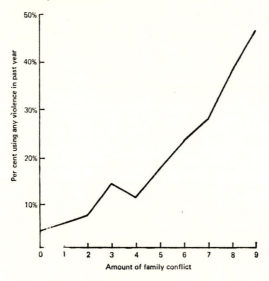

CHART 14
Severe Husband/Wife Violence by
Amount of Family Conflict

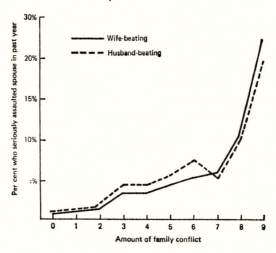

The strong tendency for violence to go up as the amount of conflict rises applies to both husbands and wives. In the non-conflict marriages, 2.1 per cent of the husbands were violent compared to 39 per cent of the husbands in the marriages with the most conflicts. Wives followed the same trend, but started with a slightly lower rate in the non-conflict marriages (1.6 per cent). The wives' violence rate then increased steadily up to the highest conflict group. Over a third of wives in these high conflict marriages had been physically violent to their husband that year.

An objection which might be made to these figures is that a certain amount of pushing, slapping, and shoving is often taken as "just one of those things" in marriage. It isn't really "violence." What about when "real violence" is involved?

Looking at this aspect we compared the non-conflict couples with the other couples using the Wife-beating and Husband-beating Indexes (see Appendix B for definition of indexes). These indexes focus on violent acts which go beyond pushing, slapping, and shoving (see Chapter 2). Chart 14 shows that the rates for severe violence of this kind are even more closely linked to the amount of conflict than the over-all violence index (see Appendix B). The rates for both wife-beating and husband-beating start out very low, then increases gradually, and then shoot up dramatically for the marriages with the most conflict. It is as though people are able to withstand a considerable amount of conflict, avoiding violence up to a certain point. Then all hell breaks loose.

ALTERNATIVES TO VIOLENT CONFLICT

Now let us return to the question of whether conflict is really a *useful* part of marriage. We found a clear tendency for the amount of violence to increase as the amount of conflict increases. That does not speak well for the presumed value of conflict. However, it is also not the last word on this issue because there is more to conflict theory than simple correlations.

One of the most important aspects of conflict theory, which has been left out of our explanation up to now, is the difference between conflict in the sense of differences in *what* people want, and conflict in the sense of *how* they go about trying to get what they want. Differences in what people want are inevitable, and somehow must be allowed for if the group is to continue.

Just *how* people go about resolving these differences is another matter. Physical violence is only one of many ways the contending parties can achieve their ends or interests. There is also reasoning and negotiation. But violence may, in the extreme, be necessary. Take the situation of a family in which there is a serious problem between a husband and wife. The husband refuses to listen, or doesn't get the message, or ignores the whole matter, sometimes for years. In desperation, the wife throws something at him or hits him. At least in middle class families, this is such a shocking event that the husband can no longer ignore the seriousness of the problem. It is like the hoisting of a danger signal which cannot be ignored (or is very difficult to ignore).

Violence is typically a sign that constructive ways of dealing with conflict have broken down. So the conflict theorists may be correct after all. Charts 13 and 14 may simply be documenting the fact that most couples attempt to suppress their conflicting interests. This leads to greater and greater resentment, and ultimately to violence.

It follows from this that just relating the amount of conflict to the amount of violence is not a satisfactory way of getting at the tremendously important issues which are at stake. Such a relation ignores whether these are conflicts that have been suppressed and are smoldering, or are, instead, conflicts that have been acknowledged and dealt with by methods less destructive than physical violence. There ought to be a difference between couples who deny or suppress conflict as opposed to couples who recognize their differences and attempt to resolve them by negotiation and reason.

The data we have dealing with the issue emphasize several points. First, there is the measure of conflict that was used in Charts 13 and 14. This indicates the number of issues the couple disagree on. It is a measure of conflict in the sense of *what* people want. But there is also data on *how* the couple tries to deal with these conflicts. This measures how often the couple used negotiation and reasoning to deal with conflicts.

The information about these two aspects of conflict bring us closer to what conflict theory is all about. Conflict theory says that conflict is an inevitable part of life, *and* that if constructive methods are used to resolve or manage it, then such conflict is beneficial. If this premise is correct, we should find that couples who use constructive tactics such as negotiation and reasoning to deal with conflict are able to avoid physical violence and also have more satisfactory marriages.

CHART 15
Per Cent of Couples Violent in Survey Year by Amount of Conflict and Use of Reasoning

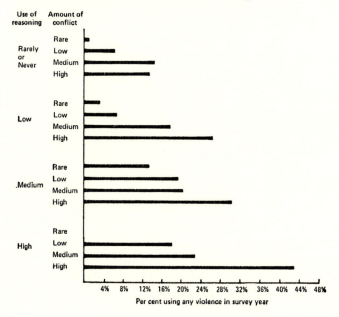

CONFLICT, REASONING, AND VIOLENCE

Chart 15 shows that the more conflict, the more violence. This is the case in each of the four parts of the chart. So we find, irrespective of whether the couple uses reasoning and negotiation, the more conflict in a marriage the more violence.

These results are exactly the opposite of what was predicted on the basis of the conflict theory! According to conflict theory, couples who bring their problems into the open, and who use reasoning and negotiation to settle those conflicts, should be the ones who do not have to resort to violence, either as a desperate measure to call attention to a grievance, or as a means of resolving the conflict. These are the couples represented by the bottom bar in Chart 15, the "High" reasoning and "High" conflict couples.[2] But instead of having the lowest rate of violence, these are the *most violent* couples in the sample. In fact, almost half of them (43 per cent) engaged in a physical fight during the survey year.

The reverse also failed to hold true in relation to the tenets of conflict theory. These people are represented at the top bar in Chart 15. They reported no conflicts and rarely or never used reasoning or negotiation. Since, according to conflict theory, it is almost impossible for there to be no conflicts in a group such as a family, these must be the couples who are repressing things, and presumably setting the stage for violent eruptions. Since they are also people who do not use reasoning and negotiation, according to conflict theory, they are the couples who will end up having to use physical force to deal with these inevitable conflicts. But, contrary to such predictions, the couples in this group have a very low rate of violence—less than 1 per cent.

No doubt even the above fairly complicated analysis does not really do justice to the subtleties of conflict theory. We continue to believe that this theory describes an important aspect of what goes on in all groups, including families. At the same time, a theory cannot remain "promising" forever. At some point, hypotheses based on the theory will have to be demonstrated or the theory abandoned.[3]

CATHARSIS AND VIOLENCE

A theory somewhat similar to conflict theory is the idea of "catharsis." The catharsis approach to avoiding violence in marriage shares with conflict theory the idea that conflict is an inevitable part of life. What it adds, however, is the idea that people have an innate aggressive drive that must somehow be expressed. If there are no avenues for expressing one's aggression in non-violent ways, then catharsis theory says that the aggression will accumulate and ultimately burst forth in severely destructive and violent ways.

The difference between conflict and catharsis theory lies in what we need to avoid "bottling up." For conflict theory it is a characteristic of the group—the presumed inevitable difference in interests between the members of the group. For catharsis theory it is a characteristic of people—their presumed aggressive drive. One theory says that groups need to face up to their internal differences; the other theory says that people need to be able to discharge their aggression in ways that are minimally harmful.

According to the catharsis theory, the way to avoid violence is to express aggression verbally or by attacking inanimate objects. In this way the aggression which is found in all of us to a greater or lesser extent is "ventilated" short of a physically violent attack on another person.

Many ways have been suggested to get rid of this built-up aggression. Psychologist George Bach advises "Get rid of your pent-up hostilities! Tell them where you're really at! Let it be total vicious, exaggerated hyperbole!" (quoted in Howard, 1970, p. 54). Others such as Bindrim, Perls, and Lowen add physical acts of symbolic aggression to their procedure for working with couples, for example, punching pillows, biting a plastic baby bottle while imagining it is someone you are angry with, and smashing a board in order to "let it out" (Berkowitz, 1973, p. 28; Howard, 1970, p. 94). Shostrom (1971, p. 176) asserts that "hurting is a necessary part of a [marriage] relationship." There is apparently a thriving sale of foam rubber bats for use in getting rid of the presumed pent-up aggression without causing physical harm. These bats have been advertised in the newsletter of the American Psychological Association (the *Monitor*), and in almost every 1976 and 1977 issue of the magazine *Human Behavior*.

Despite the plausibility of the catharsis approach, and despite its popularity with many marriage counselors, there is no scientifically valid evidence supporting it. In fact, what evidence there is overwhelmingly comes to the exact opposite conclusion: that "ventilating" aggression in minor ways makes one *more* likely to go on to further aggression (Berkowitz, 1973; Hokanson, 1970). However, none of Hokanson's experiments, and none of the studies reviewed by Berkowitz were of married couples. There was the possibility the theory could still be correct in the closed and intimate environment of a marriage. We therefore did a study of the catharsis theory using a sample of married couples (Straus, 1974a).

That study, like almost all the others using reasonably valid procedures, showed that the more ventilation the *more* violence. Still, the issue is not settled. Although our earlier study of the catharsis approach to controlling violence used a sample of married couples, the data were obtained from the couples' children. The information came from 385 university students who filled out a questionnaire about what happened in their families during the year they were seniors in high school. Therefore the sample is not representative of marriage across the country. There are problems concerning how much these students knew in the first place about fights between their parents, and how much they could remember about the circumstances of those fights.

The nationally representative sample in the present study

overcomes these limitations. Although there are still some problems, which will be explained later, it gives us a chance to take another look at this approach to family relationships.

The question is whether—as claimed by the advocates of catharsis and "creative" aggression—letting off a verbal blast at one's husband or wife helps avoid a physical explosion.

The data on our 2,143 couples suggest a resounding NO. In fact, the reverse seems to be the case. For those who engage in little or no verbal aggression, there is little or no physical violence (less than half of 1 per cent). For couples in the lower middle group in verbal aggression, the violence rate is ten times as high, but still relatively low (five per hundred couples). For those in the upper middle group of verbal aggression, nineteen out of every hundred reported a violent incident during the year. Finally, a clear majority of the top quarter who express conflict through verbal blasts were violent. The most verbally aggressive one quarter of our couples have a violence rate of fifty-six per hundred couples. Actually, the association of verbal aggression with physical aggression is even closer than these figures show. If we consider the top 5 per cent of couples in respect to verbal aggression, almost all of them (83.3 per cent) had engaged in one or more physical fights during the year we asked about.

Cause or Effect

People who advocate a catharsis or verbal ventilation approach to preventing marital violence are likely to object that our evidence does not prove that verbal violence *causes* physical violence. This is correct because our data do not tell us which came first, the verbal hurting or the physical hurting. Granting this limitation, it is still clear that verbal violence and physical violence go hand in hand. We can at least say that verbal aggression does not seem to be a substitute for physical aggression.

There is still one other aspect to consider before leaving the catharsis theory. Perhaps the association between verbal and physical assaults simply reflects the number of disagreements or conflicts between a couple. If there is a lot of disagreement, there will be a lot of both verbal and physical violence. Those who take a catharsis approach argue that we must account for this fact. It could be that the couples with many conflicts (in the sense of many disagreements) are the ones with a lot of "pent-up hostilities" who need to be able to express this agression verbally to keep it from being expressed physically.

The method we used to see if catharsis or ventilation helps couples with deep conflicts to avoid physical violence is like the method used to test the conflict theory. We divided the sample of couples into four groups according to the depth of their disagreements over money, sex, children, housekeeping, and social activities. We further divided each group into those who followed the advice of the ventilation school and expressed their pent-up hostilities by such things as swearing, insulting, smashing, or throwing objects (but not throwing things *at* their partner), and doing spiteful things. These are all verbally or symbolically aggressive acts which, if the catharsis theory is right, should allow people to rid themselves of pent-up aggression before things get to the point of direct physical attacks on a spouse.

In all four groups, the findings show that verbal aggression and physical aggression go hand in hand. In fact, the link between verbal blasts and physical blows is *greatest* for couples with the most conflicts. The irony of this is that the high conflict couples are the very ones for whom letting off steam verbally is *supposed* to be the greatest help in avoiding violence.

A Kernel of Truth

We should not go overboard in rejecting the catharsis school of thought, however. Too often when applying catharsis to the study of human relationships, people tend to overlook the reasons behind the "leveling" or ventilation. It is one thing to blow up verbally as a means of communication, but quite another if the blowup is a verbal substitute for physically hurting one's spouse (Straus, 1974a). Leveling or ventilation in the sense of getting issues out into the open, and in the sense of not hiding one's anger or disagreement, *is* a positive force in human interaction. To try to deny to ourselves and others that we feel anger is a distortion of reality which is likely to cause trouble; and to suppress issues precludes the possibility of resolving them. But leveling in the sense of acting-out one's anger by verbal or physical aggression against another is an inappropriate extension of these truths. The evidence in this chapter suggests that it leads to heightened rather than reduced aggression and is likely to produce retaliatory aggression rather than a resolution of the conflict.

THE MOST VIOLENT CONFLICTS

Even though there is little difference in the amount of conflict over money, sex, housekeeping, children, or social activities, a disagreement on one of these may still cause more trouble than a disagreement on another.

Sex and money are widely believed to be the issues which cause the most trouble. But our data show that neither of these provokes the most violence. Rather, *it is conflict over children which is most likely to lead a couple to blows.*

Chart 16 shows how close the relationship is between conflict over children and violence between spouses. The more often a couple disagree about things concerning their children, the higher the rate of violence. In fact, two thirds of the couples who said they always disagree over the children had at least one violent incident during the year of our survey! Children are a tremendous source of pride and satisfaction. Parents feel intensely about their children and their children's welfare, probably more intensely than about anything else in the fam-

CHART 16
Per Cent of Husbands and Wives
Violent in Survey Year by
Amount of Conflict about Children

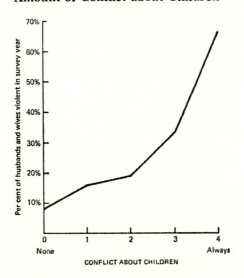

CONFLICT ABOUT CHILDREN

ily. It follows that when things go wrong with the children—as they inevitably do at some time or other—there are equal depths of despair, anguish, and conflict.

The violence rates in Chart 16 do not distinguish between mild violence, such as slaps, and severe violence, such as punching. Chart 16 also combines violent acts by either the husband or the wife. There is no need for separate charts for husbands and wives or for severe violence because we found roughly the same pattern of conflict over children leading to violence for both the husbands and wives. The same applies to violence that was severe enough to be called wife- or husband-beating: both of these increased bit by bit as the amount of conflict over children went up.

Although children rather than sex and money are the cause of conflicts most likely to produce violence, this does not mean that conflict over sex and money is unrelated to violence. In fact, conflict over all five of the issues we asked about (money, housekeeping, social activities, sex, and children) tends to produce violence between husband and wife. The main difference is that the violence rates of couples who fought over their children were higher than rates for couples whose conflicts were over any of the other four issues. For example, as conflict over social activities goes up, so does the violence rate, but it reaches a peak of "only" 50 per cent as compared to the peak of 67 per cent for the couple with the most conflict over children.

As for sex and money, we found that conflicts about money are second only to conflicts about children. Conflicts about sex and affection are on the same par for violence as conflicts over housekeeping and social activities. Our data show that the more conflict about any of these five issues, the higher the rate of violence.

SUMMING UP

It is clear that the more conflicts a couple has, the more likely they are to get into a physical fight. In fact, a persisting severe conflict over something crucial, such as disagreement over children, is almost sure to end in at least some violence. Moreover, neither recognition of these conflicts and attempts to deal with them by reason and negotiation (as advocated by conflict theorists) nor "ventilation" of one's hostility with verbal aggression (as advocated by the "creative aggression" school of family therapy) seems to help avoid the link between conflict and violence in marriage. Despite this, we think there are kernels of truth underlying both the conflict theory and the creative aggression approaches to marriage. The dynamics of what is involved, however, are too complicated to be adequately studied with our data or to be summed up in simple prescriptions to "let it all hang out."

CHAPTER 8

Violent Families:
Children, Stress, and Power

It's 5 P.M., and Mary frantically tosses potatoes and onions
into a pot of stew. Frank, her construction-worker husband, is
due home in half an hour and likes dinner on the table when
he walks in. No food and he starts yelling at the kids and sometimes at Mary. The new baby (the family's third) screams in
her crib, hungry and colicky, while the two-year-old beats rep-
etitiously on the floor with his blocks. The four-year-old adds
to the din by turning on the TV full blast, and comes whining
to his mother that there are no cartoons.

Mary turns to talk to him, and as she does, the stew boils
over down the front of the stove. Frustrated, she lashes out at
the nearest object at hand—her son—slapping and screaming
at him in fury.

The above situation, although hypothetical, is repeated with
minor variations in hundreds of American homes every day.
TV comedies and movies often resort to such scenes as the center of some supposedly humorous episode. Commercials for
headache tablets would have one believe that such behavior is
often the norm without their "tension-relieving" pills.

That many parents are unable to cope with stress without resorting to violence is overlooked by comedy writers and ad men alike.

In this chapter we will turn our analysis of violence to the structure of the family—to what characteristics of the family as a unit tend to contribute to violence.

We want to know where violence is most likely to occur.

Are parents with six children more likely to resort to beatings than those with two children? Who makes decisions in the household, and who controls the power—does this affect the family's attitude toward violence? Does violence in the home vary with the amount of stress the family has encountered in the previous year?

These are the topics we will explore in Chapter 8.

NUMBER OF CHILDREN AT HOME

> There was an old woman who lived in a shoe.
> She had so many children she didn't know what to do.
> She gave them some broth without any bread.
> And whipped them all soundly, and put them to bed.

This old nursery rhyme reminds us how long people have regarded children as causing stress and pressure—the more children, the more stress, and thus the more likelihood of parents blowing off steam with a slap, kick, or shove. The old woman who lived in the shoe had additional problems in that she apparently had no husband (at least he is not mentioned), and probably not much money (since dinner was only broth without bread).

However, anyone who has had even one child will report that the child produces stress on a marriage. Research on the impact of children on marriages consistently shows that the level of marital satisfaction and marital adjustment goes down after the birth of the first child, never to rise to its former level until the last child leaves home (Rollins and Feldman, 1970).

Other social scientists have reported that the birth of the first child is a major crisis in family life (LeMasters, 1957), and that having children rearranges family patterns and creates new conflicts (LaRossa, 1977).

The following explanation from a Massachusetts woman is one which is frequently echoed in other families:

> "The first time it happened was when I was pregnant with the first baby. He pushed me up the stairs. When the baby was christened, I had a black eye . . . When I was pregnant the second time, he kicked me. One time he took me over his knee and spanked me until I was black and blue.
>
> I never hit him back. I was afraid. To see somebody bigger than you stand over you . . . It was frightening to see this man go crazy" (Boston *Globe*, "The Story of a Battered Wife," by Nina McCain, February 26, 1978, p. A1).

Unfortunately, just as parents of only one child speak of the trials and tribulations of parenthood, they tell of major increases in chaos, stress, and crisis when the second child comes along. Evidence from social science research on the family supports the claims that having two children is more difficult than having one (Knox and Wilson, 1978).

These facts are almost self-evident. Each additional child means a decrease in time for parents to pursue their own interests or activities. Each child increases the work load in the home, creates more noise and confusion, and, as scientific research finds, often decreases marital happiness (Knox and Wilson, 1978).

So if one child is more difficult than no children, and two children are more difficult than one, are six more difficult than five? And, the most important question we ask—are the number of children living at home related to the level of violence in that household?

The survey of 2,143 American families in which the husband and wife lived together included childless families and families where there were as many as nine children. The typical family interviewed had two children. Nearly 15 per cent of the couples had no children, and less than 4 per cent had more than seven children. In terms of children who were still living at home, the average couple interviewed had two children at home. One out of five couples had no child at home, while less than 1 per cent still had more than seven children living with them.

When we examined the relationship between violence and number of children, we concerned ourselves with only the children who had lived at home during the survey year. We assumed that a child not living at home tends to cause less stress than children who are.

Child Abuse

The likelihood of a parent abusing a child increases generally with the size of a family. Parents of two children have a rate of abuse 50 per cent higher than parents who have but one child to care for (Chart 17). The highest rate of child abuse comes with five children. Thereafter, the rate goes down, but is still quite high for seven-child homes. Surprisingly, the largest families had no abusive violence toward children. Parents who have eight or nine children rarely use violence on their children.

CHART 17
Child Abuse by Number of Children
Living at Home

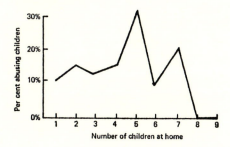

The largest families may be the least violent for a number of reasons. Perhaps parents with eight or nine children are simply too exhausted to raise a finger toward their children. But it may well be that the very largest families simply have less stress than five- or six-child homes. First, given that there is an average age span of two or three years between children, and that the odds against twins and triplets are quite high, we can expect to find that a family which has an eighth child has at least one teen-ager at home. The oldest children may be a resource for the parents. They can baby-sit, help with the chores, bring in an additional income, and minimize the impact of the last in a parade of children. Another possibility is that those people who desire to have and do raise such large families are so "child-oriented" that they will be less violent no matter how many children they have.

Our most plausible explanation for the higher rates of violence among families with four, five, and six children, however, comes down to a matter of dollars and cents—pure economic stress. Every new child means the family's economic pie is sliced smaller. As the strain on the pocketbook builds, parents' tempers tend to fray. To test this, we examined the relationship of violence and the numbers of children among different income groups. We found some important patterns.

First, among the poorest families (annual family income under $6,000), each additional child increases the likelihood of child abuse. The rate of abuse is 300 per cent greater in two-child homes than one-child households. For those families whose income is between $6,000 and $20,000 per year, the risk of child abuse increases with each child up to seven. In families with seven or more children living at home, there is no child abuse.

Finally, among the well-to-do families (above $20,000), who tended to have smaller families than those earning less money, there was no relationship between the number of children at home and the rate of child abuse.

Sibling Abuse

In families where there are more brothers and sisters living at home, there is, of course, more competition for limited physical and economic resources and for limited time and affection. Thus, larger families might reasonably be expected to have more sibling abuse. However, we found no relationship between the number of children at home and the rate of sibling abuse (see Chapter 4).

Since there is so little violence in the largest families, could it be that they actually do have more money? We looked at the relationship between family income and the number of children at home, comparing it to the incidence of sibling abuse, and again found the number of children had little to do with abuse among siblings.

Spouse Abuse

The pattern found for child abuse held up with even more precision for violence between husbands and wives. Spouse abuse was low for men and women with no children, increased with each additional child up to six, and was nonexistent in homes with six, seven, eight, or nine children (see Charts 18 and 19).

CHART 18
Wife Abuse by Number of
Children Living at Home

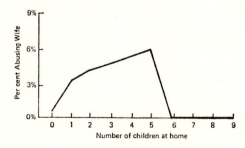

CHART 19
Husband Abuse by Number of
Children Living at Home

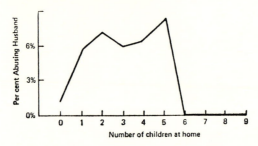

Family income was also considered. For couples with the lowest family incomes (under $6,000) the rate of wife abuse doubles from one- to two-child homes. For those in the highest income group (over $20,000), the rate of wife-battering is more than three times greater in two-child than in one-child homes.

Looking at wife-to-husband violence, the most important differences are for women living in homes with total incomes under $6,000. Here, the rate of husband-battering is three times greater in two-child than in one-child homes.

The finding that two-child homes are more violent than one-child homes for both low and high income households indicates that the presumed cause of violence is more complicated than the simple economic stresses caused by children. If the cause were economic stress, then high income families would be better able to cope with two children than low income families. This was not the case. We must look at non-monetary reasons to explain why husbands with two children at home have the highest rates of wife-battering in both the low and high income groups. The key stress which leads children to be associated with increased violence may be the social consequences of having two as opposed to one child. Two children take more time, reduce privacy, and limit the opportunities for a husband and a wife to communicate. This same argument can be applied to having three and four children, but as T. Berry Brazelton, an expert on child development says, the third child is the easiest of all to manage because parents have had so much practice (1969).

The experience of the old woman who lived in a shoe does not seem to apply very widely. The largest families do not have the most violence. In fact, the largest families are America's least violent. Having one child increases the risk of family violence. Two children living at home appears to be one of the most violent situations, and additional children (up to six) also create situations where the rates of parental and spousal violence are high.

To understand family violence we cannot assume simply that each additional child at home creates a heavier family burden which in turn translates into increased violence. There seems to be a point of diminishing return (six children) when additional children cease to produce more violence and even lessen the possibility of its occurring. We found the strain of additional children upon family income may well have a bearing on the possibility of child abuse within the home. It is interesting, however, that some types of violence—wife-battering in particular—cannot be linked to a relationship of income and the number of children living at home.

STRESS AND VIOLENCE

In the previous chapter, and in much of the rest of this book, we have explained our findings by proposing that stress is a major contributor to family violence. We have found low income, unemployment, part-time employment, and four or five children in the home are all related to violence toward children and violence between spouses. In one way or another, each of these conditions could be considered stressful or potentially stressful.

In order to get a more direct sense of how much stress the

families we interviewed were under during the survey year, we asked questions about the types of problems they had encountered in the previous twelve months. There are, of course, an infinite variety of problems that a family can encounter. Moreover, something extremely stressful in one home might be considered a mild annoyance in another. Keeping this in mind, we presented each of our families with a listing of eighteen problems or "stress" occurrences which we felt were both common and which a majority of people agreed produced stress within a family. The items were:

1. Troubles with boss
2. Troubles with other people at work
3. Laid off or fired from work
4. Arrested or convicted for something serious
5. Death of someone I felt close to
6. Foreclosure of mortgage or loan
7. Pregnant or having a child born
8. Serious sickness or injury
9. Serious problem with health or behavior of family member
10. Sexual difficulties
11. In-law troubles
12. Much worse off financially
13. Separated or divorced
14. Big increase in the number of arguments with husband/wife/partner
15. Big increase in hours worked or responsibility on the job
16. Moved to a different neighborhood or town
17. Child kicked out of school or suspended
18. Child caught doing something illegal

There was a wide range of experiences among our 2,143 families. Some individuals we talked to had encountered none of these problems in the last year. The maximum stress faced by our families was thirteen out of a possible eighteen stressful experiences. The average person we interviewed reported two stressful events in the last year.

Stress and Severe Violence

Sibling Abuse. There was no relationship between the amount of stress reported by one of the parents and the likelihood that his or her children engaged in abusive violence with one another. Thus, although a family may have experienced a great deal of stress, it appears that since this stress was encountered mainly by one or both of the parents, it played no role in increasing the chances that the children were abusive toward each other.

Child Abuse. For those parents who reported eight or less stressful events in the previous year, there was a very small relationship to the chances of their being abusive to their children.[1] For each additional stressful event, there is a slightly greater chance that a parent will be abusive. The rate of abusive violence is much higher among the few families who reported ten or more problems (Chart 20).

CHART 20
Child Abuse by Family Stress

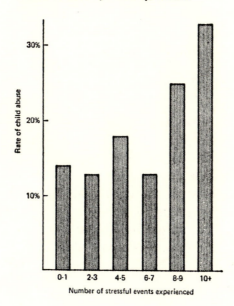

Rate of child abuse

Number of stressful events experienced

In terms of the problems which parents encounter with their children (child kicked out of school or had troubles with the law), there is a much more profound relationship between stress and the likelihood of a child being abusively struck by a parent.

Spouse Abuse. The relationship between problems reported by the individuals interviewed and the level of violence between these individuals and their spouses was quite strong.[2] Each additional problem increased the chances that there would be wife and husband abuse in a family (see Charts 21 and 22).

Our discussions with families concerning their experiences with stressful problems suggest that stress does increase the chances that a family will resort to abusive violence. However, the interviews only scratch the surface of this complicated relationship. Counting stressful events and relating the tally to percentages of violent families does support the theory, but it does not convey the reasons for the relationship. It does not give insight into how stress leads to violence. To accomplish this we must look with more detail at stress and violence.

Child-produced Stress. Most people who think about child abuse tend to regard the child as the innocent victim of his or her parents' outbursts of violence. Traditionally, people who have tried to explain child abuse have looked at the problems of the parent to understand why that parent abused the child. Overlooked, in many cases, were problems originating with the child, whether beyond its control or intentional, which precipitated the child's abuse.

Psychologists William Friedrich and Jerry Boriskin have reviewed the research on child abuse and found that in many cases the child does play a role in the abuse (1976). Premature babies, for example, have been identified as prone to abuse. Prematurity can produce a risk of abuse for a number of reasons. First, premature babies must stay in the hospital longer than their mothers. According to psychologists, this results in an inadequate "bonding" between the new baby and

CHART 21
Wife Abuse by Family Stress

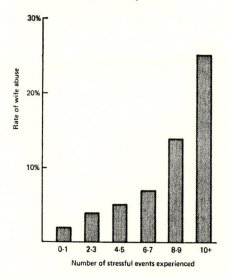

CHART 22
Husband Abuse by Family Stress

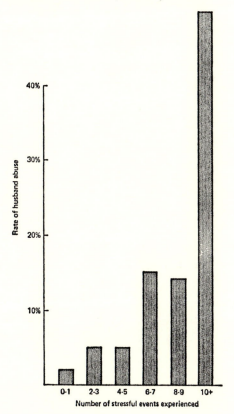

the new mother. A second reason is that once home, premature infants require more care and attention than full-term babies. Premature babies have underdeveloped nervous systems, and are likely to be hypersensitive.

Retarded children are also vulnerable to being abused. There is some question as to whether the retardation is a cause of child abuse or a product, but the evidence is there to allow us to conclude that retarded children are often responded to by physical violence.

Handicapped children are also abused by their parents. Again, these children put a greater strain on their parents, and some parents respond by lashing out at the source of the strain.

Even if the children are completely normal, they still place a stress on their parents. Our society lacks any clear standards as to what constitutes adequate parenting. (Our child abuse and neglect laws provide standards of bad parenting.) The ambiguity of what is a good parenting practice and the fact that many parents do not understand much about children and how children develop mean that just by virtue of their birth, children place strain and stress on parents. Many of the accounts of battered babies are similar to the one that follows:

> An impulsive man with a previous criminal record killed his often incontinent niece when the child had an episode of incontinence. He went into a destructive rage and, during the episode, threw the child onto the floor twice; her head hit the floor; he kicked her in the buttocks, finally throwing her against the chair (Bennie and Sclare, 1969).

Numerous incidents of child abuse and child killing involve parents striking out at their children to punish them for toilet accidents. One even hears of parents who beat a six- or twelve-month-old child for a toilet accident.

Unwanted babies seem to be targeted for physical abuse. The literature on child abuse is full of accounts of parents who beat and slew children they did not want, perhaps because they were born too soon after the birth of another child or because they could not afford them.

Having children causes stress, and this stress can be compounded if the parents are not knowledgeable in what to expect from a child. The stress is exacerbated if the child is abnormal in any way. We can see just how stressful having children is when we notice how the risk of wife abuse is raised by the wife's becoming pregnant.

Violence and Pregnancy. One of the most startling surprises in the study of family violence has been the finding that women are highly vulnerable to being physically abused during pregnancy. An earlier study of eighty families discovered that one fourth of the women who were battered by their husbands were struck during a pregnancy (Gelles, 1975b). Moreover, the character of the attacks changed during pregnancy. For example:

> "Oh yeah, he hit me when I was pregnant. It was weird. Usually he just hit me in the face with his fist, but when I was pregnant he used to hit me in the belly. It was weird" (Gelles, 1975b).

The reasons why pregnant women are beaten vary, but the central factors seem to include sexual frustration, transition, changes in the wife's temperament, and resentment and fear of the soon-to-arrive child. Although physicians tell women they can have sexual relations until the third trimester of their pregnancy, for many women, pregnancy means the end of normal sexual relations with their husbands. Women and men often fear sexual relations during pregnancy. One husband feared that if he had intercourse with his wife, the baby would bite him (Congdon, 1970).

In other instances, the battering of the pregnant wife may be an act designed to abuse the unborn child. Battering a wife to achieve a spontaneous abortion (which often happens) can be easier and cheaper than seeking a legal abortion.

Problems Outside the Home. Problems encountered outside the home are often translated into violent acts within the home. Chapter 6 presented detailed information which indicated that men who are unemployed or employed only part time are much more likely to live in violent homes than are men employed full time. One man we interviewed reported that after he lost his job he came home and blasted his shotgun throughout the house. There are many instances of family violence which are triggered by problems at work. Shortly after New Year's, 1978, six children were slain by their father as they lay in their beds in Rockville, Illinois. The father had encountered a variety of problems prior to the killing. His car had burned up, his wife had left him, and he had been out of work for six months.

The question of why a man would beat his wife or his children when he is unemployed or has a bad day at work seems to revolve around the fact that: 1) It is more socially acceptable to beat your wife and children than to hit someone at work, and 2) In a world which is growing more diverse and more impersonal, the last place where a man can be boss and control his own life is in his own home. Thus, a man who feels threatened and devalued at work may use force and violence in his home to restore his sense of being master of his life. Only a cog in a machine at work, a man can still be lord of the manor when he returns home.

Sexual Problems. Sexual problems are another common complaint voiced in violent families. Some psychoanalytic theorists claim that all battering husbands are impotent. Although there is no proof to support this theory, we have encountered many families in which the husband and wife claimed that sexual difficulties prompted violent outbursts. Husbands state their wives are frigid, while many wives say their husbands are impotent. The rate of wife and husband abuse among those who report sexual difficulties in the survey year was 300 per cent higher than the rate of abuse among those who reported no sexual problems in their relationship.

Given that sexual problems are related to violence between couples, it is not surprising that the most *deadly* room in the house is the bedroom. An estimated one out of every five deaths in the home occurs in the bedroom (Wolfgang, 1958).

Stress and Financial Resources

Couples who encounter greater than average stress are somewhat more likely to use abusive violence toward their children and toward each other. One question which we want to address is whether families with greater financial resources are better able to cope with the stresses they encounter than other families. To examine this question, we looked at the relationship between stress and violence in families at four income levels: 1) those whose total income was under $6,000 and, thus, in the poverty group; 2) those whose total income was between $6,000 and $11,999 and, thus, below the average income; 3) those whose income was between $12,000 and $19,999, and thus, could be classified as middle class; 4) and those whose income exceeded $20,000 and were comparatively well off.

Child Abuse. We found that stress among the very poor and the well-to-do has no effect in terms of increasing the chances of child abuse within these families. But for the middle income families—those with earnings between $6,000 and $20,000—increased stress does raise the risk of a child's being physically abused.

The reason why stress does not increase the risk of child abuse among the poor and well-to-do seems to be their reactions to stress. The poor, by virtue of being poor, encounter stress as a normal part of their lives. For the poor, stress is life, it is not a major crisis. An increase in stress is often considered inevitable. Second, the rates of violence for the poor are already high. It would take much more extreme crisis to push the rates higher still.

The well-to-do adapt to stress by using their financial resources to help alleviate such problems. A well-to-do family can seek counseling for a personal or sexual problem. They can afford a lawyer for a legal problem, and they can use their financial resources by drawing on savings.

This leaves us with the families making between $6,000 and $20,000. They are the ones who struggle with every stressful event. Not poor enough to get welfare or food stamps, not well off enough to have financial security, they tend to resort to violence toward their children as a reaction to increased stress.

Spouse Abuse. The patterns of stress and violence between husband and wife differ from our findings on child abuse. Only the well-to-do families who earned over $20,000 in 1975 are immune to the pressure of increased stress. For the families earning less than $20,000 additional stress increases the risk of spouse abuse. While the poor do not react to stress by striking their children, life stresses seem to produce the same increase in wife-beating and in husband-beating found in middle and high income families.

POWER AND DECISION-MAKING

One of the very first things we recognized when we began to study violence in the American family was that violence is often used as a mechanism to control the behavior of family members. Parents often use force and violence to influence and control the behavior of their children. Frequently, perhaps usually, this force is used with the best interests of the child in mind. But, in other instances, the conflict between parent and child is one of pure confrontation where only who wins matters. Violence between husband and wife is often a power confrontation. Three of our early interviews illustrate the link between power and violence in marital relations.

The simplest case was a clear-cut power struggle. The wife described her marriage as a war. She and her husband were perhaps the most violent couple we interviewed in terms of the frequency with which they hit and beat one another. When we

asked her why she was at war with her husband, she calmly explained, "Well, we both want to be the boss." Most cases, however, are more complex than this.

Another woman described how she frequently provoked her husband into violent outbursts. She would taunt him, tease him, and even hit him. The more she taunted, the angrier he got, until the episode eventually ended in the husband hitting her—sometimes beating her. Psychologists might classify her as "masochistic." But we think power, not masochism, is at the root of things. Her husband was a passive man who did not want to make decisions. Whether it was deciding what to have for dinner, which car to buy, or how to spend money, the husband left the decisions to his wife. Unfortunately, the woman said she "was brought up to believe that the man ran the family. I want my husband to wear the pants." The husband's refusal to fill the dominant decision-making role in the family was maddening to her. When asked why she taunted her husband, knowing that the end result would almost certainly be a beating, her reply was, "Well, at least then he will be doing something that a man is supposed to do."

Another interview was with a college graduate who often struck his wife; shaking her, slapping her, or pushing her out of the house to "calm down." Although the slaps, shoves, and pushes were rather common he said he was "never really violent with his wife." It was apparent that he did not want to give the impression that he was a wife-beater, but it was also just as apparent that he believed that under certain conditions it was necessary for a husband to exercise his power in the family. He told us that he only hit his wife when it was absolutely necessary to get her to do something that was in her best interest or in the best interest of the family!

Power

Although power is an easy concept to talk about, it is more difficult to define. And it is extremely difficult to measure precisely how power is distributed in the family.

One of the standard social scientific definitions of power is that it is "the ability of persons or groups to impose their will on others despite resistance" (Blau, 1964). In this case power is an enduring property which involves an ongoing process of attempting to impose one's will on other people. In addition, power also involves the ability to sanction or punish the person who resists the attempts to be controlled (Blau, 1964).

Social scientists have used a variety of techniques to measure how power is distributed in the family. The most widely used technique is based on who makes the final decision on a number of crucial issues. This method of measuring power by focusing on decision-making was pioneered in a study carried out in Detroit in 1960 by Robert Blood, Jr., and Donald Wolfe. We used the technique developed by Blood and Wolfe to measure power by finding out which family member made the final decision on six different issues. The decision issues were:

Who has the final say on . . .

1. Buying a car.
2. Having children.
3. What house or apartment to choose.
4. What job your husband/wife should take.
5. Whether you should go to work or quit work.
6. How much money a week to spend on food.

We tallied the responses to these questions to determine if the family was (1) wife dominant, where the wife makes the majority of the decisions, (2) husband dominant, where the husband makes the majority of the decisions, or (3) democratic, where the decisions are either shared or divided equally between the wife and husband.

Violence and Power

Chart 23 clearly links inequality within the American family to spouse abuse. Wife-beating is much more common in homes where power is concentrated in the hands of the husband. The least amount of battering occurs in democratic households. Husbands are more likely to be beaten by their wives in husband or wife dominant homes. Husbands in democratic homes are the least likely to be abused.

It seems that violence is used by the most powerful family member as a means of legitimizing his or her dominant position. On the other hand, less powerful members of the family tend to rely on violence as a reaction to their own lack of participation in the family decision-making process.

Inequality also may initiate a chain reaction of power confrontations running throughout the family. If the husband, for example, exerts force and violence on his wife, she may decide not to retaliate physically because she would be even more endangered. Rather than hit her husband, she repeats the pattern toward someone weaker than herself—a child. The child in turn lashes out at his brothers and sisters, with the cycle often reaching the ultimate conclusion of the youngest child abusing the family dog or cat.

The relationship between marital power and marital violence is also affected by the resources which a family member can call upon in the course of family relations (Allen and Straus, 1979). Such resources typically include the knowledge which comes from education and the prestige and income which come with a good job. Thus, men who strive to make all the decisions in the home, but who do not possess the key educational, income, and prestige resources with which to support a dominant position, tend to be more violent toward their wives and children than men who dominate decision-making and also possess the most education, earn the most money, and have the most prestigious jobs. Family members resort to physical coercion when they have power over family decision-making but have few resources to bring to bear to *legitimize* their position.

CHART 23
Marital Violence by Marital Power

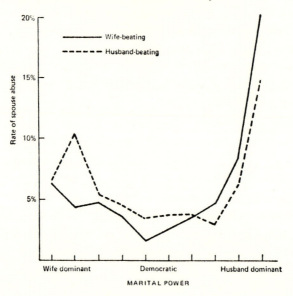

One example of such a situation occurred in a household we studied where the husband was chronically unemployed. His wife held a steady job as a waitress and raised the children during her husband's frequent absences from home. However, when the husband was home he wanted to be the boss. He frequently beat his wife and his children. On one occasion he became enraged with his five-year-old daughter and threw a fork at her, striking her beneath the eye, requiring minor surgery to repair. The precipitating event in each violent outburst was the wife's unwillingness to go along with his decisions, or her refusal to carry out his wishes. According to the wife, he lashed out when he felt he was not receiving respect from his family.

Violent outbursts, as we mentioned above, also involve spouse or child abuse by less powerful family members. Wives often claim to regret hitting their children but explain that hitting the child was the only time they felt in control of the family situation. Men or women who lack an affectional bond on which they can draw to control a child may resort to child abuse. Other times violence is used to control children and spouses because, as we saw in Chapter 5, there was a role model in the individual's past who taught the use of violence to control people and situations.

One woman, explaining her difficulties in leaving a violent husband gave this account:

> "I had four children and no money—I couldn't go on welfare because his whole family said they would fix it so I couldn't. His parents were very influential in our small town . . . His father was first detective on the . . . police force . . . His father beat his mother up for thirty years and all of his brothers did it to their wives" (Reprint from *Sister Courage*, Boston, Mass., February 1977, by the Women's Issues Program, American Friends Service Committee, Cambridge, Mass.).

We found a modest relationship between marital power and child abuse. Children are slightly more likely to be abused in husband or wife dominant families. This occurs because children are part of the family power structure. The child becomes a victim of marital power struggles when parents resort to child abuse to legitimize their power or compensate for a lack of power.

Sibling abuse is much further removed from marital power struggles. As would be expected, there was no relation between the rate of sibling abuse and who has the final say in family decision-making.

Sharing and Violence

There are two kinds of democratic families. In one type neither the husband nor wife dominates decision-making, and democracy is maintained by dividing up the decisions to be made—with the wife having final say on some things and the husband on others. In the second type of democracy, the final decision on most family matters is shared by the husband and the wife together.

CHART 24
Spouse Abuse by Per Cent of
Decisions Shared

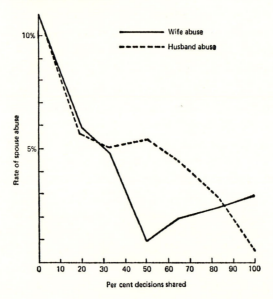

When we examined what proportion of the family decisions were shared by the husband and wife we found a rather dramatic relationship between how often decisions are shared and the likelihood of violence. Chart 24 reveals that the rate of husband and wife abuse is considerably lower in the families where all decisions are shared as opposed to the households where no decisions are shared. Child abuse and violence between siblings were not affected by whether or not the parents shared important decisions.

SUMMING UP

Thus, we found the safest homes, in terms of child abuse and spouse abuse, are those with fewer than two children where the husband and wife experience little life stress in the course of a year, and where a democratic system is used to make decisions. The highest risk of family violence occurs when there is more than one child at home, where there is considerable life stress experienced by one or both of the marital partners, and where decision-making is concentrated in the hands of one person.

These findings are both dismal and hopeful. They are dismal in pointing out the high rates of child abuse and spouse abuse which occur when families are subject to more than average amounts of stress, when they have to cope with the awesome responsibilities of children, and when (for whatever reason) the husband or the wife dominates the decision-making in a family. But they are hopeful because forces can change, and indeed are changing in the direction which our study suggests will make for less violent families in the future: people are having less children and they are eagerly participating in programs of parent education; and the trend toward more equalitarian and democratic relationships between husband and wife, while hardly a stampede, is inexorable. It is mainly in the area of stressful life events that the outlook is cloudy. Social Security, modern medicine, and unemployment insurance are examples of modern trends which reduce life stresses. But there is also geographic mobility, persistently high unemployment, changing and uncertain sex roles, and a growing feeling by parents of powerlessness to aid or control their children. All of these are examples of stresses typical of modern life. And they are the very stresses which we found are related to physical violence in the families who participated in this study.

PART V

The Future

CHAPTER 9

The Social Causes of Family Violence: Putting the Pieces Together

Human violence—be it a slap or a shove, a knifing or a shoot-out—occurs more frequently within the family circle than anywhere else in our society. That was clearly illustrated in the first four chapters of this book.

In the next four chapters we attempted to explain *"Why?"* What elements within ourselves or our society make us most hurtful to the people to whom we are closest? Although some of the factors we had assumed were related to violence turned out not to be, we found a large number which *are* substantial indications of whether or not a family is violent.

Even so, our long list does not cover all the important aspects which can affect the rate of violence within a family. Broadly speaking, our concentration centered on characteristics and circumstances within the realm of *social* causes. That is not to say we examined all the social factors which need to be studied. Nor were our methods of measuring such factors always more than barely adequate. Additionally, we made no study of the psychological make-up of individual family members within the survey. We were limited for several reasons.

First, time was an important factor. All our data had to be obtained in hour-long interviews. Had we requested longer talks with those surveyed, there would have been a substantial drop in the number of people willing to be interviewed. This, in turn, would have made the sample far less representative. We felt it better to have less data than to decrease the sampling of families.

When we had to choose what to leave out, we omitted the study of psychological characteristics of individual family members. This is because we believe that violence in the family is more a social problem than a psychological problem. Granted, psychological factors play a part, but we felt it most important to focus on what we believe to be the root and fundamental causes. Fortunately, people are not slaves of the social system. And, as we will see in this chapter, not everyone whose life circumstances point in the direction of violence is violent. Unfortunately, the reverse is also true. Not everyone whose life experiences, position in society, and family characteristics indicate lack of violence is non-violent. To explain violence in the family fully one should consider more than we were able to study. Physiological as well as psychological characteristics of the people involved, plus the social variables we were forced to omit, should be included to obtain the total picture. Having explained the study's shortcomings, the time has come to see if what we did do fits into a larger pattern. Do the factors we examined one by one add up? Some of them could really be different aspects of the same things. For example, it may not add much to know the score of a family on our Stress Index (see Appendix C) if one already knows that the total family income was under $6,000. For families living in a society where the average family income was more than double their own income, that may be more than enough stress!

EXPLAINING THE HUSBAND-WIFE VIOLENCE

Spouse Abuse "Prediction" Checklist

One way to find out if the factors, which, up to now, were considered one by one, add up to a more complete explanation of husband-wife violence is to do just that: add them up. We gave each couple one point for each of the characteristics which was found to be associated with a high rate of husband-wife violence.[1] For example, if the husband was a blue collar worker, the couple received a point. If the husband was unemployed at the time of the interview, the couple was given another point (no matter what the husband's occupation was). If the balance of power in the family was lopsidedly male dominant, another point was added. Altogether, a couple's score could range from zero, for couples who had none of the important characteristics, to twenty-five, for couples who had all twenty-five of the characteristics. The twenty-five characteristics included in the over-all checklist are:

Characteristics Important for Both
Wife-beating and Husband-beating
   Husband employed part time or unemployed
   Family income under $6,000
   Husband a manual worker
   Husband very worried about economic security
   Wife very dissatisfied with standard of living
   Two or more children
   Disagreement over children
   Grew up in family in which father hit mother
   Married less than ten years
   Age thirty or under
   Non-white racial group
   Above average score on Marital Conflict Index
      (See Appendix C)
   Very high score on Stress Index (See Appendix C)
   Wife dominant in family decisions
   Husband was verbally aggressive to wife

Wife was verbally aggressive to husband
Gets drunk but is not alcoholic
Lived in neighborhood less than two years
No participation in organized religion

Characteristics That Are Important
for Wife-beating

Husband dominant in family decisions
Wife is full-time housewife
Wife very worried about economic security

Characteristics That Are Important
for Husband-beating

Wife was physically punished at age thirteen plus by father
Wife grew up in family in which mother hit father
Wife is a manual worker

None of the families who participated in this study lived under the burden of all twenty-five characteristics. The scores ranged from zero (seven couples) to eighteen (two couples), with an average of six characteristics per couple.

CHART 25
Per Cent of Violent Couples by Spouse Abuse
"Prediction" Checklist Score

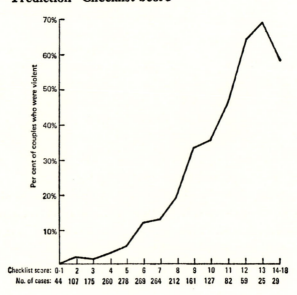

Predicting Ordinary Husband-Wife Violence

Chart 25 shows that these things do add up, and to an amazing degree. The line shows the per cent of couples who were physically violent in any way to each other during the survey year. Any couple where either the husband hit the wife, or the wife hit the husband—even if it was "just" a slap or push—was counted as having been violent that year. The rate of violence goes from zero (for the forty-four couples with none or only one of the characteristics on the checklist) to about two out of every three of the one hundred and thirteen couples who had twelve or more of the characteristics on the checklist.

Generally, the checklist score starts with only a small effect on the rate of marital violence. But then its effect doubles and keeps on doubling. Couples with up to three of the checklist characteristics have violence rates under 2 per cent. But with four of the characteristics, the rate rises to 5 per cent. With six it more than doubles, and so on.

Husband's Violence and Wife's Violence

Are the same factors associated with violence by the husband and violence by the wife? There are two sides to this coin.

They are the same in the sense that the over-all checklist score is highly predictive of both violence by the husband and violence by the wife. Also, even when we make up a different checklist score consisting of just the items most highly associated with violence by the husband, this predicts *the wife's* violence. The same applies to a third checklist consisting of only the items most highly associated with violence by wives. It also predicts violence by husbands as well.

Why? Part of the reason is that so much violence is mutual. This is true of half of the couples in this study who were violent. That is, *both* the husband and the wife had physically attacked his or her partner during the survey year. In addition, many of the characteristics contained on the checklists were factors which affected the family as a whole (such as having two or more children at home or having a low income). Thus, what was true for the husband was, in many cases, also true for the wife.

But there are also some important differences in the factors affecting husband and wife abuse. For example, a high score on the checklist for violence by husbands does a better job in identifying violent husbands than does an over-all checklist containing the items on all the checklists (An even larger percentage of the husbands with very high scores were violent [80 per cent]).

The same thing applies to violence by the wives. Ninety-two per cent of the women with scores of ten, eleven, twelve, or thirteen (the highest score) were violent to their husbands during the survey year!

Violent Husbands. It is also worth while to consider the characteristics that are particularly important for violence by each sex. There are three characteristics that are important for violence by the husband, but *not* for violence by the wife. These include: (1) the husband being dominant in family decisions, (2) the wife being a full-time housewife, and (3) the wife being very worried about economic security.

This combination bears out findings from one of our earlier investigations. That study (Allen and Straus, 1979) concentrated on families in which the husband uses physical force to maintain dominance. Lacking other resources to get his way, such as the respect which comes from earning a good income, he relies on force and, often, violence. The wife, a full-time housewife and dependent on him economically, tends to offer little resistance because the alternative may be even worse. And many such women are correct in being concerned about their economic survival if they leave a violent husband.

The sexist economic and occupational structure of society allows women few alternatives. The jobs open to them are lower in status and pay less. Despite anti-discrimination legislation, women employed *full time* continue to earn only a little more than half of what men earn. Without access to good jobs, women are dependent on their husbands. If there is a divorce, there is a good chance the husband will default on support payments after a short time, assuming he could afford them in the first place. Consequently, many women continue to endure physical attacks from their husbands because a divorce means living in poverty.

One legal assistance worker who counsels abused wives summed up the problem this way:

> . . . Many of the women who are beaten have no job experience, no marketable skills, no personal transportation and no money whatsoever to call their own. Most have children. You just can't tell a woman who can't afford carfare . . . to leave home.
>
> To a woman who has been housebound, economically dependent upon her husband and who has kids to worry about, the prospect of striking out on her own may be as frightening as another beating (New Hampshire *Times,* March 1, 1978, p. 15).

Lack of economic alternatives is one of the three main factors which Gelles (1976) found associated with beaten wives remaining with their husbands.

Violent Wives. We will now look at the three characteristics which are particularly important for violence by wives but not for violence by husbands. These are (1) growing up in a family in which their own mother hit their father, (2) being physically punished after age thirteen, and (3) being employed outside the home as a manual worker.

The first two of these identify women whose early family experience trained them to be violent. Since this childhood training is part of the wife's learning experience, it makes sense that it is not important for explaining violence by husbands.

But employment as a blue collar worker is a different matter.

Why should a waitress be more prone to violence than a file clerk? Perhaps the reason is related to the situation we described for husbands. Both husbands and wives in families where the husband is a manual worker are more often violent than when the husband does another type of work. Whatever process makes blue collar husbands more violent may also apply to wives who are manual workers.

More may be involved, however. Our earlier study found that the wife's having a job affected the balance of power in the families of blue collar husbands more than if the husband was a non-manual worker (Allen and Straus, 1979). Blue collar women who have this economic power seem to be more willing or able to take the view that "money talks," that is, to translate it into family power. This, in turn, may provoke violent resistance by their husbands, and violent retaliation by the wife.

Predicting Serious Assaults

We began this study assuming that, in principle, there is no difference between the "ordinary" violence of family life and the instances of wife-beating and child abuse which capture public attention. One is merely a more extreme form of the other. If this is the case, then the same factors which explain ordinary pushes, slaps, and throwing things should also explain serious assaults. Of course, the rates will be lower because serious assaults occur less frequently. But if our reasoning is correct, couples who have high scores on our checklist should be more likely to use abusive as well as ordinary violence.

We did find that the same set of factors is strongly related to whether or not there has been a severe assault in the family during the year. The most important difference is that it takes more of the checklist characteristics to produce an incident of severe assault than to produce pushing, slapping, shoving, or throwing things at a spouse.

CHART 26
Rate of Wife-beating and Husband-beating
by Spouse Abuse "Prediction" Checklist Score

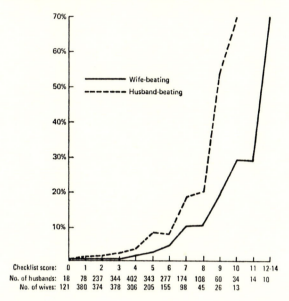

Checklist score:	0	1	2	3	4	5	6	7	8	9	10	11	12-14
No. of husbands:	18	78	237	344	402	343	277	174	108	60	34	14	10
No. of wives:	121	380	374	378	306	205	155	98	45	26	13		

Wife-beating. At this point it is important to distinguish between wife-beating and husband-beating. For wife-beating we used a checklist score consisting of only the items which were most closely associated with violence by the husbands in our sample.

Men with low to middle scores on the husband-violence checklist have about the same rates of wife-beating as men with low to middle scores on the full item checklist. Then the rates jump. There were ten husbands with twelve or more of the checklist characteristics. Although this is a small number of cases, the results are dramatic: seven out of the ten had *severely* assaulted their wives during the year.

Abusive Wives. To look at the issue of husband-beating, we made up a special checklist consisting of the items which are most closely associated with a severe assault *by a wife* on her husband. The broken line in Chart 26 shows the results. It follows essentially the same trend as we found for husbands who assault their wives (solid line in Chart 26): the more of these characteristics, the higher the rate of serious assault. Seven or more seems to be the critical turning point, even more for women than for men. The rates climb steeply from there on. When we come to the husbands and wives with the largest number of checklist characteristics, the chart shows that 70 per cent of such people severely assaulted their spouses during the year!

The ten husbands and thirteen wives with the highest number of checklist characteristics are not many cases. Still they are important because they show that the social characteristics we found related to marital violence are more than isolated findings. They explain a large part of the occurrence of wife-beating and husband-beating. In fact, the odds are seven out of ten that a household with this many of the characteristics in the checklist will be the scene of a severe assault between the husband and wife.

EXPLAINING CHILD ABUSE

Child Abuse "Prediction" Checklist

To develop a Child Abuse "Prediction" Checklist, we used the same method as for the Spouse Abuse "Prediction" Checklist. Going back through the findings we listed all the characteristics which are related to child abuse. We carried out a "discriminant analysis" to pick out the characteristics which are most highly related to child abuse (see note 1). And finally, we gave each couple one point for each item on the checklist which described that couple.

The discriminant analysis isolated the following eighteen characteristics:

Important for Child Abuse by Either Parent
  Was verbally aggressive to the child
    (insulted, smashed things, etc.).
  Above average conflict between husband and wife
  Husband was physically violent to wife

Important for Abuse by Mothers
  Husband was verbally aggressive to wife
  Husband a manual worker
  Husband dissatisfied with standard of living
  Wife a manual worker
  Wife age thirty or under
  Wife was physically punished at age thirteen plus by father

Important for Abuse by Fathers
  Two or more children at home
  Wife is a full-time housewife
  Married less than ten years
  Lived in neighborhood less than two years
  No participation by father in organized groups
  Husband was physically punished at age thirteen plus by
    mother
  Grew up in family where mother hit father

A couple could receive a score ranging from zero (those who had none of the characteristics) to sixteen (those who had all sixteen of the characteristics). Although there were two couples with a score of zero, none had sixteen. The scores ranged to a high of fourteen. The average family had between five and six (5.54) of the checklist characteristics.

Predicting Child Abuse

The higher the parents' score, the greater the rate of child abuse. The chart (27) for the Child Abuse "Prediction" Checklist shows that children whose parents had none of these characteristics, or only a few, were completely free of child abuse. On the other hand, one out of every hundred

CHART 27
Rate of Child Abuse by Child Abuse
"Prediction" Checklist Score

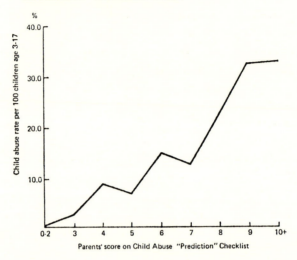

Parents' score on Child Abuse "Prediction" Checklist

children whose parents had three of these characteristics was abused severely enough to be included in the Child Abuse "Prediction" Index. Thereafter, the rate of child abuse climbs steadily. One third of the children whose parents had ten or more of these characteristics were abused during the year.

The Child Abuse "Prediction" Checklist identifies parents with rates of child abuse that range from none to thirty-three per hundred children. Clearly, the social factors included in that checklist are strongly related to whether or not parents abuse a child. The rate of child abuse for those children unfortunate enough to come from families with ten or more of the sixteen items in the checklist is staggering.

Fathers and Mothers as Child Abusers

The Child Abuse "Prediction" Checklist omitted one important characteristic associated with child abuse. This is the fact that mothers have a child abuse rate that is 75 per cent greater than the rate for fathers (17.7 per hundred children versus 10.1). This was left out because we were trying to identify characteristics of the family as a whole.

Focusing on the family group makes sense because, even though one parent may inflict the injury, the other probably knows about it. Both parents are part of a configuration of factors. The higher incidence of abuse by mothers as compared to fathers is an illustration of this point. As we noted in an earlier chapter, the 75 per cent higher rate is not because mothers are more cruel or violent than fathers. Outside the family women commit only a small fraction of the violent acts that men commit. We think it is largely because the mother has more than 75 per cent of the burden of child care in a typical American family. So, what fathers do *not* do is part of the explanation for the high rate of child abuse by mothers. Take the following case of a couple who had just had their first child:

> At home with her new daughter things quickly got out of control.
>
> "When she was only a few weeks old, I would throw her across the room in anger. Onto a bed. Never into a wall or onto the floor. I was spanking her when she was only a few weeks old.
>
> "Why? It's very difficult to remember why anymore."
>
> Her husband didn't know how to cope with her behavior. He would ask her, "Why did you do that?" when she threw the baby, but he seemed powerless to intervene (Boston *Globe*, August 27, 1978, p. A2).

The large difference between the abuse rates of fathers and mothers points to the importance of looking at other things which might differ for child abuse by men and women. It turns out that the factors which most affect child abuse are somewhat different for mothers and fathers. These differences illustrate the point we have been making about the family as a social system. The actions of the individual often reverberate through the group as a whole.

To get a clear picture of how the family operates as a system we also need data on the children, and data on how things proceed over time. But even with the data we have, using the simple method of the checklist, some insights can be gained. To do this, we computed a version of the Child Abuse "Prediction" Checklist for fathers and for mothers. We then related the fathers' Child Abuse "Prediction" Checklist to abuse by fathers and the mothers' Child Abuse "Prediction" Checklist to abuse by mothers.

The fathers' Child Abuse "Prediction" Checklist consists of the characteristics that are most related to abuse by fathers, plus the three common factors. Using this score, the results for fathers with low and medium scores are very similar to the results when the full sixteen-item checklist is used. But, as in the case of violence by husbands against wives, fathers with the most checklist characteristics had a substantially greater rate of child abuse than we found when using the over-all sixteen-item Child Abuse "Prediction" Checklist: 45 per cent of the children whose fathers had all seven of these characteristics were abused during the year!

When we used a mothers' Child Abuse "Prediction" Checklist, consisting of the six characteristics which are most important for abuse by mothers (plus the three common factors), the results were similar. Forty-eight per cent of the children of the mothers with the six checklist characteristics were abused during the year!

Neither of these rates is as high as the rate for violence against wives by the husbands with the highest scores on the Wife Abuse "Prediction" Checklist or the rate for the wives with the highest scores on the Husband Abuse "Prediction" Checklist. They are extremely high rates nonetheless. The fact that the specific versions of the Child Abuse "Prediction" Checklist are more efficient in identifying parents with a high probability of abusing a child is an additional reason for taking a closer look at the differences between fathers and mothers. We will start with the seven items in the checklist which are more important for child abuse by the father than for abuse by the mother.

Abusive Fathers. The implication of what is in that list is that the real topic of this section is not "Abusive Fathers." It is "*Families* with Abusive Fathers." Most of the seven characteristics describe family arrangements rather than the individual characteristics of the father.

Three characteristics that we would have supposed to be more important for abuse *by mothers* turned out to be most important for abuse by fathers. These are the presence of two or more children in the home, the mother being a full-time housewife, and being married for less than ten years. Each of these things also made a difference for the child abuse rates of mothers, but not nearly as great. We are not sure why this is the case. Whatever the reason, the fact that these things make a difference in the abuse of children *by fathers* is one more sign that an understanding of child abuse must be grounded in an understanding of the way families operate as social groups.

A concern with the way the family operates cannot be limited to just the interaction of family members with each other. Families do not exist in isolation from a larger community and network of relatives. This also showed up in fathers' Child Abuse "Prediction" Checklist. Fathers who lived in a neighborhood less than two years had a child abuse rate that was 137 per cent greater than in families that were longer residents (17.3 versus 7.4). Again, we are not sure why this made more difference for child abuse by fathers than it did for abuse by mothers. Perhaps it is because mothers are so much more likely to abuse a child in any case. Whatever the reason, for mothers, this sign of minimal ties to a community is associated with only a 39 per cent greater rate of abuse (21.6 versus 15.5 for mothers who lived in the neighborhood longer than three years), as compared to the 137 per cent greater rate for fathers.

There are three characteristics which describe the father himself—or rather the social relationships and family background of the father. The first of these is another indication of lack of community ties. Fathers who neither belonged to nor attended organized groups (such as clubs, unions, church groups, lodges, etc.) have a much higher rate of child abuse. This is the parental social isolation so often noted by those who write about child abuse (Garbarino, 1977; Smith and Snow, 1975).

Both of the remaining characteristics describe training in violence which these fathers experienced as children: (1) having been physically punished after age thirteen by their *mothers*, and (2) growing up in a family in which the *mother* hit the father. Violence by a man's father also makes a difference, but not nearly as much.

The fact that violence by a man's mother has the most bearing on the later abuse of his own child is fascinating. Why should the mother's violence make more difference? Our interpretation is that violence by fathers is a more accepted type of behavior than violence by mothers. If a mother is violent to her husband, or to a teen-age child, this is an indication of having grown up in a family which oversteps the bounds of "normal" family violence. It is an easy step from that to child abuse.

Abusive Mothers. The items in the mothers' Child Abuse "Prediction" Checklist supply additional evidence that what is crucial for understanding child abuse is the operation of the family as a social system in which the parts are dependent on each other.

Conflict in the family system is one such factor. If there is a high level of husband-wife conflict, this makes a difference for the rate of *child* abuse by mothers (although not as large a difference as it made in the abuse rate by fathers).

The big difference in child abuse by *mothers* hinges on

whether the wife has been hit by her husband. If so, she is twice as likely to abuse a child. The wives of violent men have a child abuse rate that is 122 per cent greater than other wives (33.7 versus 15.2). The same applies to women whose husbands were verbally abusive to them. They, in turn, physically abused their children at more than double the rate of abuse by other mothers (21.2 per cent versus 9.3 per cent).

The stress imposed by economic deprivation also seems to play a larger role in abuse by mothers than by fathers. The wives of manual workers were more often abusive, as were the women who themselves were employed as manual workers.

Women married to men who were very dissatisfied with their standard of living had a child abuse rate 77 per cent greater than other wives (22.3 versus 12.6).

Additionally, we found that mothers age thirty or under had higher rates of child abuse. Fathers surveyed showed a similar characteristic: men married for less than ten years were more prone to child abuse. Does abuse decrease after this point because parents become older and wiser? To a certain extent probably so. However, our impression of violent marriages is that they do *not* usually become less violent. Many women live in hope that this will happen, but few see that hope fulfilled. What does happen is that as time goes on, more and more such marriages break up. The longer-lasting marriages are those which were less violent from the start.

The last item in the mothers' Child Abuse "Prediction" Checklist reveals that women who were physically punished at, or after, age thirteen by their own fathers or mothers are 53 per cent more likely to abuse their children (24.2 versus 15.9 per cent). It is interesting to compare this with the effect of physical punishment during the teen-age years on the father's child abuse rates. We pointed out that such punishment made a large difference only if it was done by the mother. For women, however, physical punishment at this age by *either* parent is associated with child abuse. The same principle we suggested for child abuse by fathers may apply: for either parent to hit a teen-age girl is something which over-steps the bounds of "normal" family violence. It therefore paves the way or provides a lesson for other non-permissible violence when the daughter has grown up and has children of her own.

PREDICTING CHILD ABUSE VERSUS PREDICTING SPOUSE ABUSE

The *Spouse* Abuse "Prediction" Checklist allowed us to identify effectively groups of couples whose marriages ranged from being completely free of acts of physical violence, through groups of couples whose violence toward each other was commonplace. Homes are the scenes of violence.

The *Child* Abuse "Prediction" Checklist was also able to identify parents who are completely free of physical abuse toward their children. But it was not as effective in pin-pointing parents who are almost sure to abuse a child. This can be seen from the following summary:

	PER CENT OF THOSE IN THE CHECKLIST SCORE GROUP WHO WERE VIOLENT	
CHECKLIST	MEN	WOMEN
Marital Violence:		
Over all, any violence during the survey year	80%	92%
Wife-beating predictor items only	70%	—
Husband-beating predictor items only	—	70%
Child Abuse:		
Over all	30%	35%
Abuse by mother predictor items only	45%	—
Abuse by father predictor items only	—	48%

The rate of *spouse* abuse for people with the highest scores on the Spouse Abuse "Prediction" Checklist is about double the rate of *child* abuse for parents with the highest scores on the Child Abuse "Prediction" Checklist. Another way of seeing the shortcomings in this area is to look at the per cent of parents who were *not* child abusers despite having large numbers of the characteristics in the checklist. A rate of 30 per cent (or even 48 per cent) means that more than two thirds (or more than half) of such parents did *not* abuse a child, even though many signs pointed to the possibility of abuse.

The fact that "only" 30 to 48 per cent of children who come from families with high scores on the Child Abuse "Prediction" Checklist were actually abused during the year has two important implications. First, it means there is still a long way to go in pin-pointing the causes of child abuse. One of the most obvious things which needs to be added to a study like this is information on the child. Violence, by its very nature, is an act of social interaction. It takes two to tango and our Child Abuse "Prediction" Checklist leaves out information about one of the dancers. We may well have done better pinning down the causes of marital violence because the Spouse Abuse "Prediction" Checklist includes information on both the husband and the wife.

CAN AND SHOULD WE "PREDICT" WITH THE CHECKLIST?

A second implication of the fact that so many of the children from "high risk" families were not abused is a practical and ethical concern: People in charge of programs to prevent child abuse must be extremely cautious about attempting to use such findings as a basis for their actions.

Tempting as the possibility may be, any potential gains in preventing child abuse have to be weighed against the costs and potential dangers. An attempt to use these checklists to locate high risk parents could cause more harm than good. It could create an intrusive system of family surveillance. A second cost lies in the harm which could be caused by falsely labeling millions of parents as "potential abusers" or "high risk parents" (Light, 1973).

As we have said, there is a long way to go in pin-pointing the causes of child abuse. However, we know some of the directions in which to go. First, as explained earlier, this research is limited to the social causes of violence. There is an obvious need to include data on the psychological characteristics of the family members.

Second, as we also pointed out, little is known about *the children* who were and were not abused. This includes both their psychological and physical characteristics, as well as the patterns of interaction with their parents. For example, a parent-child conflict score similar to the husband-wife conflict score could contribute to a much higher rate of prediction.

Finally, more sophisticated methods of combining the items in the checklist could have a large pay-off. Certain groupings of characteristics might be truly "explosive combinations." The methods used in this study do not take that into account. If all three of these things were done, it might be possible to identify correctly a far larger proportion of violent families.

This survey has made a significant step in that direction. We have isolated a large number of social factors associated with spouse and child abuse. We have shown that these social characteristics do add up. Couples or parents with high numbers of the characteristics we identified also have extremely high rates of violence within their families.

CHAPTER 10

Toward Reducing Family Violence: Band-Aids, Ambulances, and Solutions

"Family Quarrel Leaves 2 Dead, 3 Hurt"
"Body of Abused Child Thrown Out with the Trash"
"Woman Shot While Fleeing Husband"
Such newspaper headlines are, unfortunately, all too common.

We all have read stories on abused children gruesomely detailing the horrors perpetrated by their parents. Provoked by anger and revulsion from such accounts, some people suggest countering violence with more violence. "A man like that ought to be shot"; or "She ought to be strung up," are often the public's response to child abusers.

If the subject is violence *against wives*, "Why doesn't she leave him—just walk out?" is the most frequently heard response.

The issue of *husband* abuse is viewed with curiosity and disbelief. Some feminists protest that there are no abused men. Violence *between siblings* is lost in the shuffle. Unless the death of a child results, most people do not take sibling violence seriously.

However, each incident of family violence which comes to public attention, each child who is beaten or battered to death, each wife who dies at the hands of her husband after having called the police for help or tried to get aid from social agencies, results in demands that something be done to prevent such incidents from occurring. Feminists, child advocates, and others plead that something be done. The question is, what?

Most social agencies and their staffs tend to view a child-abusing parent, a wife-beating husband, or a child who kills a brother or sister as mentally ill. The most frequently discussed and implemented solution is individual psychiatric care or marriage counseling for the violent person. Psychiatry or other psychological therapy is clearly needed in a small proportion of cases—10 per cent at most. For the most part, however, since the roots of family violence are to be found in the nature of the family itself, what is needed is no less than a restructuring of the relations between family members.

AMELIORATION AND PREVENTION

To make sense out of the many different (and often contradictory) proposals, it is essential to recognize that there are really two issues. The first is *amelioration*. The second is *prevention*.

Violence between family members has only recently been defined as an important problem. Victims of family violence have only recently been recognized or asked for recognition as people in need of services. Consequently, there are precious few resources and techniques available for helping victims of family violence. Such services are becoming available—slowly. But, even if there were the knowledge and the resources available to treat abused children, abused women, and abused men *after* the act of violence has occurred, these steps would not be effective in reducing the level of violence in the society. The well from which these cases are drawn seems to be inexhaustible. Treatment programs and intervention strategies designed to assist violent families are Band-Aids, emergency stopgaps, which can only be employed after a victim is identified. The *prevention* of violence in the home and the reduction of family violence involve major structural changes for both the society and the family.

Band-Aids and Ambulances

It is crucial that any program or policy designed to deal with the problem of violence between family members be capable of *protecting* the victims while preventing further violence—if possible by strengthening the family. Without both these components there is no long-term solution program.

Children and wives can leave or be removed from violent homes and still be at risk of injury or death. Most wives who leave return, and most children who are removed also are returned to their parents. Almost always, they return to a home which has the same problems which produced the original violence. There are innumerable incidents where children and husbands and wives are killed by family members after they have returned to a home which they fled or were removed from. And for children placed in foster homes, the risk of further abuse (especially sexual abuse of girls) is very high (Finkelhor, 1979).

> The police investigation of 11-year-old Dianne DeVanna's death reveals a portrait of a lonely little girl who never could do enough to please her demanding parents.
>
> Police investigators yesterday said information received from interviews with relatives, friends, former teachers and neighbors shows that the Braintree girl was repeatedly subjected to harsh disciplinary measures by her father and stepmother for minor and in some cases, manufactured infractions.

"Every time she did something wrong, like taking too long to
do the dishes or going to the bathroom too often, the mother
would put it on a list. By the time her father got home from
work the list would be enormous," an investigator said.

The only neighbor who could ever recall seeing Dianne said
she was always alone. "She didn't have anyone to play with.
She'd lie in the sun sometimes or play with a bike."

A Dedham Probate Court order returned Dianne to the custody of her father, Sylvester DeVanna, 49, of 1335 Liberty St.,
Braintree, last August (Boston *Globe*, September 28, 1978,
p. 1).

Instances of beaten women returning to the men who assaulted them are even more frequent.

Shelters

For women who are being attacked by their husbands we
believe the most important immediate step is the creation of
shelters—homes where victims are protected from further violence. Shelters do more than remove the woman from immediate danger. They also have tremendous potential for preventing further violence. This is because the woman is given the
physical, economic, and psychological support needed to
change the basis of the marriage.

Shelters often provide or make referrals to legal and marriage counseling services, help women find jobs, and above all,
help restore the sense of self-esteem which the woman has typically lost from years of psychological and physical battering.
All of this is needed if the woman is to negotiate a new and
non-violent basis for the marriage. Alternatively, when the
marriage cannot be reconstructed, these same services are
what is needed for the woman to avoid getting into the same
trap with another man.

Every shelter can document cases in which the shelter experience has changed the marriages and the lives of its residents.

Unfortunately, every shelter can also document the tragedy of a woman returning to a violent man, or going on to a new violent relationship.

The first shelter established to protect victims of family violence came about by accident. In 1971 a group of women in Chiswick, England, met to discuss rising food prices. The most frequent complaint was not food prices, however, but one of loneliness. Out of these meetings a Women's Aid project was established by Erin Plzzey. Shortly after a house was set up as Chiswick Women's Aid, it became, instead, a center for women with personal problems. The house soon began to fill up with women with a common problem—all were abused wives.

Within three years, Women's Aid of Chiswick, England, became the model for women's shelters around the world. Erin Pizzey authored one of the first books written on the subject of wife abuse, *Scream Quietly or the Neighbors Will Hear*. Her book and her personal dynamism spread the idea of women's refuges throughout England and other countries.

The concept of a shelter for victims of family violence is elementary and deals with one of the most difficult problems faced by victims of family violence—a place to go. Because family violence usually takes place on weekends, in the evening or early morning hours, there's no place for the victims to turn. Battered wives in bathrobes have spent hours on street corners in freezing weather because they had no place to go to find shelter or help. We received a letter from one woman who spent every Saturday night for two years locked inside her car in the driveway of her suburban home. We interviewed women who fled into the street without a dime to call the police. Ultimately, most of these victims must go home, and when they do, they frequently encounter more violence and torment.

A Canadian woman, for example, participated in counseling for a short time, and then decided to go home. Her counselors agreed that the time was right. Four days later she was dead (Montreal *Globe and Mail*, June 16, 1977, p. F4).

Shelters are necessary to protect the victim, or potential victim, from violent assault in his or her home. Shelters are relatively inexpensive—particularly when compared to the cost of individual or group counseling or even to the cost of police response to domestic disturbance calls. Shelters are effective in protecting victims of family assaults, and they are potentially valuable for preventing further episodes of family violence.

It is difficult to pin point exactly how many shelters are currently operating in the United States on a seven-day-a-week, twenty-four-hour-a-day schedule. Our best estimate is that in the summer of 1978 there were no more than sixty shelters in the United States (a list of their addresses and telephone numbers is provided in Terry Davidson's book *Conjugal Crime*). At the same time there are more than one hundred shelters operating in Great Britain. Although sixty shelters are an improvement over the six that existed in 1976, sixty shelters are far too few to help the millions of victims of family violence. In the United States we spend more money on shelters for dogs and cats than for human beings. If we have effective animal rescue shelters for abused dogs, cats, and bunny rabbits we should be able to spare something for people as well.

Day Care

A few years ago a Rochester, New York, shopping mall opened a child-care service in one of its vacant stores. Needless to say, the mall's rationale was economic—mothers buy more if not contending with bored and crying children. Although the child-care program drew large numbers of children, it was abandoned after a few months. According to one store manager, the mothers were "abusing" the facility. Instead of dropping the children off while they shopped, some mothers brought them in at 10 A.M. and did not return until 5 P.M.—letting the mall care for the children, while they had time for themselves.

Such incidents indicate a need for community child-care facilities which are safe, well-run, and available on a drop-in basis to mothers. This is especially true for mothers who do not work—to enable them to drop off their children and have a few hours of free time.

The day-care system in the United States does not provide such services to the population who needs them most. There are not enough day-care facilities. Some facilities are open only to mothers who work or they are too expensive for many families. Other centers cannot, and do not, offer drop-in day care.

Our findings, that mothers are most likely to abuse their children and that preschoolers are at great risk of abuse, mandate that we provide assistance to mothers who need to have periodic breaks from child care. Our culture cannot continue to assume that a woman is psychologically and socially prepared to care for children twenty-four hours a day. There is no such thing as an instinctive ability to mother. It makes no sense for a woman to feel constrained to her home and children, with no chance of escape. The danger of child abuse is understandably great when a woman must stay with her child all day, every day, with no one to help. Day care is an absolute necessity to reduce the risk of child abuse.

Child Welfare Services

It should be obvious from the data in Chapter 3 on violence toward children that if all incidents of child abuse were reported to public and private child welfare agencies, and if each reported case were fully investigated, there would be no time left to provide even minimal services to abused children and their families.

In many states, social service personnel employed in the field of child protection are burdened with case loads which are far too large to allow social workers to service the child and family adequately. Caseworkers often have case loads of fifty families or more, whereas most professionals in the field of social and human services argue that a protective worker should have no more than twenty families to serve at one time.

One Massachusetts social worker said she felt very lucky—at the moment she had only seventeen cases. Her agency said she should carry up to twenty cases. The social worker thought she could do a good job with fifteen. She had recently talked with a New Hampshire social worker who had sixty cases. "My God, sixty cases! And she had an hour travel time each way," added the Massachusetts worker (Boston *Globe*, July 16, 1978, p. A1). If there were full reporting of all the cases of abused children we documented in Chapter 3, child protective workers in the United States would have case loads exceeding two hundred families and reaching as many as five hundred families. Clearly, this situation would tax the protective service system beyond belief.

An example of the impact of full reporting occurred in Florida in the early 1970s. Florida instituted a mass media campaign to alert citizens to the problem of child abuse and at the same time installed a state-wide toll-free phone line which allowed people to report cases of abuse or neglect at any time of the day, seven days a week. The number of reports rose from 10,000 to 100,000 reports a year. Protective workers answered telephone calls seven days a week, and soon the average tenure of a protective worker was less than six months.

Of course, such doomsday forecasts of what could happen if there were full reporting are not likely to become reality in the near future. At present, child welfare services receive reports on only a fraction of the total number of cases of child abuse in the United States. Yet serving only a portion of the total population of abusing families, the child protection system in the United States shows serious weaknesses.

The overriding weakness of the current system comes down to a lack of dollars and cents. State and federal agencies simply do not have the resources to deal even with the cases of child abuse and family violence which *do* come to public attention. And when case loads are high and resources low, a number of tragic consequences are likely. In many instances, child protective workers are unable to protect their clients.

A recent Boston case sadly illustrates this fact. Two years after removing two young children from their parents on grounds of abuse, the children were returned home by a social worker with only six months' experience, none in child abuse cases. The children went home despite a number of protests from foster parents that they showed signs of abuse even after weekend visits with their natural parents. Six months later, police, acting on complaints from neighbors, found one child beaten, suffering from multiple injuries. Further investigation revealed that the other child had died after a beating, her body thrown out with the trash. The social worker had visited the reunited family only once after the children's return.

Subsequent investigations into the case revealed that 65 per cent of the state's protective service workers had less than forty hours' training in handling complex abuse and neglect cases. It also showed that two thirds of the workers currently handling such cases had less than one year's experience in protective services. Until the above case attracted public attention, the welfare department did not even require protective service workers to hold a college degree (Boston *Herald American*, July 30, 1978, p. A8).

An examination of the deaths of children at the hands of family members reveals that in perhaps 90 per cent of such cases there had been official recognition by a public or private agency (including the police) that the child was at physical risk in his or her home.

Although extreme, this illustrates the most typical "treatment" of reported cases of child abuse—*nothing* is done to help the child or the family.

Some people concerned with child abuse advocate a screening device for parents in order to predict the possibility of violence against a child. But this would only overload the system more than at present—without providing adequate protection for children.

What is needed is a properly staffed, trained, and funded child protection system.

The effects of services in some current child welfare programs are often as bad or worse than the original parental abuse. Underfunded and overburdened, many welfare agencies resort to the most direct measure of protecting the child— removing the child from abusive parents. In the short run this does protect the child, but in the long run, the risk of damage remains. First, children who are returned to their parents after a time away are at continued risk if the factors which produced the abuse are not corrected. Second, even if the child is not abused again, the very fact that he or she was removed from the home and placed in foster care produces long-term psychological problems. Most children do not know they are abused, and if they do recognize it, they often react by believing they deserved what happened to them.

A child continues to love and depend on a parent despite abuse. This is highlighted in the following social worker's account, rewritten by a newspaper reporter:

> The court session is brief. The cigarette burns on the child's face and arms are enough to convince the judge that Ried's [the social worker] recommendation that the child be placed in foster care is right.
>
> But when Ried takes her hand to lead her from the judge's chambers, the child begins to scream.
>
> "Mommy!"
>
> There is no scream like a child's separation scream. It is worse than the screams of a child in pain. This mother had hurt this child. The child's life may well be in danger. But the mother is all the child knows.
>
> "Mommy?"
>
> Ried picks up the child. As she walks through the courthouse corridors people turn to watch. The screams continue until they reach the car. Then the screams turn into sobs . . . (Boston *Globe*, July 16, 1978, p. A1).

A child who is removed from an abusing parent may think the parent is giving him away because he was bad. It is not surprising that James Kent found that abused children who are removed from their abusing parents and placed in a series of foster homes suffer from long-term, irreversible psychological damage (1976).

Besides not being a satisfactory solution for the child, the system of removing such children also ignores massive evidence that abusing parents typically proceed to have additional children, who in turn are abused. Except in the most intractable cases, what is needed is family assistance, not moving children around like chessmen.

Child welfare systems must be able to respond to problems of violence toward children quickly, effectively, and in a manner which treats the causes of the abuse, not only the symptoms. Child welfare agencies should be able to provide:

1. *Immediate Crisis Intervention for Families.* In Florida, which has one of the better reporting systems for child abuse and neglect, only 25 per cent of the reports of child abuse and neglect are responded to within one day of the report. This is too slow to protect possible victims of child abuse. A protective service system ought to be able to respond to all reports of abuse and neglect and be able to supply emergency resources for the child and the family immediately, or at least within twenty-four hours of a report.

Note the different standard we apply to violence within the family when compared with other violent behavior. A report to police of someone screaming in terror while being beaten up in a shopping center would produce an immediate response. But similar incidents occurring within family homes are often ignored or "referred."

2. *Support for Families Under Stress.* To protect a child, a welfare system must reduce the stresses which limit parents' ability to cope with their children. A child welfare system should be able to provide emergency homemaker services, a "hot line" to help parents deal with day-to-day crises, trans-

portation, child care, referrals for counseling and self-help
groups (such as Parents Anonymous), health care, clothing,
shelter, and other resources which ease the burden of child
care for parents.

3. *Education in Becoming an Effective Parent.* Studies of
child abuse frequently show that abusing parents do not know
how to cope with and manage a child. They do not understand
a child's capabilities. The abused child has literally driven
them to distraction. Experience has shown that with education
most can learn to be effective non-abusing parents (Jeffrey,
1976; Kempe and Helfer, 1974).

4. *Continuity of Care.* The average protective worker keeps
a child abuse case open for a relatively short time. In Florida,
the average case is open for less than twelve months. This is
simply too short a time really to prevent further abuse. For a
child welfare system to help families and children there must
be long-term continuity of services for the family. Too many
child abuse cases result in further abuse within the family, and
many times the abuse comes years after the initial incident.

Police and Courts

The American police officer often functions as the neighborhood social worker. The police, even more than professional
social workers or marriage counselors, bear the brunt of providing immediate services to violent families. As we pointed
out earlier, this is dangerous work. As many police officers are
killed answering domestic disturbance calls as are killed pursu-
ing armed robbers. Domestic disturbance calls are considered
neither glamorous nor prestigious. Although dangerous work,
few police officers win medals or receive promotions for effectively handling domestic violence situations.

Because family violence is dangerous for police and because
its rewards are few, police, for the most part, are reluctant actually to get involved in its prevention. In some jurisdictions
the police use a "stitch rule." They arrest an abusing husband

only if his wife has been injured badly enough to require a specific number of surgical sutures. At best, police officers offer to take the husband out of the house and walk him around the block until he calms down. At worst, they offer to remove the woman from "his" house, or do nothing, or even sympathize with the abusing man. Often, the police are frustrated by victims of abuse who, once the police have arrived, refuse to cooperate and decline to file charges.

The court system is also reluctant to get involved in the problem of domestic violence. On the one hand, prosecutors are often frustrated by wives who file charges, only to drop them later. On the other hand, the prevailing attitude of many prosecutors and judges is that family violence is a private matter and should be worked out between the husband and wife without the intervention of the courts.

Of course, part of the frustration experienced by the police and courts is their own doing. By their reluctance to get involved in domestic violence problems and by clouding the issue with legal red tape, victims of family violence are frustrated into believing that the police and courts cannot help them. It takes only one violent incident after a husband has been served a restraining order to convince a wife that such orders are worthless. A woman who calls the police only to see them walk her husband around the block and then return him to batter her more severely after they've left is not likely again to call the law.

Our recommendation is to encourage police departments to train their officers in methods of dealing with domestic disturbances. Such experimental training programs have been developed by Professor Morton Bard in New York City (1969; Bard and Zacker, 1971). Specific programs which have been implemented include training in the investigation of domestic assault cases, establishing domestic crisis teams to respond to domestic disturbance calls, and crisis intervention training.

Along with police training, there is an important need to overhaul the criminal justice system's attitude toward domestic violence. "Stitch rules" and laws mandating that a wife must be more grievously injured than a victim of an assault from a stranger in order to file charges must be eliminated. We need a court system which is seriously interested in the issue of domestic violence and is willing to take sufficient steps to protect the victims of violence in the home.

Courts must be willing and able to issue protection orders, restraining orders, and peace bonds to protect victims of domestic violence. Moreover, these orders and bonds must be enforced. Some states have passed laws to allow police to take offenders into custody if there is the threat of harm or assault. Other states have passed legislation which specifically states that spouse abuse is a crime, thus making it easier for victims to seek relief and for police officers to arrest the offending family member.

The court system must also be strengthened and streamlined to handle domestic violence cases. The bottom line of legal and police reform is the need for the entire criminal justice system to view domestic violence as a crime which requires legal action. The hands-off policy of the police and courts in dealing with domestic violence must be changed if we are adequately to protect the victims of conjugal crimes.

Family Planning

One of the consistent findings in the study of child, wife, and husband abuse was that an unwanted child is most likely to be a victim of child abuse. The stress such a child creates also increases the likelihood of spouse abuse within the home. There are many types of "unwanted children." We interviewed a number of violent family members who said that their first child was conceived before they were married and that they were rushed into marriage and parenthood without proper preparation. Other families said that an unexpected child, a child born very soon after the birth of an older sibling, or a child who taxed the financial resources of the family was the factor which seemed to ignite violence in the home. The problem of unwanted children is compounded in families which cannot afford additional or unexpected children.

One obvious step in such cases is adequate family planning programs available to all families. Such programs involve education, access to birth control devices, and abortion on demand. To advocate abortion as a treatment for child abuse may strike many as odd, since a portion of the American public equates abortion with child abuse. However, the issue transcends the philosophical debate over when a fetus becomes a human. People who do not want children or cannot afford children have extreme difficulty in becoming effective parents. Moreover, the additional stress of an unwanted child raises the risk of violence between the parents. Abortion is legal and it should be provided to *all* those who desire it.

Individual and Marital Counseling

The success of individual and marriage counseling in treating problems of family violence is mixed. Those treatment programs which base their efforts on "curing" the pathology which afflicts the violent individual have had minimal success —probably because there are no clear pathologies which make people violent. Research conducted by Berkeley Planning Associates (1978) on child abuse treatment programs funded by the federal government found that, in terms of preventing further abuse, individual counseling was the most costly and least effective. Group counseling was somewhat more effective, while lay therapy and self-help groups, such as Parents Anonymous, proved the most productive in terms of coming to grips with the problem of child abuse and preventing further occurrences within a family.

Said one woman after her first encounter with Parents Anonymous, "Just being able to tell someone I was doing this to my kids and not have them stone me to death or lock me up helped."

Psychologist James Prescott, of the National Institute of Child Health and Development, has proposed innovative methods for treating violent families. It is Prescott's contention that experiencing pleasure and inflicting pain are incompatible in human beings (Prescott and Wallace, 1976). Prescott's research found that many violent individuals did not, and had not, experienced physical pleasure. Prescott believes that if violent family members could experience physical pleasure they would be less violent. He has proposed that, instead of the numbing counseling session held in an office, counselors should take families skiing or swimming or camping. He believes that families need to learn to have fun with one another, and that if they do, there might be less violence.

Some counseling programs are not only ineffective but can, in fact, cause increased family violence. Bach and Wyden, in their book *The Intimate Enemy* (1968), propose that families are violent because they have no outlet for their aggressions. The authors' approach is to encourage family members to get mad—to release frustrations through verbal aggression or physical violence on inanimate objects (such as punching bags and pillows).

The theory behind such "let it all hang out" counseling is that verbal and mild physical aggression are cathartic and reduce the likelihood of hostilities building to violent conclusions. But as we explained in Chapter 7, our evidence shows the catharsis approach to violence actually leads to increased physical aggression in the family. Mild forms of violence tend to increase in severity, until the family is once more faced with explosive situations.

The therapy of counselors such as Bach and Wyden is based on current life-style fads. Scientific evidence points in the opposite direction. It is a sad commentary that we must caution that certain "modern" therapies often do more harm than good.

However, we must reiterate that counseling and therapy are

at most stopgap measures—temporary, as well as insufficient treatments.

TOWARD THE REDUCTION OF VIOLENCE IN THE HOME

The steps and programs just presented are necessary to protect the lives and well-being of victims or potential victims in violent homes. But implementation of such programs and policies will not break the cycle of cultural norms and values contributing to the violent nature of the family. Nor do the policies alter characteristics of the society or family which increase the chances that certain families will resort to abusive violence.

If we want to *reduce* the level of violence in the American family we must reconsider and alter some of our most fundamental values and attitudes. It is these long-standing beliefs which contribute to the high incidence and deadly nature of domestic violence in the United States.

Step 1: Eliminate the norms which legitimize and glorify violence in society and family. As long as we, as a society, continue to believe that spanking children is necessary, good, and beneficial to the children; as long as we continue to believe that physical violence is an effective way to punish people; and as long as we accept violence as a means of solving problems and expressing one's self in the family and on the street, we will have a high level of violence in our homes and in our society.

Violence cannot be reduced until we eliminate the norms and values by which it is tolerated, legitimized, and glorified.

Public awareness campaigns can outline the extent, seriousness, and consequences of violence in the family. The American public does not realize just how violent the family is. We need to convey the message that violence is more widespread than the lurid episodes of child or wife abuse seen in the occasional news story. Violence is a fundamental pattern of behavior, a way of life, to many families.

The American public needs to understand the consequences of children growing up in violent homes. We must explain that street violence is directly traceable to violence in the home, just as violence in the home is traceable to violence in the streets.

We need domestic disarmament. Those who oppose gun control argue that control of firearms cannot be expected to keep guns out of criminals' hands. True enough. But strict gun control and the elimination of easily obtained handguns will keep guns out of the setting where they do the most damage— the American household. Men and women who buy handguns for protection are more likely to use those guns on a family member than on a stranger or a burglar. Certainly, there are knives, ice picks, and other weapons in homes which combatants can use, but knives and ice picks are considerably less deadly than Saturday night specials.

Third, we must eliminate violence committed in the name of the state. The death penalty, corporal punishment in the schools, and other legally sanctioned acts of violence are of dubious value when it comes to changing behavior or deterring someone from breaking rules and laws (Bedau and Pierce, 1976). The death penalty and corporal punishment in the schools *do* teach that the ultimate acceptable punishment for incorrigible behavior is violence. Each time a student is spanked by a teacher and each time the death penalty is administered, people are taught that an effective and ultimate form of sanction is violence.

Lastly, we recommend that the extent and glorification of violence in television and other media be reduced. Certainly, individuals and families were violent before television. It would be simplistic to place the blame for violence in society squarely on the mass media. But the media reflect what is going on in the society. They also reinforce and help maintain that pattern. Violence is presented in a manner that teaches viewers that it is necessary, legitimate, and effective. Research shows that television contributes to attitudes which favor the use of violence to control and punish people. It emphasizes a macho image for males—encouraging the expression of masculinity through violent behavior.

In short, we must invalidate the hitting license and develop a social norm and culture which argues: "People are not for hitting!" We must remember that children are people too.

Step 2: Reduce Violence-provoking Stresses Created by Society. Our examination of the factors related to family violence indicated that unemployment, underemployment, poverty, and stress are all related to violence between family members. Family life is fragile enough without the added burdens of inadequate medical care, rising food costs, and lack of sufficient resources to provide a minimum standard of living.

The relationship between unemployment and violence suggests that the *elimination of unemployment* and establishment of full employment could reduce the level of violence in the family. In our society a jobless person is a stigmatized person, regardless of the reason for unemployment. Joblessness and poverty undermine an individual's self-respect and interfere with one's ability to cope with stress and strain. Eliminating poverty and guaranteeing each family adequate financial resources would not eliminate violence in the home, but it would at least reduce the potential for violence in the most violent-prone group of families.

We see a need for adequate health and dental care for all American families. Our early interviews with violent families indicated that many suffered from chronic and aggravating health and dental problems. Impacted wisdom teeth, decaying teeth, arthritis, chronic illness, all undermined family members'. abilities to cope with problems arising in their homes.

Violence is often the easiest out. A father with a toothache and a hang-over to boot is most likely not interested in reasoning with a five-year-old who refuses to pick up his toys and turn down the TV—particularly when a slap gets faster results.

Of course, we are aware that full employment, health care, and elimination of poverty would do nothing to eliminate violence in wealthier families, where such problems are not a factor. But we should take steps to ensure that the rate of violence in impoverished social groups is lowered. We cannot continue to hold out high expectations for marital happiness and good child rearing while systematically denying certain groups and families the basic resources which are necessary to be an adequate husband, wife, or parent.

Step 3: Integrate Families into a Network of Kin and Community. The joys of family life are matched only by the pain and depths of despair created by the everyday strains and the crises inevitable in being a member of a family (Gelles and Straus, 1979). People who do not have friends and relatives to turn to when these strains arise are more likely to strike out physically at others in the family. It is no wonder then that one of the most frequent characteristics of child-abusing families is social isolation. The same finding is beginning to emerge from research on spouses who abuse each other.

The reverse is probably also true: people tend to avoid association with couples who are violent to each other or to their children. Regardless of the sequence of events, violent families are often without the aid, comfort, and social approval of friends and relatives. We have seen that this is particularly true of families who are geographically mobile.

Whatever can be done to reduce the isolation and alienation of modern life is worth exploring. Many government and corporate policies, for example, push in the opposite direction. Transfers to new locations must be accepted if the young manager is to advance in the company. New factories and government installations are built in areas where land is cheap, rather than in the cities where workers are now located. Highways and urban renewal displace run-down, but long-established neighborhoods. Such actions have the unintended consequences of producing a nation in which one out of five people move each year.

Changes in such policies should be given high priority. Vice-president Mondale, while still a senator, may have been on the right track. He introduced a bill which would have required a "family impact analysis" in addition to the physical environmental impact analysis necessary for all new federal government projects.

It is not, however, merely a matter of reducing geographic mobility. French sociologist Emile Durkheim and others have repeatedly shown that membership in groups is needed to insulate individuals from alienation. The group can be a trade union, a photographic club, a social or "service" club, a neighborhood food co-operative, etc. Each group helps to include the individual in a network of other people. America is often referred to as a nation of joiners, but the fact is that most Americans belong to none of these types of groups.

Perhaps ways can be found to involve a larger proportion of the population. Some work has been done on mobilizing the extended system of family, relatives, friends, and neighbors for help during times of crisis (Rueveni, 1978). Integrating people into groups *before* a crisis may be more difficult. For example, 4-H clubs for youth and "homemakers clubs" for married women work well in rural areas. However, attempts to establish these types of groups in large urban centers (where over two thirds of Americans now live) have not been particularly successful.

The same applies to what feeble attempts there have been to preserve neighborhoods, their traditions and institutions. Public demands for low priced consumer goods have fostered the rise of supermarkets and discount department stores. In the process the local "Mom and Pop groceries" and the corner candy stores have been destroyed.

Sons and daughters opt for split level homes in the suburbs rather than the house down the street from the in-laws. Some of the old-time neighborhoods have been broken up in the name of urban renewal. People find their homes turned into parking lots. Neighborhoods in many areas are now being taken over by the rich for "restoration" as city life once again becomes fashionable. The residents become "displaced persons," unable to afford their long-time homes. Although the difficulties are great and the needed policies are far from obvious, this is clearly a high priority matter. It affects not only the level of violence, but also the "quality of life" in the most fundamental sense of that term.

Step 4: Change the Sexist Character of Society and the Family. Our examination of power, decision-making, and sharing of household tasks indicated that inequality in the home is a prime contributor to violence between family members. The family is the outstanding example of a social institution which assigns jobs and responsibilities based on a person's sex and age rather than interest, competence, or ability. As long as we expect men to head the family because they are men and women to care for children because they are women, we are going to have potential conflict and violence in homes. If women want an equal say in decisions, and do not want to give up careers and life outside the home in order to be full-time mothers, the potential strain and conflict are very high. Just because a woman wants to have children and be a good mother does not necessarily mean that she wants to, or should, be home 24 hours a day, 365 days a year. Women can be effective mothers and economically productive human beings. Society should provide day care, educational opportunities, and flexible work schedules to help them achieve this potential.

Within the home we can eliminate the sex-patterned allocation of roles and tasks. Individuals should be free to do tasks and take on responsibilities which they are capable of doing, irrespective of their sex.

Women's liberation needs to have a men's liberation counterpart. The common view of the man as head of the household should be eliminated. Sexual equality in the home should reduce the need for men to defend their supposedly superior masculine position by using violence toward their wives and children.

Sexual inequality at home and in society is the heart of the battle of the sexes, and is a part of the reason why women are more likely to abuse their children than men. The concept of "women's work" must be eliminated and with it, the implication that jobs filled by women are less important and therefore should have lower salaries. Only then can we begin to develop equity in the world of work and in the home.

Step 5: Break the Cycle of Violence in the Family. Perhaps the most disturbing chapter of our book was the chapter which demonstrated that family violence is carried over from one generation to the next. Unless this cycle of violence is broken, we can never reduce the level and toll of domestic violence.

Despite the fact that physical punishment is viewed as necessary and beneficial by the majority of American parents, and despite the fact that many parents dogmatically cling to the notion that spankings are good for children, we *must* reduce and gradually eliminate the use of physical punishment and develop alternative technologies for child rearing. It is possible to raise healthy, happy, well-behaved children without violence. Thomas Gordon has pioneered a program of Parent Effectiveness Training which provides a "no-lose" non-violent technique for raising children without force or aggression. Gordon's version of parent-child relations does not meet the needs of all parents. We mention it only as an example of the many parent-child relations now gaining popularity. Parent Effectiveness Training, education for parenthood programs, and other non-violent technologies are absolutely necessary if we are to break the cycle of violence.

We can no longer tolerate or be amused by violence between siblings. It is just as damaging as any other form of violence. It is a powerful lesson teaching that violence within the family is no different from violence outside the family. There is an added irony when parents use violence as a means of punishing sibling violence. This is one of the most outrageous and damaging examples of the cycle of violence in the family.

In short, it is possible to eliminate the sequence of early experiences which teach millions of American children to use violence on those they love.

SUMMING UP

The steps we have proposed to reduce family violence involve extremely long-term changes in the fabric of a society which now tends to tolerate, accept, and even encourage the use of violence in families.

Many of the proposals would appear to confront and challenge some of our basic notions about the privacy of the family and the belief that a man's home is his castle. Some proposals appear to be out of the question—can we ever achieve full employment? Can poverty be eliminated? Can we guarantee health care to all Americans? Clearly, some of the steps we propose are costly and some will seem completely unworkable.

However, the alternative to taking steps such as those outlined is a continuation and extension, and perhaps even an escalation, of the deadly tradition of domestic violence which:

1. Creates a cycle of violence.

2. Is one of the causes of all types of assault and homicide outside of the home, including political assassination.

3. Makes the family a source of untold misery for millions of Americans who know only violence and danger from those who should most provide love and security.

No meaningful change will take place without some drastic social and familial changes and this means a change in the fundamental way we organize our lives, our families, and our society.

NOTES

Chapter 2

1. The term "beating up" was defined by its place in the list of violence items. Specifically it came after the items dealing with kicking, biting, punching, and hitting with an object, and before the items dealing with a knife or gun. Thus, it is something more than just a single blow, but the precise meaning of the term undoubtedly varied from respondent to respondent.

2. We do not know exactly what is meant by "using a gun or a knife." In the case of the knife it could mean threw the knife or actually stabbed or attempted to stab. In respect to a gun, it could have been fired without anyone being wounded. However, the fact is that the respondent admitted employing the weapon, not just using it as a threat.

3. Most of the other standard errors were substantially below 1 per cent because of the large sample size and the fact that we are dealing with rates that are for the most part under 10 per cent. For example, the standard error for the "Kicked, bit, or hit with fist" item is .0066 (i.e., approximately .7 per cent), and that for the "used a knife or gun" item is .0042 (i.e., less than .5 per cent). Consequently, it is very likely that if all American couples had been interviewed, rather than a sample of couples, the results would have been very close to what we found.

4. See Archer and Gartner (1976) and Straus (1977a) for an analysis of the links between war and within-society violence, and Straus (1974c) for a discussion of the factors which seem to underlie the growing national concern with violence in the family.

5. The data on this issue are not as good as the importance of the

issue demands. Budget limits, and the limits of the patience of our respondents, forced us to cut out many questions. For events which happened in the previous year, we got the data separately for the husband and the wife. The questions concerning events before the previous year refer to the couple, irrespective of who did it. This was necessary because of a limit on how long an interview was acceptable to the participants and because some of the things we asked about were not easily attributed to one person or the other after the lapse of several years.

6. Another consideration is suggested by one of the pilot studies, which checked on underreporting (Bulcroft and Straus, 1975). That study shows underreporting of violence is considerably greater for violence by husbands than it is for violence by wives. This is probably because the use of physical force is so much a part of the male way of life that it is typically not the dramatic (and often traumatic) event that the same act of violence is for a woman. To be violent is not unmasculine. But to be physically violent *is* unfeminine according to contemporary American standards. So if one allows for the fact that men probably underreported their own violence, just in simple numerical terms, wife-beating is the more severe problem.

Chapter 4

1. It is important to make clear that the number of children used for categorizing families reflects only the number of children between three and seventeen who were residing at home during the survey year. Therefore, families in which children were under three years of age or older than seventeen years are not included in the analysis.

We are aware that infants and toddlers affect family relations as do teen-agers who are older than eighteen and are living at home. When we chose the minimum age we were interested in identifying an age at which a child was mature enough to select a specific conflict tactics technique. We felt that children under three would not have sufficiently developed this ability. Our second concern was selecting an upper age limit which would ensure that the child would be at home enough to interact with brothers and sisters on a daily basis. We concluded that even if older teen-agers were living at home they were very likely to be in college or employed, thus their contact with younger brothers and sisters might be minimal—too limited even to generate conflict.

2. We think the rates are higher in one-parent households because (a) The broken marriage is likely to have been one characterized by high conflict and violence. In the next chapter we will show that violence between husband and wife is associated with high rates of violence between children. (b) Mothers are usually the caretaking parent in single-parent families. Since such mothers often must have paid jobs in addition to being the housekeeper and mother, they may be less available to help their children resolve conflicts without violence. (c) Evidence from earlier studies suggests that fathers are more successful in getting children to behave. Therefore, without the father's support, a mother may have more difficulty controlling the children.

On the other hand, as we will see in Chapter 5, an unhappy home, one characterized by high conflict and violence between the husband and wife, can also increase the general level of violence in the family. Thus, a divorce in this type of family might reduce the level of sibling violence.

Chapter 5

1. This is possible, even though we talked with only one generation in each of the 2,143 families, because they answered three sets of questions. The first set was about violence in his or her own marriage, the second was about violence in the family he or she grew up in, and the third set of questions was about violence between the children of the couples we interviewed. So there is information on family violence in three generations.

The most complete and extensive information is on the couples who were actually interviewed. We simply did not have the time, nor could we expect our respondents to give our interviewers enough time to ask as many questions about their parents and about their children as we asked them about themselves. Furthermore, most people probably would not be able to give us accurate information on the finer details.

2. Data on violence by the grandfathers and the grandmothers are limited to instances which their children knew about. Consequently, both sets of data share this cause of underreporting. Data on the husbands and wives in the study are their reports of their own violence. That is where the difference may enter, because women tend to report their own violence more completely than do men.

3. Throughout this chapter when we speak of "the highest group" we mean the people who are two or more standard deviations above the mean. When charts are used, the highest group is given a score of 9 because the horizontal axis uses "Sten" scores (Canfield, 1951). Sten scores range from 0 to 9 in steps of one-half standard deviation. However, because of the importance of preserving the meaning of zero as indicating no violence, the group designated as 0 always means zero violence even if (because of skewed distributions) it is not two or more standard deviations below the mean.

4. We asked only about physical punishment when the person interviewed was a teen-ager because we do not think enough people could tell us what happened when they were younger. Of course, the number of parents who use physical punishment drops off as the child grows older (see Chapter 3). But several studies (cited in Gelles and Straus, 1979) show that about half of all parents continue to use physical punishment even on their teen-age children.

The questions about punishment by the parents of our respondents were also limited to how often each parent "used physical punishment, like slapping or hitting you?" Thus, we do not have information for the grandparents on specific acts of violence ranging from slapping to using a knife or gun. For this reason, it was not possible to compute a Child Abuse Index to compare with the Child Abuse Index computed for the parents who were interviewed.

Chapter 7

1. The answers were scored: always agree = 0, almost always agree = 1, usually agree = 2, sometimes agree = 3, never agree = 4.

2. In Chart 15 "Rare" means the couples who had scores which are more than one standard deviation below the average (mean).

"Low" means couples with below average scores, but not more than one standard deviation below average. "Medium" are the couples with scores from the average to one standard deviation above the mean, and "High" are the couples with scores that are more than one standard deviation above the average for all couples in this sample. See Appendix C for details concerning the Marital Conflict Index and Appendix B for the Reasoning Scale.

3. We think that one of the problems with the test of conflict theory in this chapter is with the way "conflict" was measured. The method used mixes willingness to recognize and engage in conflict (the aspect we want to measure) with the sheer number of problems. Conflict theory does *not* assert that the more conflict the better. It says that sooner or later there will be at least some conflicts in any group, and that attempts to ignore or suppress these conflicts will produce even further difficulties in the long run (see Foss, 1979, for the specific application of these principles to the family).

Chapter 8

1. The measure of stress used in the analysis of child abuse excluded the two items which deal with child-related stress (child kicked out of school or suspended; child caught doing something illegal). We left these items out in order to eliminate a sense of circularity implied by having child-produced stress and child abuse related to one another.

2. The measure of stress used in the spouse abuse analysis excluded two stress items which deal with conflict between couples (sexual difficulties, big increase in arguments with partner).

Chapter 9

1. The factors were selected by first carrying out a discriminant function analysis using the SPSS program DISCRIMINANT. A stepwise analysis was done, selecting those indicators which minimize Wilks's *lambda*. The items in the checklist therefore consist of those which add significantly to the identification of couples who engage in violence, and which do not significantly overlap with each other.

APPENDIX A
Sample and Interviewing

The sampling design and interviewing for this study was carried out by Response Analysis Corporation of Princeton, New Jersey. The "Response Analysis National Probability Sample" relies entirely on prior specification of locations, households, and specific individuals to be interviewed. None of the selection steps are left to the discretion of the interviewer. The sequence of steps used included:

Selection of a national sample of 103 primary areas (counties or groups of counties) stratified by geographic region, type of community, and other population characteristics.

Selection of 300 interviewing locations, or secondary areas (census enumeration districts or block groups) from the national sample for use in this study.

Field counts by trained interviewers to divide interviewing locations into sample segments of 10 to 25 housing units.

Selection of specific sample segments in each interviewing location for field administration of the survey.

Random selection of the eligible person to be interviewed using a specific scheme assigned for each sample household.

More detailed information on each of these steps is available in the methodological report prepared by Response Analysis Corporation (Weisbrod, 1976). This will be supplied at cost (write to Response Analysis Corporation, Research Park, Route 206, Princeton, N.J. 08540).

Eligible families consisted of a couple who identified themselves as married or being a "couple" (man and woman living together as a conjugal unit). A random procedure was used so that the respondents would be approximately half male and half female. The final national probability sample produced 2,143 completed interviews. Interviews were conducted with (960 men and 1,183 women).

Comparison with census data shows that this sample is representative in terms of major demographic attributes of American families, including even the same proportion of unmarried cohabiting couples as was found in a special census analysis (Yllo and Straus, 1978).

Response Analysis went to considerable lengths to secure a high completion rate, including up to four call-backs, letters, and in some cases monetary incentives. As a result, the completion rate for the survey as a whole was 65 per cent. The rate varied from a low of 60.0 per cent for metropolitan areas to a high of 72.3 per cent for non-metropolitan areas. Although we had hoped for a somewhat higher completion rate, the actual rate is still a considerable achievement in view of the sensitive nature of the topic and the fact that all surveys have encountered increasing resistance during the last decade. The average completion rate for national opinion surveys is now about 70 per cent. Consequently, we regard a 65 per cent completion rate as an important accomplishment.

APPENDIX B
Measuring Violence with the "Conflict Tactics Scales"

Chapter 1 gives the over-all definition of violence which guided this research. A more detailed discussion of the many subtle issues involved in a definition of violence is given elsewhere (Gelles and Straus, 1979). The method we used to gather the actual data on violence is known as the "Conflict Tactics Scales" (Straus, 1979). This technique was first developed at the University of New Hampshire in 1971 and was modified and used extensively over the next five years in numerous studies of family violence (see for example: Allen and Straus, 1979; Bulcroft and Straus, 1975; Steinmetz, 1977c; Straus, 1974a, 1976).

The Conflict Tactics Scales are designed to measure intrafamily conflict in the sense of the means used to resolve conflicts of interests. Three different tactics are measured: (1) Reasoning: the use of rational discussion and argument; (2) Verbal Aggression: the use of verbal and symbolic means of hurting—such as insults or threats to hurt the other; and, (3) Violence: the actual use of physical force. The Violence Scale contains eight items (items *k* through *r* in Chart 28).

CHART 28
Conflict Tactics Scales, Form N.

53. In some families where there are children, they always seem to be having spats, fights, disagreements, or whatever you want to call them; and they use many different ways of trying to settle differences between themselves. I'm going to read you a list of some things that (REFERENT CHILD) might have done when (he/she) had a disagreement with the other (child/children) in the family. For each one, I would like to know how often (REFERENT CHILD) did it in the past year.

		Q. 53								Q. 54		
		REFERENT CHILD - IN THE PAST YEAR								EVER HAPPENED		
		NEVER	ONCE	TWICE	3-5 TIMES	6-10 TIMES	11-20 TIMES	MORE THAN 20 TIMES	DON'T KNOW	YES	NO	DON'T KNOW
a.	Discussed the issue calmly	0	1	2	3	4	5	6	X	1	2	X
b.	Got information to back up (his/her) side of things	0	1	2	3	4	5	6	X	1	2	X
c.	Brought in or tried to bring in someone to help settle things	0	1	2	3	4	5	6	X	1	2	X
d.	Insulted or swore at the other one	0	1	2	3	4	5	6	X	1	2	X
e.	Sulked and/or refused to talk about it	0	1	2	3	4	5	6	X	1	2	X
f.	Stomped out of the room or house (or yard)	0	1	2	3	4	5	6	X	1	2	X
g.	Cried	0	1	2	3	4	5	6	X	1	2	X
h.	Did or said something to spite the other one	0	1	2	3	4	5	6	X	1	2	X
i.	Threatened to hit or throw something at the other one	0	1	2	3	4	5	6	X	1	2	X
j.	Threw or smashed or hit or kicked something	0	1	2	3	4	5	6	X	1	2	X
k.	Threw something at the other one	0	1	2	3	4	5	6	X	1	2	X
l.	Pushed, grabbed, or shoved the other one	0	1	2	3	4	5	6	X	1	2	X
m.	Slapped or spanked the other one	0	1	2	3	4	5	6	X	1	2	X
n.	Kicked, bit, or hit with a fist	0	1	2	3	4	5	6	X	1	2	X
o.	Hit or tried to hit with something	0	1	2	3	4	5	6	X	1	2	X
p.	Beat up the other one	0	1	2	3	4	5	6	X	1	2	X
q.	Threatened with a knife or gun	0	1	2	3	4	5	6	X	1	2	X
r.	Used a knife or gun	0	1	2	3	4	5	6	X	1	2	X
s.	Other (PROBE): _____	0	1	2	3	4	5	6	X	1	2	X

FOR THOSE ITEMS CIRCLED "NEVER" OR "DON'T KNOW" ON Q. 53, ASK:

54. I'd like you to tell me if, as far as you know, (REFERENT CHILD) *ever* (ITEM) with the other (child/children) when they had a fight or dispute.

57. Parents and children use many different ways of trying to settle differences between them. I'm going to read a list of some things that you and (CHILD) might have done when you had a dispute. Still using Card A, I would like you to tell me how often you did it with (CHILD) in the last year.

	Q. 57 RESPONDENT								Q. 58 EVER HAPPENED			Q. 59 CHILD							
	NEVER	ONCE	TWICE	3-5 TIMES	6-10 TIMES	11-20 TIMES	MORE THAN 20 TIMES	DON'T KNOW	YES	NO	DON'T KNOW	NEVER	ONCE	TWICE	3-5 TIMES	6-10 TIMES	11-20 TIMES	MORE THAN 20 TIMES	DON'T KNOW
a. Discussed the issue calmly	0	1	2	3	4	5	6	X	1	2	X	0	1	2	3	4	5	6	X
b. Got information to back up (your/his or her) side of things	0	1	2	3	4	5	6	X	1	2	X	0	1	2	3	4	5	6	X
c. Brought in or tried to bring in someone to help settle things	0	1	2	3	4	5	6	X	1	2	X	0	1	2	3	4	5	6	X
d. Insulted or swore at the other one	0	1	2	3	4	5	6	X	1	2	X	0	1	2	3	4	5	6	X
e. Sulked and/or refused to talk about it	0	1	2	3	4	5	6	X	1	2	X	0	1	2	3	4	5	6	X
f. Stomped out of the room or house (or yard)	0	1	2	3	4	5	6	X	1	2	X	0	1	2	3	4	5	6	X
g. Cried	0	1	2	3	4	5	6	X	1	2	X	0	1	2	3	4	5	6	X
h. Did or said something to spite the other one	0	1	2	3	4	5	6	X	1	2	X	0	1	2	3	4	5	6	X
i. Threatened to hit or throw something at the other one	0	1	2	3	4	5	6	X	1	2	X	0	1	2	3	4	5	6	X
j. Threw or smashed or hit or kicked something	0	1	2	3	4	5	6	X	1	2	X	0	1	2	3	4	5	6	X
k. Threw something at the other one	0	1	2	3	4	5	6	X	1	2	X	0	1	2	3	4	5	6	X
l. Pushed, grabbed, or shoved the other one	0	1	2	3	4	5	6	X	1	2	X	0	1	2	3	4	5	6	X
m. Slapped or spanked the other one	0	1	2	3	4	5	6	X	1	2	X	0	1	2	3	4	5	6	X
n. Kicked, bit, or hit with a fist	0	1	2	3	4	5	6	X	1	2	X	0	1	2	3	4	5	6	X
o. Hit or tried to hit with something	0	1	2	3	4	5	6	X	1	2	X	0	1	2	3	4	5	6	X
p. Beat up the other one	0	1	2	3	4	5	6	X	1	2	X	0	1	2	3	4	5	6	X
q. Threatened with a knife or gun	0	1	2	3	4	5	6	X	1	2	X	0	1	2	3	4	5	6	X
r. Used a knife or gun	0	1	2	3	4	5	6	X	1	2	X	0	1	2	3	4	5	6	X
s. Other (PROBE):_____	0	1	2	3	4	5	6	X	1	2	X	0	1	2	3	4	5	6	X

FOR EACH ITEM CIRCLED AS "NEVER" OR "DON'T KNOW" ON Q. 57, ASK:

58. When you and (CHILD) have had a disagreement, have you ever (ITEM)?

ASK EVERYONE:

59. Now, let's talk about (CHILD). Tell me how often in the past year when you had a disagreement (he/she) (FIRST ITEM CIRCLED). (RECORD ABOVE)

78. No matter how well a couple gets along, there are times when they disagree on major decisions, get annoyed about something the other person does, or just have spats or fights because they're in a bad mood or tired or for some other reason. They also use many different ways of trying to settle their differences. I'm going to read a list of some things that you and your (wife/partner) might have done when you had a dispute, and would first like you to tell me for each one how often you did it in the past year.

	Q. 78 RESPONDENT-IN PAST YEAR								Q. 79 WIFE/PARTNER-IN PAST YEAR								Q. 80 EVER HAPPENED		
	NEVER	ONCE	TWICE	3-5 TIMES	6-10 TIMES	11-20 TIMES	MORE THAN 20 TIMES	DON'T KNOW	NEVER	ONCE	TWICE	3-5 TIMES	6-10 TIMES	11-20 TIMES	MORE THAN 20 TIMES	DON'T KNOW	YES	NO	DON'T KNOW
a. Discussed the issue calmly	0	1	2	3	4	5	6	X	0	1	2	3	4	5	6	X	1	2	X
b. Got information to back up (your/her) side of things	0	1	2	3	4	5	6	X	0	1	2	3	4	5	6	X	1	2	X
c. Brought in or tried to bring in someone to help settle things	0	1	2	3	4	5	6	X	0	1	2	3	4	5	6	X	1	2	X
d. Insulted or swore at the other one	0	1	2	3	4	5	6	X	0	1	2	3	4	5	6	X	1	2	X
e. Sulked and/or refused to talk about it	0	1	2	3	4	5	6	X	0	1	2	3	4	5	6	X	1	2	X
f. Stomped out of the room or house (or yard)	0	1	2	3	4	5	6	X	0	1	2	3	4	5	6	X	1	2	X
g. Cried	0	1	2	3	4	5	6	X	0	1	2	3	4	5	6	X	1	2	X
h. Did or said something to spite the other one	0	1	2	3	4	5	6	X	0	1	2	3	4	5	6	X	1	2	X
i. Threatened to hit or throw something at the other one	0	1	2	3	4	5	6	X	0	1	2	3	4	5	6	X	1	2	X
j. Threw or smashed or hit or kicked something	0	1	2	3	4	5	6	X	0	1	2	3	4	5	6	X	1	2	X
k. Threw something at the other one	0	1	2	3	4	5	6	X	0	1	2	3	4	5	6	X	1	2	X
l. Pushed, grabbed, or shoved the other one	0	1	2	3	4	5	6	X	0	1	2	3	4	5	6	X	1	2	X
m. Slapped the other one	0	1	2	3	4	5	6	X	0	1	2	3	4	5	6	X	1	2	X
n. Kicked, bit, or hit with a fist	0	1	2	3	4	5	6	X	0	1	2	3	4	5	6	X	1	2	X
o. Hit or tried to hit with something	0	1	2	3	4	5	6	X	0	1	2	3	4	5	6	X	1	2	X
p. Beat up the other one	0	1	2	3	4	5	6	X	0	1	2	3	4	5	6	X	1	2	X
q. Threatened with a knife or gun	0	1	2	3	4	5	6	X	0	1	2	3	4	5	6	X	1	2	X
r. Used a knife or gun	0	1	2	3	4	5	6	X	0	1	2	3	4	5	6	X	1	2	X
s. Othe. (PROBE): _____	0	1	2	3	4	5	6	X	0	1	2	3	4	5	6	X	1	2	X

79. And what about your (wife/partner)? Tell me how often she (ITEM) in the past year.

FOR EACH ITEM CIRCLED EITHER "NEVER" OR "DON'T KNOW" FOR BOTH RESPONDENT AND PARTNER, ASK:

80. Did you or your (wife/partner) *ever* (ITEM)?

The administration of the Conflict Tactics Scales involves asking the respondents what they did when they had a disagreement with their spouses. This list of possible actions starts with those low in coerciveness (such as discussing the issue). The items gradually become more coercive and physically violent, ending with whether the respondent ever used a knife or gun on his or her spouse. This sequence enhances the likelihood that the subject will become committed to the interview and continue answering the questions. Analysis of response to the items indicates that there was no noticeable drop in the completion rate of items as the list moved from the Reasoning Scale questions to the most violent modes of conflict resolution.

ACCEPTABILITY TO RESPONDENTS

The husband-wife Verbal Aggression Scale and, even more, the husband-wife Violence Scale ask about highly sensitive and normatively deviant types of behavior. This can lead to respondents being antagonized, to self-defensively distorted responses, or to refusing to continue the interview. All of these can result in invalid data. The question of validity is discussed later. However, before one can even consider validity, the data must be obtained. Experience with the CTS indicates low refusal and antagonism rates. For example, in the national survey, the "completion rate" was only slightly lower than is currently typical of such mass surveys. Four factors seem to account for the acceptability of the CTS.

First, the instrument is presented in the context of disagreements and conflicts between members of the family and the ways in which such conflicts are resolved. Since almost everyone recognizes that families have conflicts and disagreements this serves as the first step in legitimizing response.

Second, as previously explained, the items start with conflict tactics which most respondents value positively and then gradually increase in coerciveness and social disapproval. The respondent is, therefore, given a chance first to present the "correct" things which he or she has done to resolve the conflict. In the context of a society in which there is a widespread approval of violence "if all else fails," this serves to legitimize reporting the use of violence.

A third factor is the sequence in which the data on behavior in different family roles are obtained. The CTS begins with the items concerning child-to-child relationships. This sequence was deliberately selected because the use of physical force between family members is most legitimate in this relationship. Next, the CTS items are presented for conflicts between parents and children. Since hitting children by parents is also widely accepted, respondents are again being asked about behavior which, although not liked, is also not threatening to their self-esteem.

A final factor which seems to account for the willingness of respondents to provide data on acts of physical violence between themselves and their spouses is that, by the time the husband-wife cycle of items is reached, they are familiar with the questions which will be asked. Having responded to these questions previously, the strangeness of responding to a question about throwing things or hitting someone else has sharply diminished.

Although this "practice effect" seems, on the face of it, to be important, the evidence from the Bulcroft and Straus (1975) study shows that it is far from essential. In that study, mail questionnaire versions of only the spousal role section of the CTS were used. These were completed and returned by 72 per cent of the parents of a sample of university students to whom questionnaires were sent.

VIOLENCE RATES

The rates used to indicate violence are the percentage of the sample (or groups within the sample) who carried out one or more violent acts during the twelve months preceding the interview. They are therefore annual incidence rates per hundred. For example, the incidence of parents throwing something at a child is the percentage of respondents with a child age three to seventeen living at home who said they did this during the previous twelve months. In addition, at a few places we report data on whether a given type of violent act or group of acts had *ever* occurred.

VIOLENCE INDEXES

For the most part attention in this book is focused on indexes which take into account several different types of violent acts. This is because we think that the important thing is to know if a family member has assaulted another member of his or her family, irrespective of whether the attack was in the form of throwing something or slapping the other person.

However, it is important to distinguish between the milder forms of family violence and the more serious violence. This is because the milder acts of violence have at least some normative legitimacy, and also because they pose less danger to the physical well-being of the person attacked. Consequently, for each family relationship we computed two different indexes: an over-all violence index and a severe violence index.

The *over-all violence indexes* consist of the eight items labeled *k* through *r* in Chart 28. The *severe violence indexes* exclude the items k, l, and m (throwing something at another person, pushing, shoving, or grabbing, and slapping or spanking). It is restricted to the more serious and dangerous acts of violence: kicking, biting, punching, hitting with an object, beating up, threatening with a knife or gun, and the use of a knife or gun.

We measured violence between seven different pairs of family members. There is both an over-all violence index and a severe violence index for each of these pairs. There were a total of twenty-one different violence indexes. The names given to these indexes are:

OVER-ALL VIOLENCE INDEXES (Items *k* through *r*)	SEVERE VIOLENCE INDEXES (Items *n* through *r*)
Husband-to-wife Violence Index	Wife-beating Index
Wife-to-husband Violence Index	Husband-beating Index
Couple Violence Index	Spouse Abuse Index
Father-to-child Violence Index	Father's Child Abuse Index
Mother-to-child Violence Index	Mother's Child Abuse Index
Parent-to-child Violence Index	Child Abuse Index A (includes "hitting with object")
	Child Abuse Index B (excludes "hitting with object")
Child-to-father Violence Index	Father Abuse Index
Child-to-mother Violence Index	Mother Abuse Index
Child-to-parent Violence Index	Parent Abuse Index
Sibling Violence Index	Sibling Abuse Index

To illustrate how these indexes were computed, let us consider the over-all Husband-to-wife Violence Index and the Wife-beating Index. A husband would be counted as having been violent to his wife if he carried out any one or more of the acts described in items *k* through *r*.

Suppose a respondent reported that he had slapped his wife, or did any of the other things in items k through m, but did *not* do any of the more serious things included in items *n* through *r*. He would be counted only in the Husband-to-wife Violence Index, and not in the Wife-beating Index. If a husband punched his wife, then he would be counted in both the over-all Husband-to-wife Violence Index and also in the Wife-beating Index.

These indexes, like the individual items, are reported in the form of incidence rates per hundred husbands, wives, or children. They differ from the rates for the individual items because they tell us the rate at which any of the violent acts included in the Conflict Tactics Scales were used (for the over-all violence indexes), or the rate at which just the more serious acts of violence occurred (in the case of the severe violence indexes).

The same procedure was followed for all the indexes listed above. However, in the case of child abuse, we encountered objections to including hitting a child with an object as an indicator of child abuse. Although we ourselves consider this abusive violence, we recognize that our view is contrary to the way most people think about child abuse, and is also contrary to what would be counted as child abuse by most social service agencies. We therefore computed Child Abuse Index B to omit this item. This allows for the fact that, in many cases, the object is the traditional strap, paddle, clothes brush, etc., and may be violence carried out in the tradition of "strict discipline" rather than an out-of-control assault.

RELIABILITY

The internal consistency reliability of the Conflict Tactics Scales was examined by two techniques: item analysis and the *Alpha* coefficient of reliability. The details are given in Straus, 1979. The mean item-total correlation is .87 for the Husband-to-wife Violence Index and .88 for the Wife-to-husband Violence Index. These figures are based on an earlier pilot study sample of 385 couples. For the present sample of 2,143 couples, the *Alpha* coefficients are .83 for the Husband-to-wife Violence Index, .82 for the Wife-to-husband Violence Index, and .88 for the Couple Violence Index.

VALIDITY

We examined three different aspects of validity: concurrent, content, and construct validity.

Concurrent Validity

Evidence of "concurrent validity" (Straus, 1964) is reported in a study by Bulcroft and Straus (1975). The CTS was completed by students in two sociology courses. The students responded for a referent period consisting of the last year they lived at home while in high school. They were asked to indicate, to the best of their knowledge, how often during that year their father and mother had done each of the items in the CTS.

Each student was also asked to fill in a separate form with the names and address of their parents so that a similar questionnaire could be sent to them. Participation was voluntary and students were assured that they would not be mentioned in the letter to the parents, and that as soon as the mailing was completed the names and addresses would be destroyed and all documents identified by a number only from then on. Of the 110 students present in these classes, 105 completed the questionnaire. Of the 168 questionnaires sent to the mothers and fathers (each was sent separately with its own return envelope) 121 or 72 per cent returned the questionnaire. A comparison of parent reports with student reports in this study, and also with student reports from a previous study (Straus, 1974a), is given in Chart 29.

CHART 29
Correlation of Spouse Report CTS Scores
with Student Report CTS Scores

| CONFLICT TACTICS SCALE | CORRELATION (r) FOR: | |
	HUSBANDS (N=57)	WIVES (N=60)
Reasoning	.19	−.12
Verbal Aggression	.51	.43
Violence	.64	.33

The correlations shown in Chart 29 are difficult to interpret. First, the pattern is varied. The correlations are low for the Reasoning Scale and high (relative to typical concurrent validity results for most social psychological tests and scales) for the Verbal Aggression and Violence Scales. An analysis by Bulcroft and Straus (1975) suggests that the higher correlations for the two aggressive modes of conflict are due to such acts being more dramatic and emotionally charged and, therefore, better remembered.

Another way of examining the concurrent validity of the CTS is to compare incidence rates for violence as reported by each spouse, and also as reported by students for their parents. The rates are shown in Chart 30. The chart shows a tendency for the students to report somewhat more violence by husbands than the husbands themselves reported, but to report less violence by wives than the wives themselves reported. One does not know which data (the student report or the reports of the spouses themselves) are more accurate since each has its own potential source of bias. It could be that these discrepancies might be the result of the small size or other characteristics of the sample used in that study, since the results obtained by student report for the larger sample (the Straus, 1974a study—third row) are almost identical with the violence rates reported by the nationally representative sample of spouses shown in the last row of Chart 30.

Content Validity

Fortunately, it is not necessary to evaluate the validity of the CTS solely on the basis of the data just presented. First, the violence items have a degree of "face" or content validity since they all describe acts of actual physical force being used by one family member on another.

CHART 30
Percentage of Respondents Reporting
One or More Acts of Physical Violence

	% VIOLENT IN LAST YEAR	
SOURCE OF DATA	HUSBANDS	WIVES
Spouses*	9.1	17.9
Students*	16.7	9.5
Students**	11.3	11.4
Husbands***	12.8	11.3
Wives***	11.2	11.7

* From Bulcroft and Straus, 1975 (Husband N=57, Wife N=60).
** From Straus, 1974a (N=385).
*** From national sample described in this book.

Construct Validity

The results of a number of analyses using the CTS measure of violence may be taken as providing at least some evidence of "construct validity." The following are examples of the meaningful results obtained with CTS data:

1. There is a consistency between findings using the CTS and a large body of evidence concerning the "catharsis" theory of aggression control (Straus, 1974a).

2. The CTS are successful in obtaining high rates of occurrence for socially undesirable acts of verbal and physical aggression. These high rates are consistent with previous in-depth interview studies (Gelles, 1974).

3. The CTS data on the extent to which patterns of violence are correlated from one generation to the next (in Chapter 5 and in Steinmetz, 1977a, 1977b) are consistent with previous empirical findings and theory on familial transmission of violent behavior (Carroll, 1977).

4. Numerous correlations exist between CTS scores and other variables in five independent studies (Bulcroft and

Straus, 1975; Jorgensen, 1977; Mulligan, 1977; Steinmetz, 1977b). Although these are not replications of previous empirical findings, they are consistent with relevant theory. Examples include the repeated findings (using the CTS with different samples) of a negative correlation between socioeconomic status and violence (Chapter 6 and Straus, 1974a); high violence when the conjugal power structure is either extremely husband dominant or (especially) extremely wife dominant (Straus, 1973); and the finding that the lower a husband's economic and prestige resources relative to his wife, the greater his tendency to use physical violence to maintain a male-dominant power position (Allen and Straus, 1979).

VIOLENCE RATES BY SEX OF RESPONDENT

Chart 31 gives the violence rates for each of the violence indexes. This chart is a convenient summary of our descriptive findings. It also provides some indirect evidence on the reliability and validity of the violence measures. The chart makes it possible to compare violence rates that are based on interviews with husbands with those based on data provided by wives. This lets us know the extent to which one source of bias (the sex of the respondent) affected the results.

Generally speaking, the sex differences in reporting rates are minimal. However, one needs to keep in mind that these are aggregate statistics, not figures based on interviewing pairs of husbands and wives. In each family we interviewed either the husband *or* the wife. Consequently, there are no data for this sample on agreement between specific spouses. We can only say that one gets roughly the same over-all rates of violence from interviews with men that one gets from interviewing women.

CHART 31
Summary of Violence Indexes by Sex of Respondent

FAMILY ROLE RELATIONSHIP	VIOLENCE INDEXES Sex of Respondent			SEVERE VIOLENCE INDEXES Sex of Respondent		
	MALE	FEMALE	BOTH	MALE	FEMALE	BOTH
Husband-to-wife	12.8	11.3	12.0	3.5	4.1	3.8
Wife-to-husband	11.2	11.7	11.5	5.1	4.3	4.6
Couple	15.8	15.3	15.6	6.2	6.0	6.1
Father-to-child	57.9	*	*	10.1	*	*
Mother-to-child	*	67.8	*	*	17.7	*
Parent-to-child	*	*	63.5	*	*	14.2
Excluding hit with object						
Father-to-child	—	—	—	2.7	*	*
Mother-to-child	—	—	—	*	4.4	*
Parent-to-child	—	—	—	*	*	3.6
Child-to-father	13.7	*	*	7.5	*	*
Child-to-mother	*	20.2	*	*	11.1	*
Child-to-parent	*	*	17.7	*	*	9.4
Sibling-to-sibling	69.5	78.5	75.5	43.8	52.2	48.4

* = Data not available because parent-child questions were asked only about the respondents.
— = Not applicable because these rows are concerned only with severe violence.

APPENDIX C
Indexes Used to Measure Conflict, Power, and Stress

MARITAL CONFLICT

There are an almost infinite number of things which can be the basis of husband-wife conflict. They range from putting the cap on the toothpaste to how to deal with a delinquent child. Within the context of the need to gather information on many variables in a one-hour interview, we could not even attempt to list and gather data on all of these possible conflicts. If we used open-ended questions and simply asked what conflicts occurred in the last year, some respondents would focus on one or two issues and not mention others which were also sources of conflict during the year. Therefore, as a matter of practical necessity and to assure having the same information on all the couples in the sample we adopted the strategy of asking everyone about five issues which, in our opinion, are frequent sources of conflict. The specific question was:

> I am going to read a list of things that couples do not always agree on. For each of them, please tell me how often you and your (husband/wife/partner) agreed *during the past year*. First, take managing the money. Did you and your (husband/wife/partner) always agree, almost always agree, usually agree, sometimes agree, or never agree about managing the money?

	ALWAYS	ALMOST ALWAYS	USUALLY	SOME-TIMES	NEVER
a. Managing the money	1	2	3	4	5
b. Cooking, cleaning, or repairing the house	1	2	3	4	5

	ALWAYS	ALMOST ALWAYS	USUALLY	SOME-TIMES	NEVER
c. Social activities and entertaining	1	2	3	4	5
d. Affection and sex relations	1	2	3	4	5

IF RESPONDENT HAS CHILDREN AT HOME OR NOT AT HOME, ASK:

	ALWAYS	ALMOST ALWAYS	USUALLY	SOME-TIMES	NEVER
e. Things about the children	1	2	3	4	5

The Marital Conflict Index consists of the sum of these five items, divided by four if there were no children at home and by five if there was at least one child at home. The resulting index was then converted to Z scores. The charts in Chapter 7 are in units of a half a Z score, starting with 0 for couples whose score is two or more standard deviations below the mean, and ending with 9 for those two or more standard deviations above the mean.

An item analysis of the index produced the following item-to-total correlations: a = .75, b = .73, c = .75, d = .76, e = .72. The over-all coefficient of reliability, as measured by Cronbach's *Alpha*, is .87.

DECISION POWER

There is hardly any aspect of the family over which there is greater controversy among social scientists than the balance of power between husband and wife. This applies both to the very meaning of power and to methods of measuring whatever aspect of power is of interest (Cromwell and Olson, 1975, Safilios-Rothschild, 1970). Every measure used has been severely criticized.

The most extensively used (and therefore the most extensively criticized) measure is the one developed by Blood and Wolfe (1960) to index the decision power of husbands and wives. We used a modified version of the Blood and Wolfe index because: (1) It combines convenience with the theoretical merit that it consists of indicators in which power is likely to be most evident: who has the final say in relation to a series of important and typical family decisions. (2) Its wide use in the past decade and a half permits comparability with many previous studies. (3) The many correlates of power as measured by this method provide what is, in effect, "construct validation" evidence, and a recent paper by Straus (1977c) provides evidence of concurrent validity.

Although for convenience in exposition, we follow the convention of applying the term power to the particular aspect which was measured, the reader must bear in mind that this refers only to who has the final say on certain decisions. The specific decisions used for this study were obtained by asking:

Every family has decisions to make—such as where to live, whether or not to buy a car, and so on. We would like to find out how you and your (husband/wife/partner) make some of these kinds of decisions. Let's start with buying a car. Who in your family actually does have the final say about

	WIFE ONLY	WIFE MORE	HUSBAND & WIFE SAME	HUSBAND MORE	HUSBAND ONLY
a. Buying a car	1	2	3	4	5
b. Having children	1	2	3	4	5
c. What house or apartment to take	1	2	3	4	5
d. What job your (husband/wife/ partner) should take	1	2	3	4	5
e. Whether you should go to work or quit work	1	2	3	4	5
f. How much money to spend per week on food	1	2	3	4	5

The Decision Power Index was obtained by summing items and transforming the resulting scores to standard deviation units as described for the Marital Conflict Index.

An item analysis of the index revealed the following item-to-

total correlations: a = .53, b = .44, c = .48, d = .36, e = .59, f = .52. The over-all coefficient of reliability, as measured by Cronbach's *Alpha,* is .58.

STRESS

There has been a vast debate on the concept of stress (Mechanic, 1962; Lazarus, 1966; Levine and Scotch, 1967; McGrath, 1970; Scott and Howard, 1970; Selye, 1956). For example, one issue is whether stress is a property of the situation (such as illness, unemployment, family conflict, getting married, or getting promoted to a new job) or whether it is a subjective experience. For some people a new set of job responsibilities is experienced as stress, whereas for others, lack of such responsibility is a stress.

The definition of stress which we favor treats stress as a function of the interaction of the subjectively defined demands of a situation and the capabilities of an individual or group to respond to these demands. Stress exists when the subjectively experienced demands are inconsistent with response capabilities.

In fact, there is a gap between the definition of stress just given and the method used to measure stress in this book. This is because our data are restricted to "stressor stimuli." To use this data as a measure of stress one must therefore *assume* that (1) some life event, such as having a child, produces a certain but unknown degree of demand on parents, (2) that on the average this is subjectively experienced as a demand, (3) that the capabilities of parents to respond to these demands will not always be sufficient, and (4) that the result is a certain level of stress.

On the basis of these assumptions, it is then possible to investigate the relationship between such events and the level of violence in the family using a modified version of the Holmes and Rahe stressful life events scale (1967). Because of limited interview time, the scale was restricted to the eighteen items listed in Chart 32. The scores on this scale ranged from zero to 18, with a mean of 2.4 and a standard deviation of 2.1.

CHART 32
Per Cent Experiencing 18 Life Stresses During Survey Year

LIFE EVENT	PER CENT (N=2,143)
1. Troubles with the boss	17.0
2. Troubles with other people at work	20.3
3. Got laid off or fired from work	7.7
4. Got arrested or convicted of something serious	1.3
5. Death of someone close	40.0
6. Foreclosure of a mortgage or loan	1.6
7. Being pregnant or having a child born	12.4
8. Serious sickness or injury	17.6
9. Serious problem with health or behavior of a family member	26.3
10. Sexual difficulties	11.6
11. In-law troubles	11.-
12. A lot worse off financially	13.7
13. Separated or divorced	ᴜᴜ
14. Big increase in arguments with spouse/partner	8.8
15. Big increase in hours worked or job responsibilities	21.9
16. Moved to different neighborhood or town	16.8
17. Child kicked out of school or suspended	1.6
18. Child got caught doing something illegal	2.8

The Stress Index used in this study actually differs in other ways than length from the Holmes and Rahe scale. (1) In selecting items from the larger original set we eliminated stresses which have a "positive cathexis." This was done on the basis of methodological studies which show that it is the "negative" items which account for most of the relationship between scores on the Stress Index and other variables (Gerstein, Langner, Eisenberg, and Orzek, 1974; Paykel, 1974). (2) We modified some items and added some which are not in the Holmes and Rahe scale to secure a set of stressors which seemed best for the purpose of this research. (3) The Holmes and Rahe weights were not used in computing the index score for each respondent. This was based on research which found that the weighting makes little difference in the validity of scales of this type (Straus and Kumagai, 1979), and of the Holmes and Rahe scale specifically (Hotaling, Atwell, and Linsky, 1979).

REFERENCES

ALLEN, C. M., and M. A. STRAUS 1979. Resources, power, and husband-wife violence. In *The Social causes of husband-wife violence*, M. A. Straus and G. T. Hotaling, eds., Chapter 12. Minneapolis: University of Minnesota Press.

AMERICAN HUMANE ASSOCIATION 1974. *Highlights of the 1974 national data*. National Clearinghouse on Child Neglect and Abuse. American Humane Association, Denver. Mimeographed.

ARCHER, D., and R. GARTNER 1976. Violent acts and violent times: a comparative approach to postwar homicide rates. *American Sociological Review* 41 (December):937–63.

BACH, G. R., and P. WYDEN 1968. *The intimate enemy*. New York: Avon Books.

BAKAN, D. 1971. *Slaughter of the innocents: a study of the battered child phenomenon*. Boston: Beacon Press.

BALL-ROKEACH, S. J. 1973. Values and violence: a test of the subculture of violence thesis. *American Sociological Review* 38 (December):736–49.

BARD, M. 1969. Family intervention police teams as a community mental health resource. *The Journal of Criminal Law, Criminology, and Police Science* 6o (2):247–50.

BARD, M., and J. ZACKER 1971 The prevention of family violence: dilemmas of community intervention. *Journal of Marriage and the Family* 33 (4):677–82

BEDAU, H. A., and C. M. PIERCE 1976. *Capital punishment in the United States*. New York: AMS Press.

BELL, N., and M. BENJAMIN 1977. *Explaining domestic murder*.

Paper presented at Conference on Violence in Canadian Society, March 12, 1977.

BENNIE, E. H., and A. B. SCLARE 1969. The battered child syndrome. *American Journal of Psychiatry* 125 (July):975–78.

BERKELEY PLANNING ASSOCIATES 1978. Executive summary: evaluation of the joint OCD/SRS national demonstration program in child abuse and neglect. Mimeographed.

BERKOWITZ, L. 1973. The case for bottling up rage. *Psychology Today* 7 (July):24–31.

BILLINGSLEY, A. 1969. Family functioning in the low income black community. *Social Casework* 50:563–72.

BLAU, P. 1964. *Exchange and power in social life.* New York: John Wiley and Sons.

BLOOD, R. O., JR., and D. M. WOLFE 1960. *Husbands and wives.* Glencoe, Ill.: Free Press.

BLUMBERG, MYRNA 1964. When parents hit out. *Twentieth Century* 173 (Winter):39–44.

BOHANNAN, P. 1960. *African homicide and suicide.* New York: Athenium.

BOOTH, A., and J. N. EDWARDS 1976. Crowding and family relations. *American Sociological Review* 41 (April):308–21.

BOUDOURIS, J. 1971. Homicide and the family. *Journal of Marriage and the Family* 33 (November):667–77.

BRAZELTON, T. B. 1969. *Infants and mothers.* New York: Delacorte Press.

BREMNER, R. H., ed. 1970. *Children and youth in America: a documentary history.* Vol. I. Boston: Harvard University Press.

BRIM, O. G. 1958. Family structure and sex-role learning by children. *Sociometry* 21 (March):1–16.

BRONFENBRENNER, U. 1958. Socialization and social class throughout time and space. In *Readings in social psychology,* E. E. Maccoby, T. M. Newcomb, and E. L. Hartley, eds., pp. 400–25. New York: Holt.

———. 1974. The origins of alienation. *Scientific American* 231:53ff.

BROWN, C. 1965. *Manchild in the promised land.* New York: New American Library.

BULCROFT, R., and M. A. STRAUS 1975. Validity of husband, wife, and child reports of intrafamily violence and power. Mimeographed.

Bureau of the Census 1970. *Statistical abstract of the United States* 91st edition. Washington, D.C.

———. 1975. Estimates of the population of the United States by age, sex, and race, *Current population reports,* Series P-25, No. 614. 1970–1975. Washington, D.C.: Government Printing Office.

BUTTON, A. 1973. Some antecedents of felonious and delinquent behavior. *Journal of Clinical Child Psychology* 2 (Fall):35–38.

CAFFEY, JOHN 1946. Multiple fractures in the long bones of infants suffering from chronic subdural hematoma. *American Journal of Roentgenology, Radium Therapy, and Nuclear Medicine* 56:163–73.

CALHOUN, P. B. 1962. Population density and social pathology. *Scientific American* 206:139–46.

CALVERT, R. 1974. Criminal and civil liability in husband-wife assaults. In *Violence in the family,* S. K. Steinmetz and M. A. Straus, eds., pp. 88–90. New York: Harper and Row.

CANFIELD, A. A. 1951. The "Sten" scale—a modified C-scale, *Educational and Psychological Measurement,* 11 (2):295–97.

CARROLL, J. C. 1977. The intergenerational transmission of family violence: the long-term effects of aggressive behavior. *Aggressive Behavior* 3 (Fall):289–99.

———. 1979. A cultural consistency theory of family violence in Mexican-American and Jewish-American subcultures. In *The social causes of husband-wife violence,* M. A. Straus and G. T. Hotaling, eds. Minneapolis: University of Minnesota Press.

CHRISTIAN, J. 1960. Factors in mass mortality of a herd of sike deer. *Chesapeake Science* 1:79–95.

———. 1963. The pathology of overpopulation. *Military Medicine* 128:571–603.

COHEN, S., and A. SUSSMAN 1975. *The incidence of child abuse in the United States.* Unpublished manuscript.

CONGDON, T. 1970. What goes on in his head when you're pregnant? *Glamour* (December):102ff.

CROMWELL, R. E., and D. H. OLSON, eds. 1975. *Power in families.* Beverly Hills, Calif.: Sage Publications.

CURTIS, L. 1974. *Criminal violence: national patterns and behavior.* Lexington, Mass.: Lexington Books.

DAVIDSON, T. 1978. *Conjugal crime: understanding and changing the wifebeating problem.* New York: Hawthorn.

DE MAUSE, L., ed. 1974. *The history of childhood*. New York: The Psychohistory Press.

——. 1975. Our forebearers made childhood a nightmare. *Psychology Today* 8 (April):85–87.

DEXTER, L. A. 1958. A note on selective inattention in social science. *Social Problems* 6 (Fall):176–82.

ERLANGER, H. B. 1974a. The empirical status of the subculture of violence thesis. *Social Problems* 22 (December):280–91.

——. 1974b. Social class and corporal punishment in childrearing: a reassessment. *American Sociological Review* 39 (February):68–85.

FINKELHOR, D. 1979. *Sexually victimized children*. New York: Free Press.

FITHIAN, P. V. 1945. *Journal and letters of Philip Vickers Fithian, 1773–1774*. Princeton, N.J.: Princeton University Press.

FLATO, C. 1962. Parents who beat children. *Saturday Evening Post* 235 (October 6):30ff.

FONTANA, V. J. 1973. *Somewhere a child is crying: maltreatment—causes and prevention*. New York: MacMillan Publishing Co., Inc.

FOSS, J. E. 1979. The paradoxical nature of family relationships and family conflict. In *The social causes of husband-wife violence*, M. A. Straus and G. T. Hotaling, eds., Chapter 8. Minneapolis: University of Minnesota Press.

FRIEDRICH, W. N., and J. A. BORISKIN 1976. The role of the child in abuse: a review of the literature. *American Journal of Orthopsychiatry* 46 (October):580–90.

FRODI, A., J. MACAULAY, and P. R. THOME 1977. Are women always less aggressive than men? A review of the experimental literature. *Psychological Bulletin* 84 (July):634–60.

GALDSTON, R. 1965. Observations of children who have been physically abused by their parents. *American Journal of Psychiatry* 122(4):440–43.

GALLE, O. R., et al. 1972. Population density and pathology: what are the relations for man? *Science* 176:23–30.

GARBARINO, J. 1977. The human ecology of child maltreatment: a conceptual model for research. *Journal of Marriage and the Family* 39:721–35.

GASTIL, R. D. 1971. Homicide and a regional culture of violence. *American Sociological Review* 36 (June):412–27.

GELLES, R. J. 1974. *The violent home: a study of physical aggression between husbands and wives.* Beverly Hills, Calif.: Sage Publications.

——. 1975a. The social construction of child abuse. *American Journal of Orthopsychiatry* 45 (April):363–71.

——. 1975b. Violence and pregnancy: a note on the extent of the problem and needed services. *The Family Coordinator* 24 (January):81–86.

——. 1976. Abused wives: why do they stay? *Journal of Marriage and the Family* 38 (November):659–68.

——. 1978. Methods for studying sensitive family topics. *American Journal of Orthopsychiatry* 48 (3):408–24.

GELLES, R. J., and M. A. STRAUS 1979. Determinants of violence in the family: toward a theoretical integration. In *Contemporary theories about the family,* W. Burr, R. Hill, F. I. Nye, and I. Reiss, eds., pp. 549–81. New York: Free Press.

GERSTEIN, J. C., T. S. LANGNER, J. G. EISENBERG, and L. ORZEK 1974. Child behavior and life events: undesirable change or changes per se. In *Stressful life events: their nature and effects,* B. S. Dohrenwend and B. P. Dohrenwend, eds., pp. 159–70. New York: John Wiley and Sons.

GIL, D. G. 1970. *Violence against children: physical child abuse in the United States.* Cambridge, Mass.: Harvard University Press.

——. 1975. Unraveling child abuse. *American Journal of Orthopsychiatry* 45 (April):346–58.

GILLEN, J. L. 1946. *The Wisconsin prisoner: studies in crimogenesis.* Madison: University of Wisconsin Press.

GINGOLD, J. 1976. One of these days—pow right in the kisser. *MS* 5 (August):51ff.

GOLDSTEIN, M. 1977. When did you stop beating your wife? *Long Island Magazine* (*Newsday,* September 18):9ff.

GORDON, T. 1970. *Parent effectiveness training.* New York: Wyden.

HOFFMAN, F. 1925. *The homicide problem.* Newark: Prudential Press.

HOKANSON, J. E. 1970. Psychophysiological evaluation of the catharsis hypothesis. In *The dynamics of aggression*, E. I. Megargee and J. E. Hokanson, eds., pp. 74–88. New York: Harper and Row.

HOLMES, T. H., and R. H. RAHE 1967. The social readjustment rating scale. *Journal of Psychosomatic Research* 11:213–18.

HOTALING, G. T., S. G. ATWELL, and A. S. LINSKY 1979. Adolescent life changes and illness: a comparison of three models. *Journal of Youth and Adolescence*. In Press.

HOWARD, J. 1970. *Please touch: a guided tour of the human potential movement*. New York: Dell Publishing.

HUGGINS, M. D., and M. A. STRAUS 1979. Violence and the social structure as reflected in children's books from 1850 to 1970. In *The causes of husband-wife violence*, M. A. Straus and G. T. Hotaling, eds., Chapter 4. Minneapolis: University of Minnesota Press.

HUMPHREYS, L. 1970. *Tearoom trade: impersonal sex in public places*. Chicago: Aldine.

IANNI, F. A. J. 1972. *A family business: kinship and social control in organized crime*. New York: Russell Sage Foundation.

JEFFREY, M. 1976. Practical ways to change parent-child interaction in families of children at risk. In *Child abuse and neglect: the family and the community*, R. E. Helfer and C. H. Kempe, eds., pp. 209–24. Cambridge, Mass.: Ballinger.

JORGENSEN, S. R. 1977. Societal class heterogamy, status striving, and perception of marital conflict: a partial replication and revision of Pearlin's contingency hypothesis. *Journal of Marriage and the Family* 39 (November):653–89.

KEMPE, C. H. 1971. Pediatric implications of the battered baby syndrome. *Archives of Disease in Children* 46:28–37.

KEMPE, C. H., and R. E. HELFER, eds. 1974. *Helping the battered child and his family*. Philadelphia: Lippincott.

KEMPE, C. H., et al. 1962. The battered child syndrome. *Journal of the American Medical Association* 181 (July):17–24.

KENT, J. T. 1976. A follow-up study of abused children. *Journal of Pediatric Psychology* 1 (2):25–31.

KINSEY, A., C. WARDELL, B. POMEROY, and C. E. MARTIN 1948. *Sexual behavior in the human male*. Philadelphia: W. B. Saunders Co.

Knox, D., and K. Wilson 1978. The difference between having one and two children. *The Family Coordinator* 27 (January):23–26.

LaRossa, R. 1977. *Conflict and power in marriage: expecting the first child.* Beverly Hills, Calif.: Sage Publications.

Lazarus, R. S. 1966. *Psychological stress and the coping process.* New York: McGraw-Hill.

LeMasters, E. E. 1957. Parenthood as crisis. *Marriage and Family Living* 19 (November):352–55.

Levine, S., and N. A. Scotch 1967. Toward the development of theoretical models: II. *Milbank Memorial Fund Quarterly* 45 (2):163–74.

Levinger, G. 1966. Sources of marital dissatisfaction among applicants for divorce. *American Journal of Orthopsychiatry* 36 (October):803–7. Also reprinted in Steinmetz and Straus, 1974.

Light, R. J. 1973. Abused and neglected children in America: a study of alternative policies. *Harvard Educational Review* 43 (November):556–98.

Maccoby, E. E., and C. N. Jacklin 1974. *The psychology of sex differences.* Stanford: Stanford University Press.

Martin, D. 1976. *Battered wives.* San Francisco: Glide Publications.

Maurer, A., 1976. Physical punishment of children. Paper presented at the California State Psychological Convention, Anaheim.

McGrath, J. E., ed. 1970. *Social and psychological factors in stress.* New York: Holt, Rinehart and Winston.

Mechanic, D., 1962. *Students under stress: a study in the social psychology of adaptation.* Englewood Cliffs, N.J.: Prentice-Hall, Inc.

Mulligan, M. A. 1977. *An investigation of factors associated with violent modes of conflict resolution in the family.* Unpublished M.A. thesis, University of Rhode Island.

Nagi, S. Z. 1975. Child abuse and neglect programs: a national overview. *Children Today* 4 (May–June):13–17.

Newberger, E. H., et al. 1977. Pediatric social illness: toward an etiologic classification. *Pediatrics* 60:178–85.

O'Brien, J. E. 1971. Violence in divorce prone families. *Journal of*

References

Marriage and the Family 33 (November):692–98. Also reprinted in Steinmetz and Straus, 1974.

Osgood, C., G. Suci, and P. Tannenbaum 1957. *The measurement of meaning.* Urbana, Ill.: University of Illinois Press.

Owens, D. M., and M. A. Straus 1975. The social structure of violence in childhood and approval of violence as an adult. *Aggressive Behavior* 1:193–211.

Palmer, S. 1962. *The psychology of murder.* New York: Thomas Y. Crowell Company.

Parnas, R. I. 1967. The police response to the domestic disturbance. *Wisconsin Law Review* 914 (Fall):914–60.

Paykel, E. S. 1974. Life stress and psychiatric disorder: applications of the clinical approach. In *Stressful life events: their nature and effects,* B. S. Dohrenwend and B. P. Dohrenwend, eds., pp. 135–49. New York: John Wiley and Sons.

Pediatric News 1975. One child dies daily from abuse: parent probably was abused. *Pediatric News* 9 (April):3ff.

Pittman, D. J., and W. Handy 1964. Patterns in criminal aggravated assault. *Journal of Criminal Law, Criminology, and Police Science* 55 (4):462–67.

Pizzey, E. 1974. *Scream quietly or the neighbors will hear.* London: Penguin Books.

Pokony, A. D. 1965. Human violence: a comparison of homicide, aggravated assault, suicide, and attempted suicide. *Journal of Criminal Law, Criminology, and Police Science* 56 (December):488–97.

Prescott, J. W., and D. Wallace 1976. Developmental sociobiology and the origins of aggressive behavior. Paper presented at the 21st International Conference of Psychology, Paris.

Radbill, S. X. 1974. A history of child abuse and infanticide. In *The battered child* (2nd ed.), R. E. Helfer and C. H. Kempe, eds., pp. 3–24. Chicago: University of Chicago Press.

Rollins, B. C., and H. Feldman 1970. Marital satisfaction over the family life cycle. *Journal of Marriage and the Family* 32 (February):20–28.

Ross, C. J. 1977. *Society's children: the care of indigent youngsters in New York City, 1875–1903.* Unpublished doctoral dissertation, Yale University.

RUEVENI, U. 1978. *Networking families in crisis.* New York: Human Sciences Press.

SAFILIOS-ROTHSCHILD, C. 1969. Honor crimes in contemporary Greece. *The British Journal of Sociology* XX (June, No. 2): 205–18.

———. 1970. The study of family power structure: a review. 1960–1969. *Journal of Marriage and the Family* 32 (November):539–52.

SARGENT, D. A. 1972. The lethal situation: translation of the urge to kill from parent to child. In *Dynamics of violence,* J. Fawcett, ed., pp. 105–14. Chicago: American Medical Association.

SCOTT, R., and A. HOWARD 1970. Models of stress. In *Social stress,* S. Levine and N. A. Scotch, eds., pp. 259–78. Chicago: Aldine.

SEARS, R. R., E. E. MACCOBY, and H. LEVIN 1957. *Patterns of child rearing.* Evanston, Ill.: Row, Peterson, and Company.

SELYE, H. 1956. *The stress of life.* New York: McGraw-Hill.

SHOSTROM, E. L. and J. KAVANAUGH 1971. *Between man and woman.* Los Angeles: Nash Publishing.

SHOTLAND, R. L. and M. K. STRAW 1976. Bystander response to an assault: when a man attacks a woman. *Journal of Personality and Social Psychology* 34 (November):990–99.

SMITH, D. L., and R. SNOW 1978. Violent subcultures or subcultures of violence. *Southern Journal of Criminal Justice* 3 (Fall):1–13.

SMITH, S. M. 1975. *The battered child syndrome.* London: Butterworths.

SOUTHWICK, C. 1955. Regulatory mechanisms of house mouse populations: social behavior affecting litter survival. *Ecology* 36:72–83.

STARK, R., and J. MC EVOY III 1970. Middle class violence. *Psychology Today* 4 (November):52–65.

STEELE, B. F. 1977. Psychological dimensions of child abuse. Paper presented at the annual meetings of the American Association for the Advancement of Science, Denver.

STEELE, B. F., and C. B. POLLOCK 1974. A psychiatric study of parents who abuse infants and small children. In *The battered child,* R. E. Helfer and C. H. Kempe, eds., pp. 89–134. Chicago: University of Chicago Press.

STEINMETZ, S. K. 1971. Occupation and physical punishment: a response to Straus. *Journal of Marriage and the Family* 33 (November):664–66.

———. 1974a. Occupational environment in relation to physical punishment and dogmatism. In *Violence in the family*, S. Steinmetz and M. Straus, eds., pp. 167–72. New York: Harper and Row.

———. 1974b. The sexual context of social research. *American Sociologist* 9 (August):111–16.

———. 1977a. The use of force for resolving family conflict: the training ground for abuse. *The Family Coordinator* 26 (January): 19–26.

———. 1977b. Wife-beating, husband-beating—a comparison of the use of physical violence between spouses to resolve marital fights. In *Battered women*, M. Roy, ed., pp. 63–96. New York: Van Nostrand Reinhold.

———. 1977c. *The cycle of violence: assertive, aggressive and abusive family interaction.* New York: Praeger Publishers.

———. 1977d. Assertive, aggressive, and abusive patterns of family interaction: U.S. and Canadian comparison. Paper presented at Conference on Violence in Canadian Society, March 12–13.

STEINMETZ, S. K., and M. A. STRAUS, eds. 1974. *Violence in the family.* New York: Harper and Row (originally published by Dodd, Mead and Co.).

STRAUS, M. A. 1964. Measuring families. In *Handbook of marriage and the family*, H. T. Christenson, ed., pp. 335–400. Chicago: Rand McNally.

———. 1971. Some social antecedents of physical punishment: a linkage theory interpretation. *Journal of Marriage and the Family* 33 (November):658–63.

———. 1973. A general systems theory approach to a theory of violence between family members. *Social Science Information* 12 (June):105–25.

———. 1974a. Leveling, civility, and violence in the family. *Journal of Marriage and the Family* 36 (February):13–29, plus addendum in August 1974 issue.

———. 1974b. Cultural and social organizational influence on violence between family members. In *Configurations: biological and cultural factors in sexuality and family life*, R. Prince and

D. Barrier, eds., pp. 53–69. Lexington, Mass.: Lexington Books-D. C. Heath.

———. 1974c. Foreword to *The violent home: a study of physical aggression between husbands and wives,* by R. J. Gelles. Beverly Hills, Calif.: Sage Publications.

———. 1976. Sexual inequality, cultural norms, and wife-beating. *Victimology* 1 (Spring):54–76.

———. 1977a. Societal morphogenesis and intrafamily violence in cross-cultural perspective. In *Issues in cross-cultural research,* L. L. Adler, ed. New York: Annals of the New York Academy of Sciences 285:717–30.

———. 1977b. A sociological perspective on the prevention and treatment of wife-beating. In *Battered women,* M. Roy, ed., pp. 196–239. New York: Van Nostrand Reinhold.

———. 1977c. Exchange and power in marriage in cultural context: a multimethod and multivariate analysis of Bombay and Minneapolis families. Paper read at the 1977 meeting of the Association for Asian Studies, New York. Mimeographed.

———. 1979. Measuring intrafamily conflict and violence: the conflict tactics (CT) scales. *Journal of Marriage and the Family* 41 (February):75–88.

STRAUS, M. A., and G. T. HOTALING, eds. 1979. *The social causes of husband-wife violence.* Minneapolis: University of Minnesota Press.

STRAUS, M. A. and F. KUMAGAI 1979. An empirical comparison of eleven methods of constructing indexes. In *Indexing and Scaling for the Social Sciences with SPSS,* M. A. Straus. Book in preparation. Mimeographed copy available from first author.

TINBERGEN, H. 1952. The curious behavior of the stickleback. *Scientific American* 187:22–26.

United States Senate 1973. Hearing before the subcommittee on children and youth of the committee on labor and public welfare. United States Senate, 93rd Congress, First Session. On S.1191 Child Abuse Prevention Act, 1973. U. S. Government Printing Office.

WEISBROD, S. A. 1976. *Physical violence in American families: a methodological report for a national survey.* Princeton, N.J.: Response Analysis Corporation. Mimeographed.

WELSH, R. S. 1976. Severe parental punishment and delinquency: a developmental theory. *Journal of Child Clinical Psychology* 35 (1):17–21.

WOLFGANG, M. E. 1957. Victim-precipitated criminal homicide. *Journal of Criminal Law, Criminology, and Police Science* 48 (June):1–11. Also reprinted in *Studies in homicide*, M. E. Wolfgang, ed., pp. 72–87. New York: Harper and Row.

———. 1958. *Patterns in criminal homicide*. New York: John Wiley and Sons.

YLLO, K., and M. A. STRAUS 1978. Interpersonal violence among married and cohabiting couples. Paper presented at the 1978 meeting of the National Council on Family Relations. Mimeographed.

INDEX